P9-BYK-104

The Royal Winnipeg Ballet

The First Forty Years

The Roya

Winnipeg Ballet
The First Forty Years

MAX WYMAN

1978

Doubleday Canada Limited, Toronto, Ontario

Doubleday & Company, Inc., Garden City, New York

ISBN: 0-385-14009-6

Library of Congress Catalog Card Number 78-1228

Copyright © 1978 by Max Wyman
All rights reserved

First edition

The photographs of Arnold Spohr on pages 201-06 are by
Michael Wesselink.

Printed in Canada by the John Deyell Company

Designed by Robert Burgess Garbutt

Canadian Cataloguing in Publication Data

Wyman, Max, 1939-
    The Royal Winnipeg Ballet, the first forty years

Includes index.
ISBN 0-385-14009-6

1. Royal Winnipeg Ballet — History. I. Title.

GV1786.R75W94   792.8'0971274   C78-001462-6

for my parents

Foreword

What matters most, of course, is what happens on the stage. That's what a dance company exists for. Everything else—history, happiness, heartbreak—is extra: the process before the product. This book is an attempt to unravel some of the threads of process in one of the last great prairie sagas, the story of the Royal Winnipeg Ballet.

The book is neither puffery nor hatchetry; it is an affectionate exercise in curiosity. For help in its preparation, I have many persons to thank. Gweneth Lloyd and Betty Farrally, the company's originators, and Kathleen Richardson, one of its principal benefactors, made me welcome in their homes, and gave generously of their time. Arnold Spohr, the company's artistic director, spent hour after patient hour responding to my questioning; David Yeddeau, Richard Rutherford, Bonnie Wyckoff and David Moroni also provided particularly valuable perspectives. I am grateful, too, for personal viewpoints from a large number of individuals, many of whom have been or are still in some way connected with the company—among them David Adams, Salvatore Aiello, Woodrow Bennett, Ruthanna Boris, Shirley (Russell) Bracken, Jim Cameron, Hilary Cartwright, Marina Eglevsky, Aileen Garland, Peter Garrick, John Graham, Benjamin Harkarvy, R. A. Kipp, Sol Kanee, Linda Litwack, David Y. H. Lui, Doreen Macdonald, Jean McKenzie, Sheila Mackinnon, Marilyn (Young) Marshall, Hugh Pickett, Edward Reger, Bill Riske, Viola (Busday) Robertson, Sergei Sawchyn, Linda Lee Thomas, and Ken Winters.

In the early years I have quoted occasionally from the writings of the late   *vii viii* Frank Morriss (who signed his early columns F.A.M.) of the Winnipeg *Free Press,* and Roy Maley (S.R.M.), of *The Winnipeg Tribune*. Both were responsible for general arts coverage in Winnipeg for several decades (Morriss wrote a popular column under the title "Here, There and Hollywood") and their reactions to the fledgling ballet and its works is perhaps as honest an indication of public response and interest as we are likely to find.

Kind assistance in clarifying points of detail came from J. C. K. Madsen, associate director of the Banff Centre; Barbara H. Clark, executive officer of the senate at the University of Calgary; R. LaPage, consultant in physical education at the Manitoba Department of Education; K. C. Vidruk, consultant to the Winnipeg School Division; and the city secretary of Cambridge, England. I must also thank the members of the company staff, particularly Jill Smith, Lendre Rodgers, and Elspeth MacRae, for their patience with my pestering. And I am indebted to the publishers of *Spectrum Magazine of the Arts,* of Portland, Oregon, for permission to use extracts from Bonnie Wyckoff's *Spectrum* article, "Dancing, Dreams, and Reality," in my chapter titled "On the Road."

My employers at *The Vancouver Sun* kindly allowed me time away from my duties as critic to undertake the necessary research for this book; the Canada Council generously provided financial support during that time.

And throughout it all there was Susan, for whose unflagging encouragement, advice, and assistance I cannot properly express my gratitude.

Contents

The Royal Winnipeg Ballet

The First Forty Years

Introduction

In a leafy suburb of London, in the last years before the first world war, a sturdy, studious, hockey-playing schoolgirl developed a teenage passion for her gymnastics teacher.

In blustery Bradford, Yorkshire, a brewer's daughter failed her Latin tests and was forced to abandon plans for a career as a veterinary surgeon.

Much later, in Winnipeg, Manitoba, the skinny son of a Lutheran minister saw his first dance performance—the Ballet Russe—and was spellbound.

The meetings and moments that led to the Royal Winnipeg Ballet are part of the casual, clicking interlock of particular persons at particular times that we call, according to our personal visions of the world's unfolding, chance, or coincidence, or serendipity, or fate. They are cogs on a tiny, turning wheel; the leaning wheel engages a notched spindle, the spindle turns and waits and turns again, the small gear shifts.

The cable address of the Royal Winnipeg Ballet is CANDANCE, and that means a 9 P.M. Varig flight from Rio to Lima, a midnight bus from Sault Ste. Marie to Timmins, an 8:50 A.M. Western flight from Calgary to Boulder, a 6 A.M. bus from Jalapa to Mexico City. It means the Ranchman Hotel in Medicine Hat, the Howard Johnson in Santa Clara, the Shalom Tower in Tel Aviv, the Westward Ho in Grand Forks. It means the Centennial Auditorium in Brandon, the Colón

Theatre in Buenos Aires, the Operetta Theatre in Moscow, the comprehensive-school auditorium in Swift Current.

It means anywhere and everywhere, one night, two nights, three nights, a week, for six months a year—whistling round the world on buses and planes, cut off, untouched, *dancing*.

The Royal Winnipeg Ballet has been dancing for forty years; only one North American ballet company (the San Francisco Ballet) is older. It has brought the experience of dance to thousands of people who *still* have no idea where Winnipeg is. ("Zees Royal Winnipeg Ballet," said the director of the Théâtre de la Ville in Paris as he signed the booking contract in 1970. "Is it from Toronto or Montreal?")

The name of the wheat strain that was developed specifically to thrive in the climatic extremes of the Canadian prairie is No. 1 Northern, and that name might be appropriated as an epithet for the RWB itself. Prairie grain money made it grow, and it survived, in the spirit of Western pioneering, by guts, grit, and an indomitable belief in possibility. Today the Royal Winnipeg Ballet is Manitoba's most important export after wheat.

The odds the company has faced have always been long; it seems always to exist on the fine edge that precedes hysteria. For all its portability it is too small for its own comfort. For years the quality of its dancers was low; they never stayed long enough for a proper style to develop; for the first three decades it didn't even have a school. It has always been weak in the classical style. It has a board of volunteer directors whose fingers poke everywhere. Once, a fire almost closed it down for good; other times, it was money.

And yet, and yet . . . the RWB goes on going on, putting on a show. Its catalogue of "firsts" is impressive, if those things impress you—first "royal" company in the Commonwealth, first Canadian company to Russia, Europe, Australia, South America, the U.S., and so on—but ambition and pride have never been allowed to override practicality. This has always been a company for the people, and come flood, 'flu or howling blizzard they're always there, quivering-ready to dance, as if that's all the world was made for. They project an innocent excitement, and that is something an audience can smell. There's something about the RWB that warms your heart.

Like many world-class ballet companies, the Royal Winnipeg Ballet was founded by a woman. It is and always has been a *contemporary* ballet company. The fence that separates classical ballet and modern dance is still up, despite the attempts of the "Third Stream" modernists of the 1960s and 1970s to break it down, but the people who have choreographed for the RWB have always had a habit of straddling it, plucking flowers from either side, offering colourful (if not

always long-lasting) bouquets. The company has certainly erred from time to
time in the direction of trendiness and "pop" dance, but it has never fallen into
the trap of artsy pretentiousness. Through its repertoire it celebrates life as a
wide-eyed adventure, everything endlessly possible. Other companies may
have *The Green Table,* or *Rodeo,* or *Meadow Lark;* other companies have their
Rites of Spring, their *Nutcrackers,* their Balanchine and Neumeier and Butler
works, their Smuins, their "after-Petipa" pieces. Few other companies have
them all together, pell-mell in a mix. Some see this diversity as a mirror of the
popular concerns of the times through which the company has passed; others see
it as an indication of an essential lack of seriousness about the dance art on the
part of the RWB; Arnold Spohr, the artistic director, looks on it as a library in
which everyone should be able to find something to enjoy.

Inevitably, this range demands a special kind of dancer. There is a popular
belief in some corners of the dance world that ballet dancers are no
good as dancers of anything else—folk dance, tap dance, rock dance,
disco—because they spend their entire working lives mastering the narrow
specifics of a single aspect of the art. In Winnipeg, they have to do *everything.*
And because of the company's size, each dancer, ideally, must be a recognizable individual, contributing to the total RWB image. In this company, there's
no taking it easy in the back row of the swans. Everyone works; Spohr makes sure
of that.

Spohr is a gregarious and enthusiastic man whose instincts about what the
public will want to buy have had a significant influence on the RWB's fortunes
for 20 years. From him comes the innocence that gives the company, still, its
power in the theatre. The innocence, *and* the knowingness. "You're only as good
as your last show," he once told me. "I'm always terrified, every show . . .
whether it's going to have that magic that is theatre. I want us to do something
worthwhile in dance. I want us to do something that's honest. Maybe the success
that we've had, maybe those words like freshness and vitality, words that have
been used to death about us, maybe that has to do with our honesty. We were
youngsters, still finding our own identity. But we communicate, and that's
theatre."

The company's 40-year progress has embraced the double turning of a
20-year cycle. Early struggles, innocent striving, happy success, and then an
acceptance, a settling, and a slight souring as the financial realities hit

4   home—the cycle has a classic simplicity. The first time they ran it through, they were new to the business, professionalism was just a concept, and a fire mercifully brought it all to a shuddering halt. The second time, they had a double underpinning—professionalism, and real money. The second cycle has come complete; there has been no fire. It is time, now, for the company to break out and up. Bonnie Wyckoff, a dancer who came to the company in 1974, is one of those who think it can.

"It feels like a very *evolved* organization now, which may be something to do with where we are, at the centre of the continent, far from the blocks of stress that afflict society—a place where this delicate thing can flower. New York supports a lot of dance, but in a very violent way. Here, I get a sense of gentle power that brings the company a real easiness. When it goes finally to the top it's not going to do it with a big splash and then go nowhere. It's simply going to get there and sit there and *glow*."

The City

If the Royal Winnipeg Ballet didn't exist, you would be hard pressed to invent it. Why Winnipeg after all? The city is a lonely place, a brave ring of an encampment in the remote centre of the desolate Canadian prairies. It has no suburbs; the city pulls its boundaries tight in on itself, like a wagon-train. Seated at the confluence of the Red and the Assiniboine rivers, it is almost exactly at the centre of the North American continent, closer to Los Angeles and New York than it is to the cities at the extreme east and west edges of Canada. It is a city very much unto itself. The Winnipeggers' sense of isolation is bred into their bones—they live, they like to say, $150 from anywhere—and what they have, they make for themselves; what they make they value.

Winnipeg's name is derived from the Cree Indian words for muddy water, *win nipee*; the city grew out of the fur trade. French voyageur Pierre de La Vérendrye established the first trading post on the site that is now Winnipeg in 1738, and called it Fort Rouge. The North West Company built Fort Gibraltar there in 1804, and in 1821 the Hudson's Bay Company founded Fort Garry. Today, tourists are offered comfortable river cruises along the routes of the early fur-traders.

Winnipeg was chosen as the provincial capital when Manitoba was founded in 1870, and was officially incorporated in 1873. Before the railways came the city thrived as the focal point of the largest inland waterway system in North America, but its most significant growth began with the advent of the Canadian Pacific Railway in 1885. The Winnipeg Grain Exchange is now one of the continent's chief grain markets, and the city is the funnel through which all Canada's east-west overland trade must pass. Many persons stop off in the city en route elsewhere; few of them stay. Winnipeg is a way-station to more important places.

It is not a major metropolitan capital. Even today, its population numbers only slightly more than half a million (and many Winnipeggers are grateful for that—the city is big enough to feel comfortably "involved" in, they say, but not big enough to be intimidating). Those who love it claim it has the healthiest climate in the western hemisphere, and perhaps it has. It is a city of space and air; expatriates dream of returning to its limitless horizons. They talk longingly—I have heard them—of walks in fields in summer moonlight, of the warmth of harvest, of spellbound nights spent watching the aurora borealis as it decorates the north-east sky, of hearing frost split a tree trunk in winter at 40 degrees below zero.

Others will never be able to understand the charms of the prairie—its flat dullness, its muggy summer days, its mosquitoes, the rigours of its winter. (In winter, if you are foolish enough to walk more than a couple of dozen yards out of doors, your nose turns to ice and your cheeks go blue; the moisture on the surface of your skin freezes you to whatever metals flesh touches. In winter there are no stray animals.)

Winnipeg has been called a "classless society," perhaps because of the ethnic mix its industries have brought. Almost half the population of Winnipeg is of British origin. One in eight is of German ancestry; one in nine has Ukrainian roots. Its principal moral influence has been a stern Protestantism, but the sister town of Saint Boniface, a French enclave that exists within Winnipeg's walls, is enthusiastically Catholic.

The receptiveness to the arts that many of the immigrant European families brought with them to Winnipeg probably played a crucial part in the remarkable success of the ballet in its middle years. It is certainly true that the company first took firm root thanks to the support of a small group of members of the Winnipeg social elite that grew out of and around the grain trade and the university. But it quite clearly survived not because it was "the thing to do," the way it might have survived in other small cities, but because the people of the city as a whole wanted it to. (In a city in which survival is still a battle, there is, too, automatic appreciation of tenacity from fellow survivors.)

This is not to suggest that Winnipeg is a particularly arts-conscious town, though it has its art gallery, its orchestra, its theatre and opera companies

—all of which, no doubt, have benefitted to a greater or lesser degree from the city's cosmopolitanism. Before the ballet came, the best-known dance in town was the traditional Red River Jig. Today, still, three of the city's most popular public events are the curling bonspiel, the rodeo, and Folklorama, a pageant of the folk-art talents of the city's many nationalities.

The rise and fall and rise and fall and rise again of the RWB has been linked in no small way with its continuing desire to be a knit-to-fit company for the city that houses it—a company of and for the prairies. Winnipeg has always liked novelty in the arts, and the company's repertoire through the years is spattered with fluff and fashion. But in recent years the ballet's international successes have underlined the need for more sophisticated programming. What Winnipeg is happy with is not always what New York wants, and the conflicting demands of audiences at home and abroad have taxed and strained the company's creative ingenuity.

1 *The Chronology*

Beginnings

There exists a picture of Gweneth Lloyd as a child of six in a white dress so frilly and flowery around the neck and shoulders it might have been designed by a confectioner trying to think up ways of using leftover icing. She is holding aloft in one hand a paper flower; with the other, she is attempting to be dainty with her hem. No one, gazing on that chubby face and its expression of confident glee, on those plump hands, those sturdily-positioned legs, no one, not even someone who loved the child dearly, could have imagined, then, that she would one day launch and give character to Canada's first ballet company.

There exists another photograph of Gweneth Lloyd taken 35 years later, the company not long begun. There is a serenity—almost visionary—about her eyes and her high and open brow. Her best work is still ahead of her, but already, challenge and adversity have set her lower lip firm and tight.

In the years in which she built the company, she was a forceful, dominant, single-minded woman, of great charm when the need arose (though no one, I think, ever looked on her as sweet and gentle). Bred to be an achiever, she never married, and she regrets that mildly. Still, she says, she wasn't that sort of person, really; anyway, she says, she has been very fortunate in her life.

Gweneth Lloyd, aged six.

Gweneth Lloyd was born in Eccles, an industrial town four miles west of Manchester, in the northwest of England, on September 15, 1901. She was conceived in the dying days of the Victorian era, but born and raised an Edwardian. Her father, Joseph Charles William Lloyd, was an inoffensive, ineffectual man who ran a modest automobile engineering business and fancied himself an inventor.

Gweneth's maternal grandmother, a driving and ambitious woman who was married to a prosperous linen draper in Cambridge, argued that it would surely be better for *her* to bring up the child, with all the advantages of linen-drapery wealth, than to leave her at the mercy of the financial vagaries of the, ah, Vulcan Engineering Shop. Mrs. George Stace was accustomed to having her way (she had the satisfaction of seeing her merchant husband installed as the mayor of Cambridge in 1906 and again in 1910) and at the age of five the child was whisked off to Cambridge, given into the charge of a full-time nurse-governess, and enrolled as a day student at the university city's foremost primary-education establishment, the Perse School.

The parents visited the girl regularly, motoring down in elaborate box-on-wheels contraptions of James Lloyd's own design and construction. But in place of parental guidance and affection, the significant influences of Gweneth Lloyd's childhood were Miss Berry, the governess, who took the girl to and from school each day and supervised her leisure-time bicycling, and her grandmother. Her grandmother insisted on success in everything. "You *should* be first, you *can* be if you want to be, so *be* first"—it was drilled into her like prayers. All homework was checked before it was handed in, and if something was wrong she was made to tackle it again until it was right. The drive for success became a habit, and so did the seriousness of purpose; they were to serve her handsomely in later days.

By the time Gweneth was 13, her parents and her younger sister, Enid, were living in Pinner, to the northwest of London and Gweneth and Enid were enrolled at a nearby boarding school, Northwood College. Enid hated it; she wept throughout the start-of-term hackney-cab journey to the college. Gweneth loved it; she wept all the way back. So much to do, so much to discover! She was an ambitious, probably a horrible child—confident, bossy, popular, and successful at everything (hockey, music, French, netball, English, mathematics, science, nighttime dormitory pillow-fighting . . .)

It wasn't until she reached Northwood that she began to take dancing seriously. An assistant of one Mrs. Wordsworth, "dance teacher to the British royal family," taught a weekly class in skirt dancing (what was then called "fancy-dancing") and at the end of each term Mrs. Wordsworth herself would conduct her inspection. She would sweep into the room, a short, majestic figure with a glass eye and a feathered hat, wearing a silk cape and carrying a walking stick, and bark commands to the waiting, quaking girls.

Gweneth loved dancing better than anything, and she became determined to make it her career—a determination strengthened by her first experience of theatrical dance, a performance by Diaghilev's Les Ballets Russes, at the London Coliseum. It was September of 1918, the autumn of Gweneth's seventeenth birthday. Those Ballet Russe performances of the immediate post-war years revolutionized the theatre's approach to the use of colour—it was one of the company's most important legacies—and Gweneth recalls: "Everything had been pastel before, and suddenly there was all this brilliance. I knew nothing of ballet as such, because I'd only done fancy-dancing, but I knew this was what I liked. I must have absorbed an awful lot of ideas on construction and shade and climax and so on, because otherwise how could I have made all the ballets I did?"

She was not to start to make all those ballets—three dozen of them—for more than two decades. Her hopes of becoming a dancer were never to come to much. For one thing, she was too old. A man of 17 just beginning might have a chance of forging a decent dancing career with unrelenting hard work (certainly a number of men made the effort in the company's early years) but the likelihood of a 17-year-old girl with no significant previous training being able to make dance her career has always been small.

For another thing, it was not an idea that would have found much favour at home; what was the point of granny spending all that time and money on refinement if Gweneth was going to become a performer in public spectacles?

But what, if not dance? The decision was, in a sense, made for her. In the way that schoolgirls will, Gweneth adored, passionately, her gymnastics mistress at Northwood, Miss Bertha (Bunty) Knowles. By her last year of school, the girl was eager to follow her idol's footsteps along the path to higher learning.

The Liverpool Physical Training College was certainly not regarded at that time as one of England's more distinguished teaching establishments, but Bunty Knowles had been one of its first five pupils, and what had been good enough for Miss Knowles was good enough for Gweneth. She took up studies there in the autumn of 1919.

There was no actual building—the students lived in row houses and went to a public gymnasium for classes—but work was beginning on the conversion of property bought by the school's proprietor, and the girl students were roped in to help clear the land. They were trained like Amazons, turned into tough young women who could take anything; a breed apart. At best, conditions were primitive; when an epidemic of influenza hit the college during Gweneth's first winter in residence, the girl in the next bed to Gweneth in the basement sickbay died. Gweneth thrived. She emerged, after two years, with a first-class teaching diploma and the year's plum job—second-in-command of the gym program at the Jersey Ladies' College, in St. Helier, the main town on the tiny market-garden island of Jersey, 13 miles off the coast of France.

She fell in love with the island. It was her first contact with so much raw natural beauty, and she spent three innocent and happy years there, cycling in her free hours from St. Helier to the north beaches, climbing the high cliffs, and swimming alone in the deserted bays. She shortened her skirts, and one Christmas on her way through London to spend the break with her family she had her hair bobbed, but she was never a flapper, champagne was never drunk from her slipper at madly gay parties at the Savoy. The roaring twenties passed her by.

In St. Helier, she renewed her contact with dance. A teacher from the mainland had opened a studio specializing in "the revived Greek dance," a system of movement based on ancient Greek forms, introduced in London about a decade earlier by the English dance teacher Ruby Ginner. More thorough in her researches than Isadora Duncan, and far more disciplined in her methods of codification, Ginner had laid down a solidly practical technique. She went into dance-school partnership in London with the mime specialist Irene Mawer shortly after the end of the first world war, and in 1923 she established the Association of Teachers of the Revived Greek Dance, later to become the Greek Dance Association. The Ginner method was exactly what Gweneth needed. At the end of three academic years in St. Helier, she gave up her job and in the fall of 1924 enrolled as a student-teacher at the Ginner-Mawer school.

For the next three years she raced around London supplementing her basic Greek training with tuition in character dancing, national dancing, and, in particular, ballet—first under Margaret Craske, a famous Cecchetti specialist, and then with instructors in the teaching techniques of the Royal Academy of Dancing (then quite new and known as the Association of Operatic Dancing of Great Britain).

Gweneth graduated from the Ginner-Mawer school in the summer of 1927, at the age of 25, and she and Doris McBride, one of the school's younger teachers, decided to open a school of their own. But where?

Enter, for the second significant time, Bunty Knowles. By now she was married, and her husband, Robert Jarman, was established as an organizer of physical education for Leeds, an ugly clothing-industry town in the West Riding of Yorkshire. At the suggestion of the Jarmans—who undertook to sponsor Gweneth and her colleague and see them started—they moved to Leeds.

Betty Hey was born into brewing money in Bradford, Yorkshire, 20 miles from Leeds, on May 5, 1915. Hey's Nut Brown Ale had made the family rich; at the age of seven the child was packed off to Harrogate Ladies' College for the education befitting a young lady of her social position. Spoiled by indulgent parents from her infancy, she was not ideal material. In the first week, she was almost expelled for threatening to punch another little girl in the nose. In her senior years, she used to lead her fellow students on midnight ghost hunts through the school grounds. When she left at 17, the only social graces she had acquired were a good lacrosse game and an ability to eat dessert gracefully.

Her parents didn't expect her to do anything significant with her life; for them it would have been enough for her to "come out" with the appropriate ceremony (which she did) and settle down to a lifetime of pouring tea at the appropriate moment and perhaps doing Good Works. Betty had other plans. Originally, she badly wanted to be a veterinary surgeon, but her poor academic record dashed any hopes of that. To be a vet you needed Latin, and her Latin was abominable. So she settled for what she considered to be the next-best thing. Dancing.

It was 1932, she was 17, and with all the headstrong determination that was eventually to make her the terror of her dancing charges during her Winnipeg days, she demanded to be allowed to go to London to follow her chosen career. To her parents, the prospect was unthinkable. They enrolled her, instead, at Gweneth's new school in Leeds.

Betty was driven back and forth between Bradford and Leeds each day in the family limousine. Betty found nothing unusual in that. What she did object to, however, was having to muck in with the other students and take her turn at washing the staff's luncheon dishes. She particularly hated cleaning sauce-pans—she didn't know *how* to—and she'd hide them in cupboards instead.

A vivacious and charming young woman of distinct character, she was a good performer, because she was so outgoing, and she was always winning prizes in regional competitive dance festivals. But to Gweneth and her partner, who aimed to provide a fully-rounded dance education for serious students, Betty hardly qualified. "Greek dancing was our main subject, and I thought it was hilariously funny, having to go round with an imaginary bow shooting imaginary animals. I wasn't a good student, because I didn't take it seriously." But because she wanted to prove to her family and her teachers that she could do something with her life, she stuck it out for the full four years—all the Greek dancing, the mime, the British and Russian techniques of classical ballet, ballroom, musical comedy, tap, anatomy—and was duly awarded a teaching certificate.

Her parents now expected her to retire to a life of languor. But Betty, goaded by everyone's lack of faith in her, found a teaching post in Gainsborough, Lincolnshire: thirty shillings a week, plus room and board. The "room and board" was straight out of Dickens: the bath was so filthy she couldn't get it clean, she was issued one set of sheets in her first six weeks on the premises, and the kitchen proved to be the permanent living quarters of a mentally deficient grandmother. The job was no better. Engaged to teach dancing, she soon found herself teaching everything, and handling all the administrative problems as well. After a full school year she decided she had made her point with dignity, and resigned.

She returned to Leeds that fall, and was taken on at the school as a teacher. It was a fateful move. She had already established strong ties of friendship with Gweneth during her four student years. Now, a member of the school teaching staff, she was an equal. The friendship ripened and blossomed.

Gweneth, meanwhile, had been growing restless. She had been teaching for close to 10 years; the school was coasting along successfully; the excitement of the early days was over—perhaps it was time for a move.

Enter, for the third significant time, the former Bunty Knowles. In 1928, the year after Gweneth Lloyd and Doris McBride had hung out their shingle in Leeds, Robert Jarman had been invited to Winnipeg, "on loan for six months" to introduce and establish a system of physical education in the Manitoba schools. It soon became obvious that the program would need a permanent director, and in September of 1929 he took up the dual position of Director of Physical Education in Manitoba and the Winnipeg schools—a post he held until 1938, when he resigned from the provincial position to devote his energies solely to physical education in the city's schools.

The Jarmans invited Gweneth to visit them in their new home, and she travelled to Winnipeg in the summer of 1937. After the smoke and grime of 10 years in Leeds the clean openness of the prairie city was a revelation. The possibilities for growth seemed endless. One day, taking the air in a city park, she fell into conversation with a woman sharing her bench. "Is there much going on in the way of ballet in the prairies?" she asked. "Ballet?" answered the woman. "I've never heard of it." Gweneth's lower lip set in that determined way that it has. "You will," she said. "You wait and see." She returned to England to set about making that promise come true.

Betty proved to be a fine and thorough teacher, but she had difficulty fitting the image. She preferred to be riding a horse (hardly the most suitable of hobbies for someone closely involved with dancing) or out at a party. Intelligent and witty, she was rarely without a suitor.

One day early in 1938 Gweneth took Betty aside and mentioned casually that she was thinking of moving to Canada. "Are you really?" said Betty, equally casually. "Well, if you want any help, I wouldn't mind giving you a hand. I'm ready to take a look at the rest of the world."

In fact, she was smarting from the wounds of a recently-broken romance—her preferred young man of the moment had given up the relationship to become a monk—and she welcomed the suggestion of new horizons. Within a week, their passages were booked.

It was a decision that was to change the lives and shape the careers of them both, and it was to unite the two women into a lifelong, mutually supportive team. Without Gweneth's urging, says Betty, she would probably not have left England. Without Betty's drive, says Gweneth, she would probably never have persevered with the company (and, indeed, when Betty married and left the company briefly in 1944, production activity was suspended until her return).

Effectively, Gweneth and Betty were on their own, with no one but each other for support, from the moment they stepped off the Liverpool dock and onto the gangplank of the Canada-bound steamship, *Empress of Australia*. Betty was barely 23. Gweneth was 36. It was late spring, 1938.

1938-41 First Flowers

These were the pioneer years, when they cleared the land, broke the ground, sowed the seeds. If anyone had told Gweneth Lloyd and Betty Hey, then, that they were preparing the way for a major ballet company that was to be toasted on four continents, they would have hooted with derision. Their little group?

But seeds, sown and nurtured, grow. Thirty years, almost to the day, after she first set foot on Canadian soil, Gweneth Lloyd put on an academic's cloak and stood on a carpeted platform in Banff, Alberta, to receive an honorary doctorate from the University of Calgary. Donald Cameron, delivering the eulogy, called her Canada's "Mr. Ballet"—"to her, more than any other single person, Canada owes a debt of gratitude for creating the wide acceptance of ballet as an art form in this country." Did she smile at that, thinking back? I wonder.

Gweneth and Betty were not *quite* on their own on that 1938 Liverpool-Montreal crossing. With them to Winnipeg went Gweneth's Cairn terrier, Garry Strathpeffer Lloyd. Gweneth and Betty travelled modestly; they had bought third-class tickets but there were so many tourists that they were bumped down to steerage, where the accommodation consisted of "glorified horse-boxes" somewhere far below the waterline. The dog, on the other

Backstage 1897.

hand, travelled in style: shipboard regulations would not allow him to travel with his owner, so he spent the entire trip in the company of the ship's butcher.

It was a rough crossing; both spent most of it being seasick. When they finally reached Montreal, they threw financial caution to the winds and took a private drawing-room on the train to Winnipeg. The journey quite revived their spirits.

They arrived in Canada on the tail-end of the depression, just over a year before the outbreak of the second world war. But they never doubted the rightness of their move. Canada was exciting, and different. The sky seemed bluer than anything poor, grimy Leeds had ever been able to show them; the farms, by contrast with the farms of England, were immense. After the seeping moistness of the northern English weather, they found Winnipeg bracing, its air fresh. Romantic escapees, they identified with the spirit of the prairie pioneers. Everything had such a sense of potential.

It was summer, of course; their first experience of a prairie winter was still ahead of them.

It would be misleading to suggest that Winnipeg was entirely without exposure to ballet before Gweneth and Betty arrived. A number of individuals made a modest living running the toe-tap-and-acrobatic type of dance academy, and while Paddy Stone, the company's first male star, talks of most of them as being of the "let's-have-fun-and-dance" variety, David Yeddeau —a significant contributor to the company's growth in its first decade —remembers some "extremely good work." But dance in Canada was just beginning. Good teaching was rare across the land. June Roper, from Texas, was making a name for herself in Vancouver. Gwen Osborne (the original teacher of Nesta Toumine and Patricia Wilde) was establishing herself in Ottawa. Melissa Hayden's first teacher, the Russian-born Boris Volkoff, was active in Toronto.

As far as actual performance was concerned, Volkoff had been running an amateur group in Toronto since 1930 (it had performed at the Berlin Olympics in 1936, and became the Volkoff Canadian Ballet two years later) but Canada's only exposure to professional dance was via the touring companies that passed through on their North American jaunts—the various Russian ballets, the Jooss Ballet (which came through in the late 1930s with *The Green Table*, a Jooss work that was later to become a successful addition to

the RWB repertoire), the Trudi Schoop company, the early Denishawn and
Martha Graham groups. For the most part, however, dance in Canada was a
rare and exotic flower. Transplanting it to the prairies was not going to be
easy.

Gweneth and Betty rented a small studio at the top of a building at 333
Portage Avenue, right on the city's main shopping street, named it, bravely,
the Canadian School of Ballet, and placed advertisements in the city's two
daily newspapers. After a week of sitting anxiously by the telephone, they
had six pupils. Well, it was enough to get them started.

Little by little, they began to break through. Part of it was their presence—enormously energetic, enormously enthusiastic. But the raw drive
was tempered by their breeding. They had such *charm*.

Gweneth had learned from her experiences in Yorkshire that one sure way
of getting one's name talked about as a dance teacher in the circles that
mattered was by hiring out one's talents to the schools for the children of the
wealthy and influential. In those early months in Winnipeg, she did such a
fine job of persuading people that the "revived Greek dance" was the latest
thing in London that two of the private girls schools made it a compulsory
subject, with Gweneth in charge.

One of her pupils from that first year recalls: "We had to make green
tunics, and bunches of rowanberries out of orange material with a little wad
of cotton and wire, and then we'd skip, skip, skip across the lawn
—barefoot, of course. I hated it. But it was compulsory. She had us all
whirling about. We were disciplined, of course, and nobody was not going to
do what she said—she demanded attention—but not in the way that Betty
did. Betty came later on; she stamped and yelled at people. But Gweneth had
great, well, style." Granny's upbringing in Cambridge was paying dividends
at last.

Gweneth and Betty taught everything—classical ballet, "modern" dancing, tap, social dancing. By 1940, students were being prepared for examination by London's Royal Academy of Dancing.

Within months of their arrival in the city, Gweneth and Betty also founded
the Winnipeg Ballet Club—free concentrated tuition for all students accepted, and an opportunity for sustained and steady progress as performers.
Although she says now that she never imagined the club turning into the
internationally famed company that the Royal Winnipeg Ballet is today,
Gweneth admits she did see the potential for the eventual creation of a

repertory ballet company of entirely local origin. There was no way, she realized, that she was going to be able to build such a company from the thin ranks of the school. But by offering intensive free tuition to anyone who passed the auditions for her club, she was more likely to come up with at least the beginnings of the raw material she would need.

The advertisement announcing the formation of the club brought 200 responses—150 seniors (teenagers and persons in their early twenties) and 50 juniors—and the response from the established teachers in the town, who saw their bread and butter dwindling fast, was like something from a western movie. One of the locals phoned the new studio and threatened darkly that the two interlopers would be run out of town (a posse on *pointe*?) if they didn't withdraw these offers of free classes. Gweneth, in her most regally British manner, drew herself up and declared: "If I wish to give away a pound of butter with every lesson, it has nothing whatsoever to do with you. I shall do exactly what I want to do. Good day to you." Later, the resident dance-teaching establishment tried to form a rival club of its own, but it fell apart—no one could agree on who should teach what when. From the start, they were outclassed by a pair of smart operators.

The auditions were simple, but effective. Applicants were first tested on their abilities in a simple ballet class (the only person who could demonstrate, of course, was Betty, and she did "so many *pliés* and *grands battements* I couldn't stand up for a week"), then on their potential for mime ("You have just arrived at the station after a long journey—how would you act?") and finally on their understanding and appreciation of music.

The only senior male applicant to be accepted was a 16-year-old named Paddy Stone, part of a tap-dancing brothers act called the Stepping Stones.

One of the juniors chosen was a shy newspaper boy of nine. Yes, he said, when he arrived for the audition, he wanted to dance. No, he had never seen any dancing. No, he wouldn't take his clothes off, and if it was all the same to them he'd rather keep his moccasins on, too. The audition showed he had enormous potential, but he left without giving his address. It took Betty an afternoon of dogged telephoning to track him down. She thought he had said his name was David Allen, but she couldn't be sure because he had mumbled so, and when she drew a blank with every Allen in the telephone book, she simply began to work right through from the beginning of the A's. By early evening she had found the lad—a major break for the company, as it turned out, and, for the youngster, a particularly fateful call. Without it,

David Adams might never have gone on to become a star of Britain's Royal
Ballet.

In all, about two dozen seniors and juniors were accepted for the club. More members were recruited from private-school classes (Jean McKenzie, later to become one of the company's stars, was one of those) and others moved over from the paying classes at Gweneth and Betty's new school.

Gweneth soon realized that if she ever hoped to attract an audience to the ballet in Winnipeg, she was going to have to de-mystify the business. So on the second Sunday of every month, "useful" people were invited to attend lecture-demonstrations at the studio. The presentations showed the kind of work that went into the making of a ballet dancer, and illustrated the process of putting together a ballet. Everything was laid out very simply and clearly—girls in short green tunics, brown tights, white socks and head-bands, the men in white shorts, black tights and white socks, first running through some simple demonstration exercises, with narration by Gweneth, then performing a simple finished sequence or two. The presentations were modest—there was no talent to allow them to be anything else—but they aroused great interest, and an awareness of a new and potentially exciting dance presence in the city began to grow. Certain individuals in particular began to take a keen interest in the club's affairs.

One of these was Lady Tupper, wife of Sir Charles Stewart Tupper, a prominent lawyer and grandson of Sir Charles Tupper, one of the fathers of Canadian Confederation.

Madge Tupper was not rich, but she was powerful in her connections and her enthusiasms, and she had an unquenchable thirst for the arts. Born Margaret Morse, in Shelburne, Nova Scotia, in 1887, she was the only daughter of Charles Morse, a prominent Ottawa lawyer. She began a career as an amateur actress at the age of 11, playing Alice in Wonderland. (It was an inauspicious beginning: someone threw a pack of cards at her as part of the theatrical effect and broke her nose.) She was married in 1910, settled in Winnipeg, and promptly set about reorganizing the city's arts scene according to her own wishes and expectations.

This was the era when amateur theatricals were commanding national attention—there was, after all, no Canada Council to bolster self-styled professionals with comfortable cushions of public funds—and Madge Tupper was one of the driving forces in the founding of the Dominion Drama Festival. The Winnipeg Little Theatre was Madge Tupper's consuming interest for many years, but she eventually found it necessary to withdraw because of "irreconcilable differences" with the then director, John Craig. She subsequently formed her own group, the Players' Guild, but the strain of two companies was too much for the Winnipeg theatre scene to take, and in the late 1930s they both expired. It was Robert Jarman—he had done some amateur acting with the Players—who alerted her to the arrival of Gweneth and Betty in Winnipeg, and to the launching of the ballet club. She took to the two Englishwomen immediately, and began to organize busily on their behalf. Gweneth welcomed the help, but was not without her misgivings. What if this woman wanted to boss the whole works?

One of the first things Madge Tupper did for them was organize a cocktail party at which everyone who might be useful to the furtherance of the ballet-club scheme was brought together to meet the newcomers. In attendance was David Yeddeau, a busy young man-about-Winnipeg-theatre. Born in Winnipeg, he sold newspapers to put himself through theatre school, and abandoned plans for a University of Manitoba arts course when a stage-management job with the touring Chautauqua Theatre Company presented itself. After he returned to Winnipeg in the 1930s he became involved as an actor, director, stage manager and scene painter in the amateur theatre movement. He directed productions of the University of Manitoba dramatic society for many years, staged Gilbert and Sullivan for the university Glee Club, taught drama at night classes, did make-up for things like the Winter Carnival and the local operettas, and even staged dance recitals for some of the city's ballet teachers. "The people I associated with were extremely cultivated people from other parts of the world," he recalls. "They came to this godforsaken place for the grain trade, and they used the theatre as their means of social stimulus. I didn't know then how fortunate I was, but everything was first class. They were miles ahead in many things."

He recalls that first party clearly, "I wasn't very impressed with these ladies, and they were certainly not impressed with me. We were polite to each other, but we just didn't register. When we first began to register was when they had a party in their first studio, on New Year's Eve. They had the right Scotch, the right gin, the right food and the right glasses and I thought . . . ah."

Ah, indeed. The Lloyd-Hey-Yeddeau team was later to be described by Arnold Spohr as the "Holy Trinity" that gave the company its distinctive character and success in those early years.

As significant in the company's development and growth as the members of the "Holy Trinity" was John Russell. His official post was dean of architecture at the University of Manitoba, but working in the theatre was his hobby and his passion; at one time, in fact, his wife actively encouraged him to give up architecture and devote himself to a career of theatrical design. He, too, had his finger in everything: musical comedy at the Playhouse, the university's Gilbert and Sullivan, a ball in the Crystal Ballroom of the Royal Alexander Hotel, the Players' Guild—if it needed sets or designs, John Russell was available. Undergraduates in his architecture department were all expected to be members of the Ancient and Honourable Guild of Stagecraftsmen, which meant taking an active part in both university theatricals and off-campus activities, painting scenery, designing backdrops, sewing curtains. Later, they were given credits for it—a system that exists to this day.

Gweneth and Betty hit it off immediately with Russell, but Yeddeau and Russell were never close. They were from different ends of town, with different views of the business. Yeddeau was a self-made man, with a strong streak of the circus in him. (His grandfather owned and ran the city's opera house in the days when opera house meant bawdy burlesque.) In the theatre, he had the common touch, and the chief value of his contribution to the enterprise was going to be the thorough professionalism of his staging and presentation, and the populist balance he provided at the planning sessions. Russell was drawn to the theatre not because he needed to exist from it but because he enjoyed it and felt there were things he could contribute. City businessman Bob Kipp, who played a significant role in RWB activities for many years, remembers Russell as "a Christian Scientist, a quiet, soft-spoken, nice guy, without rancour." He was well-placed socially, and when the company was eventually taken over by a board of well-meaning do-gooders, Russell was able to slip easily into their pattern. Yeddeau, resenting their interference and by nature unwilling to accept their kind, left for Toronto.

The Club thrived, but the Canadian School of Ballet was slow to become a profitable operation. A yearly stipend of one hundred pounds from Gweneth's grandmother was a help, but there were still days when they would have to wait for someone at the studio to pay a bill before they could buy food. At one point they were living on porridge. But Gweneth and Betty didn't mind. They were pioneers, and pioneering meant privation. They walked each day from their small apartment to the studio; when the weather grew cold they knitted little booties and a turtleneck sweater for Garry, the terrier, and he would sit at the door of the studio office and bite people. "He always knew the end of a class," says Betty. "When people did their *grands battements* he'd come out of the office and stretch himself and then we knew it was time to go."

In the spring of 1939, not quite a year after their arrival in Winnipeg, Gweneth and Betty were approached by civic officials. King George VI and his queen, Elizabeth, were coming to town; a pageant commemorating La Vérendrye was to be held; would the Ballet Club be in a position to stage a little something? Of course, said Betty and Gweneth; they'd be delighted. What sort of thing, exactly? Well, said the city fathers, how about two ballets, on prairie themes? Make one about grain, they suggested, and the other about the coming of hydro-electric energy to the province—nothing fancy, nothing too long, let's say five minutes each, and plenty of leg.

Oh, and one other thing, they asked. Would it be, ah, possible for Gweneth and Betty to teach the city fathers and their wives how to bow and curtsey for the royal visitors? "It wasn't easy," Gweneth recalls. "This was no *corps de ballet* we were confronting. We had to close the doors at city hall to keep away the curious."

The pageant—*Happy and Glorious* was its title—was produced by John Craig, and given seven performances at the Playhouse Theatre in June, 1939. The club contributed two pieces—*Grain*, which depicted the grain cycle from the sowing and reaping of early times to the modern-day harvesting and the activity of the grain exchange (a lot of mimetic bodies waving in the wind), and *Kilowatt Magic*, which chronicled the social improvements that the coming of electricity brought. (Manitoba's power was at that time the cheapest in the world.)

As far as performance was concerned, it was amateur night. One observer remembers *Kilowatt Magic* as "a great deal of cellophane and some earnest young men flailing their arms in symbolism of the wheels of industry." Gweneth had had to work with what she had been able to recruit. One male dancer, called on for a rapid costume change, made an entrance fastening his fly.

The King and Queen did not in fact attend the first performance by the organization their daughter was to dub "royal" 14 years later, but no one in the company seemed to mind. "We thought we were doing fantastic things," said Paddy Stone much later. "And maybe we were. After all, we were starting dance in Canada."

In those early days the war seemed far from Winnipeg, though Gweneth and Betty both felt pangs of guilt at their absence from their homeland. "We felt like

deserters," says Gweneth. "Of course, we had made our decision to move to   27
Winnipeg long before it happened, but I know I had a bit of a conscience at the
time. You couldn't help it."

The club continued to grow steadily. Among the women there were clerks,
teachers, stenographers, debutantes, a figure-skating champion, and a competitive diver. Among the men, a carpenter, an insurance executive, and a customs
clerk. Soon the male contingent numbered 10. It has been a common complaint
of dance companies in small towns that the task of recruiting male dancers is
complicated by social prejudice; Arnold Spohr kept the fact of his becoming a
dancer a secret for a year, for fear that his sports-enthusiast friends would turn
against him. However, Gweneth claims there was never much of a backlash
against the male dancer in Winnipeg. Winnipeg's cosmopolitan population
included large numbers of Eastern Europeans, to whom dancing was second
nature, an expression of one's manliness, "so people took it for granted. There
wasn't the kind of prejudice you get now."

Gweneth ran the club like the private girls' schools in which she had been
raised. It was genteel, and she was always a lady (she has a silky queenliness and
a real refinement), but she was also a stern disciplinarian. Betty was the
noisemaker. There is a fiery vitality about her presence that has daunted dance
students for decades. Since neither suffers fools well, they made a fine
team.

Gweneth was not in any special hurry to see the ensemble grow. She knew that
making dancers—getting bodies ready, building responses in, watching security develop—was all a matter of patience and unremitting labour. Even so, by
1940 they had a nucleus of people they could decently show. Paddy Stone was
very promising; Jean McKenzie, who had studied ballet in Vancouver before
moving to Winnipeg with her family as a child, was his partner. Along with Betty
Hey, they were the company's first stars.

Once the decision to perform had been made, Gweneth set programming
policies that gave broad guidance to the company for four decades. "Ballet," she
declared, "is no longer a champagne and caviar treat. Ballet is a beer-and-skittles entertainment." Lofty art was out. If prairie audiences were to be held
beyond the initial novelty, she reasoned, she would have to offer dance everyone
could enjoy—something pretty and white for the ladies, something comic to
amuse the reluctant husbands, something "modern" to appeal to those who
considered themselves avant-garde. Any attempt to re-create the traditions of
the European companies, she argued, would be ridiculously out-of-place.

The early ballets were no doubt homespun and unsophisticated, but Gweneth was determined that the company would present a thoroughly "professional" front. That meant sets, an orchestra (recorded music was unthinkable), costumes, make-up, a hall. That meant money.

The club itself was hardly wealthy, but in a spirit of family togetherness that was to characterize its first decade and a half, the club members took on the responsibility of raising $10 each for the performance kitty. They held raffles, silver teas, whist drives, dances. They sewed, knitted, cooked, made coffee to sell to each other at rehearsal breaks. David Adams, who lived on the outskirts of town, went out to the fields each day during spring and picked bunches of crocuses to sell on Portage Avenue. Lady Tupper, wholly committed to Gweneth's principle of professionalism, turned over to the club's operating fund a balance of $165 left in the account of her now-defunct Players' Guild. She also began to do some vigorous twisting of arms among her influential acquaintances (a task that would occupy her increasingly as the years passed). In many instances, however, there was a feeling that the group should prove it could deliver the goods before commitments were made involving hard cash.

Well, delivery date was set: June 11, 1940.

June 11, 1940, was the two hundred and eighty-sixth day of the war. Nazi forces crossed the Marne and advanced to within 20 miles of the Arc de Triomphe, Egypt broke off relations with Italy, the Allies blocked the Suez Canal and the U.S. Senate voted 67 to 18 to support President Roosevelt's plan to ship U.S. army and navy supplies to the Allied forces—effectively ending U.S. neutrality. It was a beautiful day in Manitoba. Farmers delivered 320,000 bushels of wheat to country elevators (more than twice the amount delivered on the same date the previous year), and that evening the Winnipeg Ballet Club launched its first full-scale presentation, at the Playhouse Theatre: a series of seven *Divertissements*—"interpretations in the classical style of the music of Tchaikovsky and Arensky"—plus a three-act comedy ballet, *The Wager*, and an expanded *Kilowatt Magic*.

It was very much a family affair. Gweneth had done the choreography, John Russell had designed "decorations" for *The Wager* and *Kilowatt Magic*, James Robertson, whose Miniature Musicale radio program was a coast-to-coast favourite, had been hired to conduct a 34-piece orchestra, David Yeddeau was in charge of the technical side and the make-up, and Betty, who had drilled the company, was one of the stars. ("I was the wrong shape but I was a good performer, and since there wasn't anybody better, naturally I had to do it.")

Listed on the program as Honorary Patron of the historic event was the Lieutenant-Governor of Manitoba. His name was William Johnston Tupper, and he was Madge Tupper's father-in-law's brother. Manning the box-office at the Playhouse Theatre, her duties as choreographer complete, was Gweneth Lloyd.

The general consensus was one of high approval. "Local dance history was made," said F. A. M. in the Winnipeg *Free Press*. "It was definitely a triumphant evening and there is every indication that the club will go on to even greater achievements." *The Winnipeg Tribune* prophesied: "Winnipeg is not yet ballet-conscious but a few performances by the Winnipeg Ballet Club . . . would change that thoroughly. The three ballets proved one long succession of thrills to the lover of visible music."

The ink that followed was even better. In the *National Monthly*, Ray Darby called the show "a milestone along a trail that is comparatively unexplored in Canada." He wrote: "Amid the chaos of war and upheaval, an art new to Canada has lifted its head proudly, confident that the grinding heel will only serve to make it the more beautiful and inspiring by contrast."

And in the *Free Press*, an editorial by K. M. H. enthused: "A great event has happened in Winnipeg, and that event is the performance of the Ballet Club. It was not a perfect performance, it was not a smug performance . . . it was a performance that held evidence that those who took part . . . knew they held in their hands not any such tawdry thing as an extension of their own ego, but that they served a great art; that it was fire, white fire they sought to light . . . to say that this Club has begun well is to present it with an ovation."

But audiences were small. A war was on. Manitoba's spring had begun. Holidays were near. The city was still smarting from a decade-long depression. Attendance estimates had been far too enthusiastic, and the club found itself with a large deficit.

The bake sales were revived. Lady Tupper continued to twist arms. Gweneth campaigned for club memberships. A major fund-raising help at this time proved to be the city's Women's Musical Club, an association of arts-minded ladies who met regularly to listen to good music and to drink post-performance tea with the players. Helping the ballet pay its bills was the kind of project they liked to be involved in, and they put their elegant shoulders to the wheel. By way of recompense, the ballet club performed *Divertissements* and *The Wager* at the club's annual meeting the following March (1941), and the press was even more enthusiastic than before. According to S. R. M. in *The Tribune*, Gweneth and

Betty had "revolutionized Winnipeg's conception of what an amateur group can achieve."

On hand for that performance was Adeline Genée, president of London's Royal Academy of Dancing. Then in her early sixties, and not to become a Dame of the British Empire for almost another decade, she was in town to conduct RAD examinations at Gweneth's school. It was not at all normal for Genée to do the examining, but she had been trapped in New York at the outbreak of the war, she on one side of the ocean and her panel of regular examiners on the other, and she was making the best of a bad job. Gweneth had to sit next to her and guide her discreetly through the procedure.

Genée had not danced professionally for more than 20 years, but she could still shame everyone in the studio with her technical control. Betty remembers her standing "in an absolutely perfect fifth position, flat, her legs straight, and then she picked her foot up and did a *developpé* right up the front, and her extension was right up there." One of the examination candidates was Paddy Stone. "She made him do a *couru* from the corner on half-*pointe*," says Betty, "and he looked at her and said, 'But I'm a boy, I don't have to do that.' And she said, 'You never know when you might have to teach it, go to the corner and do it,' and he did, and she passed him."

The club's second major presentation took place three months later, on June 6 and 7, 1941, with a 40-piece orchestra under Geoffrey Waddington. Patrons now included the new Lieutenant-Governor of Manitoba, R. F. McWilliams (merely following, of course, the precedent set by his predecessor, Tupper), the premier of Manitoba, and the mayor of Winnipeg. Sticking to her beer-and-skittles policies, Gweneth programmed three ballets that offered something for everyone—comedy *(Backstage 1897)*, novelty *(Triple Alliance)*, and *ballet blanc* or abstract classical ballet in which the female dancers wore the traditional white tulle tutu, or skirt *(Les Preludes)*.

Triple Alliance, which contrasted bar scenes in Canada, England, and the U.S., was "one of the funniest pieces of nonsense one has ever seen perpetrated in ballet," according to S. R. M. in *The Tribune*. "Altogether, it was the kind of show that tempts one to spill adjectives," said Frank Morriss in the *Free Press*, proceeding to succumb. "Triumphant is the word to describe the impression that the Winnipeg Ballet Club made on an audience that almost packed the Playhouse Theatre . . . it's a glowing example of what an amateur group can accomplish under the firm guidance of a professional."

Backstage 1897 ("a ballet pantomime") had choreography by Gweneth, with

Betty providing the scenario and Yeddeau the decor. The music was Glazunov's
Scènes de Ballet, and the work was one of those peep-behind-the-curtain affairs that appeal to anyone intrigued by the glamour of the theatre. Frank Morriss called it "a piquant affair . . . from the group of gay coryphées, like ethereal ponies in their prancing movements, through the bored stage-hands, the haughty ballerina, the coy maître de ballet, and the impetuous balletomanes, the performance was sparkling."

Les Preludes was the sop to the audience members who liked the white-ballet conventions of *Les Sylphides* and *Swan Lake* (the two ballets most used as a yardstick by commentators in those years—they were, after all, the only ballets most people had ever heard of). Danced to Liszt's symphonic poem, it followed "as nearly as possible" the program Liszt took as his inspiration for the work. A note that Gweneth must have written for the program-note writer (Yeddeau?) explains that the music was inspired by French poet Alphonse de Lamartine's statement that "the varied phases of life such as love, happiness, courage or glory are all a prelude to eternity," and she says "the ballet will portray the journey of man through life, and his reaction to the emotional incidents in which he becomes involved. A single individual [Paddy Stone] interweaves with groups representing Conflict, Happiness, and Strength; soloists representing Love and Courage are never far from his side." She adds, in a telling footnote: "I expect you saw *Présages*? The same type of thing, all very symbolic-cum-abstract-cum-Dali!!" (*Les Présages* was a much-imitated ballet by Léonide Massine to music of Tchaikovsky, depicting man's struggle with his destiny. It was first performed in the spring of 1933 in Monte Carlo and must have been performed in Winnipeg by the Ballet Russe in the late 1930s.)

Russell's set ("a vivid blue sky, full of stars and constellations" according to *The Tribune*'s S.R.M.) was "stunning," said Morriss. Russell himself always remembered the ballet with embarrassment—"the backdrop was a deep midnight blue on which were indicated the starry heavens cut diagonally by the milky way," he wrote in a 1950s reminiscence. "In the centre, a great nebula of greenish white dominated the heavens. Imagine my chagrin, on the opening night, to realize that this nebula looked for all the world like a great 'R'. . . . It was months before my friends ceased accusing me of blatant self-advertising."

Five days later, the *Free Press* editorial writer K.M.H. was back in action again. "The important, the exciting, the fascinating thing about the performance of the Winnipeg Ballet Club," he wrote, "is not that it has arrived —not that it has produced the Ballet Winnipeg, but that it is on its way. Last year produced a beginning so full of promise as to shock the audience into the trembling belief that a new art was being born on the prairies. This year's production adds faith and hope to that belief. It was more finished than last year's, more sure, less shy of ranging itself in the company of a great art. And it still holds to its heart the knowledge that ballet is a great art, and to aspire to it is to stand on the threshold of one of the loveliest kingdoms of the spirit of man."

This was marvellously flattering, of course, (it was also, we should remember, probably highly indulgent in the nicest possible way), but the realities of day-to-day life continued to press. Despite the "almost packed" house described by Morriss, the production again ran at a considerable loss. Gweneth's dream of building a company that could exist and support itself from box-office receipts alone was noble, but unrealistic. As the treasurer's report made clear, it was time to bring out the begging bowl again. A fall season had already been planned, but if money was not forthcoming in a hurry, it was likely that the company would no longer exist by the time fall came around. It was time for something more drastic than a bake sale. Gweneth went to the Richardsons.

1941-45 Growing Years

From the top of the Richardson Building, 30 floors above Lombard Place, at the heart of the city, you can see Winnipeg's perimeter, and the green, flat lands beyond. What vantage point could be more appropriate? The Richardsons—grain people, financiers, politicians—have been a significant force in Winnipeg's growth since the descendants of grain merchant James Richardson from Kingston, Ontario, opened up shop at the turn of the century.

Grain was the foundation of the family fortunes, but it was James A. Richardson, nephew of the original James, who expanded the enterprise into the massive empire of retail stocks and investments, grain elevators, feed, fertilizer, insurance, oil and gas pipeline construction, accounting systems, land-clearing equipment, road-building, shipping, cattle-breeding, oil exploration, and real estate.

When James A. Richardson died in 1939, his wife, Muriel Sprague Richardson, took over as president, and ran the entire organization brilliantly, until 1966, when the appointment of her son James A. as chairman and her son George T. as president was announced simultaneously. The Richardson family fortune has been estimated at not much short of $500 million, and it rests, via family trusts, on the four children—James, George, Kathleen, and Agnes.

Muriel Sprague Richardson arrived in Winnipeg as a bride in 1919. It would be wrong to suggest that she immediately turned the Richardson family into prairie Medicis—it would be misleading, indeed, to suggest that that is what the family   35

Viola Busday and Bill McGrath in Finishing School, *choreographed in 1942.*

has become—but her involvement in the world of the fine and performing arts in the city grew steadily. She became an indefatigable worker for the theatre, the art gallery and, eventually and most significantly, for the ballet.

Attitudes to the well-provided-for are always mixed in the impoverished arts. Cynics might suggest that the family's involvement in charitable work in the city is merely a manifestation of rich-man's guilt; others will call it a businessman's investment in the future, a purchasing of long-term goodwill; still others might see it as dabbling of the most pernicious kind, bored socialites playing games.

In other cities and other circumstances, any of these allegations might hold truth; one has only to look at the erratic history of the Harkness Ballet, for instance, to see the dangers inherent in chequebook manipulation of the arts. But in Winnipeg it is generally agreed that the Richardsons have "done well by" the ballet. From the beginnings, they have always quietly enabled it to continue— "whenever the ballet gets in a deep financial hole," someone connected with the company once told me, "the Richardson family bails us out."

Their financial involvement has not been as large as is popularly supposed in Winnipeg, and is certainly nothing like the $3 million-plus that U.S. writer, critic and department store heir Lincoln Kirstein is reliably said to have put into the company he co-founded with George Balanchine, the New York City Ballet (though the NYCB's budget, of course, is four or five times larger than the RWB's). But it has, equally certainly, been consistent, and has often made a crucial, life-saving difference. The regular grants and donations come today from various sources—Kamarin Investments, a holding company for Kathleen Richardson's personal investments, the Mrs. James A. Richardson foundation, the Richardson group of companies, and family individuals. But, in addition, there have always been quiet gifts in times of pressing need, help in the form of hospitality, and, occasionally, the discreet paying-off of individuals who have in one way or another become a burden to the organization.

But the Richardson involvement with the RWB has always been more than financial, just as Kirstein's has been with the NYCB. From the start, they have given encouragement and guidance and artistic advice—first Mrs. Richardson, in her early involvement with Gweneth and Betty, and, since 1955, her daughter Kathleen. Kathleen Richardson served a brief tour of duty as president, a position she has retained in an honorary capacity ever since, and she has been for two decades an active member of the company's production committee (the artistic decision-making arm). Today, she is probably as influential in the company's overall direction as any other single individual. She sees the company as "part of

what makes Winnipeg," and she sees her role in its continuance and development
almost as a duty. It is the old-fashioned principle of patronage—recognizing
something worth preserving, and having the time and money to do something
about it.

Both she and her mother have kept the family's giving discreet—neither have
wanted the company to become known in any way as the "Richardson ballet"—
and she is modest today about the financial support she gives. "It just seems that
the ballet, if it needs something, it steps around, or else sometimes I think of it first,
and it works out very well."

When Gweneth "stepped around" to the Richardsons' big old house on Wellington Crescent in the aftermath of the June, 1941, disaster, she was in desperate straits. Without money, the company would be unable to continue. Yet collapse would be unthinkable. The company had come so far, so fast. . . .

Mrs. Muriel Richardson was sympathetic, understanding. She had seen the company's performances, she had bought charter memberships the previous season for herself and two of her children (Kathleen and George), she was entirely convinced of the worth and the civilizing effect of the things Gweneth and Betty were trying to do. Perhaps she made a discreet suggestion or two regarding the company's future plans, possibly she hinted at means of cutting costs while maintaining quality, she may even have suggested other homes on the crescent to go to for help. What is certain, however, is that she personally undertook to take care of at least part of the debt the company had incurred. Mrs. Richardson was not the only monied and influential citizen Gweneth and Lady Tupper called upon. But her gift was an example, and others followed it.

Yet another editorial appeared in the *Free Press*, extolling the virtues of the company and making strong arguments for the perpetuation of ballet as a force for social improvement.

Plans for a fall season went ahead—modified, sensible, cost-cutting plans: a smaller theatre (the Dominion, on which site the Richardson tower now stands), only one new ballet, and no orchestra, which meant ticket prices could be reduced.

For the first time, the company offered different programs on consecutive nights in what was, with the exception of the new ballet, a company retrospective. The new work, set to extracts from William Walton's Façade suites, was described in the program as "a satirical ballet based on superficial nonsense in seven divertissements."

Walton's controversial and highly successful Façade, a setting of 16 poems by the abstractionist Edith Sitwell, had first appeared in 1922 as a "melodrama for reciting voice and seven instruments." Later, Walton revised and expanded the score and eventually published two separate suites from the complete work. Gweneth was by no means the first to make a ballet to this music—Frederick

Façade Suite

Ashton's, for instance, was premièred for the Camargo Society in London in 1931—but she made a point of making her own selection of music from the suites, shuffled to suit her own purposes. Her ballet was intended as a satire on the various social dances of the day and the characters included Scottish maids, Gibson girls, gentlemen "mashers,"a shepherdess, two lambs, and a cow. One writer who witnessed a dress rehearsal for the October show described the ballet as "allusive and sarcastic, witty and colourful . . . these parodies are seminal, they sprout ideas (and chuckles) like a lilac bush sprouts suckers. The perfume is, unquestionably, *lilac sec*—harsh and dry. I thought the Gibson girls were almost cruel, for the Gibson girl was queen when I was young."

Every ticket was sold for both performances (would-be audience members were actually turned away at the door) and when the accountant's reckoning was complete the club was able to declare its first financial surplus. It was a cheerful start to the third season, and many believed it signified the end of the company's troubles.

The Ballet Russe de Monte Carlo played two nights at the Walker Theatre the following January. The visit is significant as something of a turning point in two careers.

Paddy Stone, by now dancing principal roles for the Winnipeg group, auditioned for Léonide Massine, the artist director of the Ballet Russe, and was engaged to dance two small roles with the company during its Winnipeg stay. He particularly impressed Massine with his work in a duet with Tanya Orlova, Massine's wife, in a ballet called *The New Yorker*—so impressed him, in fact, that later that year, when Massine switched form the Ballet Russe to the recently formed Ballet Theatre (later to become American Ballet Theatre) he recommended that Stone be hired for the company.

In the audience the night the Ballet Russe performed *The New Yorker* was a tall, nervous young Winnipegger named Arnold Spohr. He was an athlete, a keen basketball player, and a musician, but no ballet fan. He had never seen a ballet company in his life.

"I was dragged there by my sister, Erica. She cried for two hours about wanting to go, so I went, to please her. I saw the show and I was in another world. I didn't know what had happened to me. We were way back, but it was magic." Two years were to elapse, however, before Spohr followed up on that first intimation of his future.

Jean McKenzie goes Through the Looking Glass *as Alice. Pat Litchfield (left) is Tiger Lily.*

The next major presentation, the following March (1942), was again given at reduced prices to recorded music (there would be no more live orchestra until 1948). New works included a children's ballet, *Queen of Hearts*, an adaptation of the Alice story, titled *Through the Looking Glass* (later known simply as *Alice*), and *Ballet Blanc*, a further set of *divertissements* to music of Arensky.

Through the Looking Glass was nine little scenelets from Lewis Carroll's tale, to music of Deems Taylor. Jeanne McKenzie (she stuck the extra letters on the end of her first name in those years apparently to add distinction) was Alice, Paddy Stone was the White Knight, and two dozen others impersonated canterbury bells, chattering daisies, slithy toves and the rest of the population of Alice's improbable world. The slithy toves, wearing bodysuits and pointed headgear, did a lot of weaving about with their arms, palms pressed together above their heads in Oriental prayer style. The daisies wore feathery ruffs to signify petals; the canterbury bells wore bells on their heads.

Queen of Hearts, in part a vehicle to display the talents of the junior members of the club, was seen in a pre-performance première by the loyal members of the Women's Musical Club, and one of those singled out by *The Tribune*'s S.R.M. for special praise was David Adams, playing the knave—"in a difficult role for a little boy, (he) was most realistic and proved a fine actor." This was not Adams's first stage appearance—he had been seen in *Triple Alliance* the previous June—but the review seems to have been the first written notice of his career as a dancer. He was 13.

The club had become very much a happy-families situation in a way that has never been duplicated since. People volunteered to help because they enjoyed being part of what was going on. For the dancers, unpaid and for the most part unsung, it was a time of total dedication.

"Today," says Yeddeau, "you couldn't buy that experience, it was so marvellous. But then, we had no sense of the future—we were simply doing shows to entertain the public. We were a big success, you see—we'd finish one show and immediately start work on the next. The ballet was our life."

David Yeddeau as he looked in the 1940s.

Officially, Yeddeau was listed in the program as the stage manager; unofficially, he was taking over publicity, program design, scenario-writing, costume and scenic design. He found himself an office area at the studio, and soon he was spending at least part of each day there, a kind of unpaid jack-of-all-trades manager. He was exactly what Gweneth and Betty needed at that time—a thoroughly practised expert in theatrical arts.

Programming decisions were made by the three of them in consultation, Spohr's "Holy Trinity." The way Yeddeau describes it, "it was a combination of Gweneth's high musical taste, me pulling her down slightly, and Betty's good judgment. Gweneth was Bach and Mozart and Beethoven. I am Puccini and Tchaikovsky and Rachmaninov. My point was that Winnipeg didn't know too much about ballet, and while there is always a group who travel in the Mozart-Beethoven class, the general mass—the people we were trying to get to the theatre—they needed something my style. We were always able to work it out. We all knew when a thing was right. Gweneth contributed the choreography, Betty was invaluable for getting them into shape and making them work, and I staged them."

Whenever a new ballet was needed, Gweneth would sift through her music, choose something suitable, and then sit down and make the ballet. "She churned them out like sausages, really," says Betty. Unlike many choreographers, who like to work out their ideas with the dancers on the studio floor, Gweneth always came to the studio fully prepared. She created according to an unvarying routine. As soon as she had conceived her idea for the ballet, she would get hold of the music—either a score or a recording—and write the ballet out, move by move, in science notebooks, lined paper on one side, blank paper on the other. On the lined page, she wrote a verbal description in longhand of what was to occur, marked off bar by bar according to the music, and on the other page she drew pictures of little lettered stick-men with swirls and lines to indicate the directions in which they were to move. Then she went to the studio, selected the dancers, gave them letters according to her designs, and laid the ballet out.

Her favourite place to compose was in bed, listening to the music over and over again, and scribbling her directions and drawings in the books. Once, when a new ballet was needed in an emergency during a company tour, she was locked in the lavatory of the train on which the company was travelling and was not allowed out until the ballet was complete. They gave her a windup gramophone to work with and checked every hour or so to see how she was progressing.

Gweneth never remembered the details of her work—"it took her a long time to get the things written out," says Betty, "but then, when it was finished, that was it. It was blotted. She didn't remember anything about it any more, and I suppose that was how she was able to go on making them. That was why I always learned the ballets, so that someone would know them properly."

More and more, in fact, Betty was moving into the role of ballet mistress. She was an enthusiastic teacher and coach, and a fearsome disciplinarian. She had never been a great dancer—she had started too late in her career (the familiar RWB complaint) and her legs were too short and sturdy for the elegances of classical ballet. But her lively, volatile nature equipped her well for character roles.

"They were a marvellous team," says Marilyn Young, then a student and later to become a principal dancer with the company, "Betty was the one who yelled and screamed at you—she got all the beats right and all the heads turning at the same time and all the feet doing exactly the same thing—and then Gweneth would come in for a run-through, and Gweneth was the one who could make you *dance*."

Betty also served as a kind of den mother. She advised her kiddies on their diets, she gave them sage advice when they were in love trouble, she helped them find lodgings or part-time jobs, she nursed them if they were sick. The club was a family, and no one personified that more than Betty.

Her vitality and gregariousness made her a popular young woman. In the early 1940s she fell in love with one of the Royal Air Force officers sent to Canada to assist in training pilots for the Royal Canadian Air Force. Flight Lieutenant John Farrally proposed, they were married in 1943, and in 1944 Betty gave birth to their son, Richard Blaise. She continued to dance several months into her pregnancy—so far, in fact, that her role as one of the foolish girls in a performance of the ballet *The Wise Virgins* seemed to be given an altogether unexpected significance—but around the end of 1943 she moved away from Winnipeg to be with her husband, first in Carberry, about 100 miles west of the city, and then at the air base in Vulcan, Alberta. But life as a flying instructor's wife bored her, and when John was posted to Greenwood, Nova Scotia, she went back to Winnipeg to teach and dance. It is a measure of Gweneth's dependence on Betty's organizational drive that the company's performing activities had been largely suspended in her absence.

Not long after Betty's return to Winnipeg, her husband was posted back to Europe to fly the famous Mosquito fighter plane. In the course of one hedge-hopping operation his aircraft was badly hit, and he was ordered to put down in British-occupied territories in northern France. His plane collided on landing with a fire-truck sent out to stand by for a crash landing. There were no survivors. The son, Richard, was 10 months old.

The story of the evolution of *The Wise Virgins*, an abstract interpretation of the New Testament parable, illustrates the way the company worked at that time. Gweneth, Betty, Yeddeau, and Russell spent an evening in the fall of 1942 listening to the music Gweneth had chosen for her new ballet—an arrangement of Bach chorales by William Walton—and out of a chance remark by Yeddeau ("Can't you just see them coming over the brow of a hill and winding down among tall cypress trees?") came the idea for the set: a hillside surmounted by cypresses, Winnipeg's first experience of a raked (slanting) stage. Costumes

Dale Clark and Paddy Stone (standing, centre) as Spiritual Apotheoses in The Wise Virgins. *Betty Farrally, four months pregnant, is the second prostrate figure from the right.*

and lighting—a cool, clear, blue-green moonlight—were designed to empha-
size the mood. "Perfection in balance of form and force is the fitting apotheosis of
the human desire for a long-awaited spiritual visitation" said the program note.
In Yeddeau's view this was Gweneth's best ballet ever, though it was by no
means the most popular.

It was introduced in November, 1942, on the same program as *Finishing
School*, a one-act comedy. *Finishing School* stayed in the active repertoire, by
public demand, for close to a decade. The scenario for this simple tale of high
jinks in the Paris of 1870 was credited to "Josephine Blowe"—Betty's pseud-
onym whenever it seemed her name might be appearing in a program too
often.

Working hard on those November nights was David Adams. He was not quite
14, and you can see him in the background of a 1942 souvenir-program picture
of the junior club at class. At centre is Gweneth at her most English,
straightening the foot of a young girl valiantly trying to hold an *arabesque*.
Leaning against the *barre*, an expression of bored seriousness on his face, is
Adams, the very image of crewcut pre-teen nonchalance. He was small, but
Gweneth used that to advantage, re-choreographing a role in the English pub
sequence of *Triple Alliance* to accommodate him (a Bookmaker was
transformed to a Jockey). He was game for anything they could throw at
him.

In mid November, Paddy Stone received a cable from Ballet Theatre, asking
him to report to the company in Detroit. He was 19, and eager. He said his
goodbyes. But when he reached Detroit, he found himself without a job. Massine
had been going around the country promising work to dancers the company
didn't want. Sadder but wiser, he returned to Winnipeg.

On the weekend of May 7 and 8, 1943, the Winnipeg Ballet (the word "club"
had now been eliminated) offered its ninth major production. There were two
new works—*Russalki*, a folksy piece about jolly Russian peasants joined in
their Whitsuntide celebrations by golden-haired wood nymphs (a disaster), and
Etude, the newest *ballet blanc*, to music of Chopin (received with raptures—"a
peak in the company's bright career").

Again the editorials rhapsodized: "The Winnipeg Ballet is an outstanding
artistic achievement . . . an achievement for all of Canada . . . on its shining
way to greatness." But not everyone reads the editorial pages, and Yeddeau was
smart enough to plant a series of pop-journalism picture features for the more
general reader. "Constant training in turning out the knee gives all the girls a

Betty Farrally (left), Paddy Stone, and Jean McKenzie in An American in Paris.

curious duck-like walk," one picture caption asserted. Under a picture of two male dancers looking particularly effeminate ran the warning: "They may wear hair-nets, but the men are rugged athletes. Never risk calling one a pantywaist."

The fall of 1943 featured the première of Paddy Stone's choreographic debut, *Zigeuner*, a story-ballet about gypsies to music of Kodaly. "A vivid sense of colourful movement," said Morriss, though Stone "does need a restraining hand at times when he is apt to be more Minsky than Massine." The comment might have been a prophecy for Stone's future.

Other new works that fall were Gweneth's comedy, *An American in Paris*, and her setting of part of Holst's suite, *The Planets*. Both were designed by Russell. The backdrop for *An American in Paris* was a striking panorama of Paris as if seen from the air. Part of the design was a poster for the Folies Bergères, and sharp-eyed members of the audience might have spotted something odd about the chorus-line—they had ten legs in the air and only nine on the ground.

The Holst work was another semi-mystical piece featuring such characters as The Will to Survive, Tranquillity and Tragedy. Its main interest today lies in the

fact that it was the first ballet in which Arnold Spohr ever danced. Three months
earlier, he had been taken to Gweneth and Betty's studio (by his brother this
time) to learn social dancing. His background in music and athletics gave him an
ideal base on which to build, and he took to dancing right away. "They needed
boys and before I knew it I was involved with the company. I never did do much
ballroom, but I got into the ballet in my first three months. Because they were
short of boys you really had a chance—and you progressed quickly, out of
necessity." His first stage appearance was as a member of the corps in *The
Planets*. He wore green tights and he remembers putting up his fist to signify
strength. His next was in *Zigeuner*—"I lifted one girl in that, and learned my
partnering very quickly and well . . . she was 138 pounds."

Late in 1944, after a year of consolidation and retrenchment, the company
announced its first "tour"—two performances at the Ottawa Technical School
auditorium in February, 1945, as part of a "celebrity series" sponsored by the
Civil Servants' Recreational Association. This was a significant move. No
western ballet company had ever ventured east before (there had never been a
western ballet company to try). The capital loved them.

"Out of the west rode the Winnipeg Ballet, to lasso the hearts of Ottawa
balletomanes and the public at large," wrote W. B. Gladstone, in a special
report to the *Free Press*. "Something beautiful, sincere, and genuinely artistic
has come out of the west to delight lovers of the aesthetic in the capital city," said
Isabel C. Armstrong, in the Ottawa *Citizen*. And a *Citizen* editorial suggested:
"Perhaps this visit can be taken as a good omen for the future, when Canada shall
receive encouragement in the arts as a national policy stemming from the
dominion government."

Both performances were sold out—itself a novel experience for the series
presenters. In the audience were capital-city notables of the usual sort
—foreign ambassadors, the nation's chief justice, highly positioned civil
servants—and everyone gushed. "Marvellous!" exclaimed L. Arvardo, a
diplomat from Peru, his eyes no doubt gleaming with Latin enthusiasm. "I
believe they are even better than the Volkoff Canadian Ballet of Toronto. The
girls have much better figures and are so neat." Boris Volkoff himself made the
trip from Toronto to Ottawa specially to see the company. His verdict:
"Winnipeg can be proud of its talent." He said he thought the company's
reputation would spread Winnipeg's name far—and in that, he was not far
wrong. Just a decade or so premature.

1945-49 Stepping Out

"The thing about the ballet was that it was fun," says David Yeddeau. "That was why we did it. For people who thought ballet was all white tutus."

This was one of the happiest periods in the company's history. Winnipeggers looked upon it warmly, but national success had not yet arrived; inevitably, success was to sour the atmosphere—bickerings, power plays, and outright fights, all the concomitants of small-time, small-town arts-organization growth, would change for good the family feel. There would be other times of innocence, but there would never again be quite the freedom and spontaneity, the gaiety, that was felt during those immediate postwar years. There was no money to fight over; there was no power to speak of, apart from Gweneth's, and her word was the unquestioned law; there was no real prestige to gain. The dancers—by now about two dozen of them—danced for the love of it, and it showed; they were caught up in the sheer, glamorous pleasure of it all. Arnold was always too long to fit the sleeping-car bunks: what a laugh. The auditorium floor in Saskatchewan turned out to be mud: what a lark. In Alberta your make-up froze: what a joke.

"We were like the early crusaders," says Spohr. "We moved on against whatever obstacles—famine or feast . . . mostly famine. Cecil B. de Mille couldn't have done better with his major epics. But he at least made money."

You danced no matter how you felt; you never expected not to dance. The pressure weeded the weak ones out, and created a strong rapport among those who remained. Many of the dancers from those early years have stayed close friends, and several are still involved with the company: Jean McKenzie is now director of 49

Arnold Spohr (left), Betty Farrally, and David Adams in Kaleidoscope.

the company school; Viola Busday teaches alongside her; Marilyn Young is on the company board and an active member of the production committee.

Viola was a Winnipeg Ballet girl from the beginning. She saw Through the Looking Glass *as a child, and it left her awestruck. Years later, as a junior member of the company, she danced the ballet's lead role, Alice. She was one of the original "mooky dooks," as Betty dubbed the first team of* Swan Lake *cygnets; she was David Adams' first* Bluebird *partner. Her husband, Dave Robertson, now a television producer with CBC Winnipeg, remembers spending whole evenings— evenings when he had booked a* date—*leafing through the magazines and books in the studio waiting room, waiting for the rehearsals to end. They never did. Not in time.*

Marilyn Young took ballet lessons because "I had these long, gangly legs I didn't know what to do with." Almost immediately, the child was dancing —as a Lamb in Façade—*and she remembers standing, open-mouthed, in the wings, watching Jean McKenzie in* Chapter 13—*"she was the most gorgeous thing I'd ever seen on the stage . . . and I wanted to be one of the gum-chewing babes in the chorus, with padded sweaters and their hair in nets. I thought they were super." By the time she was 15, Marilyn was touring with the company. There is a picture of her in her early teens—slim legs going on for ever, and a kind of innocent knowingness about the face. No wonder the stagehands bought her meals when she wept at losing 75 cents playing poker on the long, touring train rides.*

Well, 75 cents was important. There was still no money, and wouldn't be for some years. Everyone did what they could to survive. Spohr supported himself with a daytime job teaching piano; evenings and weekends went to class and rehearsal. He was all skin and bones and hollow face, but it taught him stamina. "I'd teach all day, then we'd rehearse all night, and because Gweneth was always a procrastinator she'd do all her choreography the two or three days before a show, and those times we'd be working until 2:30 or 3:00 in the morning, and we got the grand prize of Chinese food brought in."

These were the days before the board was constituted, and none of the non-dancer volunteers thought twice about pitching in. The woman who was to become Marilyn Young's mother-in-law would turn up at the studio to sew sequins. Schoolteacher Aileen Garland, later to become the first chairman of the ballet's women's committee, used to sell programs at the performances, wandering up and down the aisles, smiling bravely and trying to make it look as if the theatre was filling.

It was an innocent, carefree time, though inevitably the company settled into something approaching a formal structure. By 1948, Gweneth was officially known as director, Betty was ballet mistress, and Yeddeau, whose duties included stage direction and some set design, had the catch-all title of manager. The term artistic director was taken literally and bestowed on two designers: John Russell, who had been with the group from the start, and Dorothy Phillips, whose first designs for the company were for The Queen of Hearts and Finishing School in 1942.

From its first full year of operation, the group had regarded its "season" as running from fall to spring, in line with standard performing-arts company practice. Initially, two main sets of performances were given in each season —one in the fall and one in the spring—with a scattering of additional single performances, generally "benefits" for groups such as the Women's Musical Club (by now a significant supporter of the ballet) and the Chinese War Relief fund. By 1945 the pattern was changing as the company took its first tentative touring steps, and two years later the Winnipeg appearances were extended to three sets of performances a season—fall, late winter and early spring.

With the exception of Paddy Stone's Zigeuner in 1943, all the ballets danced by the company in its first decade were created by Gweneth. She had a clear-eyed understanding of her audience's need for novelty (at her peak she was turning out ballets at the rate of four or five a year) and she had a creative facility that allowed her to choreograph in many styles—comic, abstract-modern, narrative. She also knew her own limitations. As a sop to the fans of the romantic nineteenth-century style of ballet, and in the interests of balanced programming, she regularly produced ballets in the classic style (Divertissements, Les Coryphées, and Etude are three examples), but attempts at actual, familiar classics did not begin to appear in the repertoire until David Adams' return from London in 1948. Today, many of Gweneth's ballets would no doubt be considered naïve creations, probably quite clumsy in their symbolism and "modernity." But in their time they were exactly what the company (and Winnipeg) needed. They made the dancers look good, they made no extreme technical demands, and they were—for their audiences—marvellously entertaining. This knit-to-fit tradition became a major factor in the company's continuing existence.

The Ottawa trip cost $3,600. The fee the company received was $1,200. The difference was covered by pre-tour benefit performances—"It was really Winnipeg who paid us to go and entertain Ottawa," Gweneth told an interviewer that spring, "but that can't go on. Winnipeg has a right to see new ballets, but a new ballet costs about $2,200. Private enterprise on that scale is an awful headache." It was time, she said, for state support, and the creation in Canada of a National Ballet. Though she never voiced her hopes in print, it was plain on whose company she thought a National Ballet should be founded.

Encouraged by the success of its first venture out of town, the company headed west in November of 1945—to Regina, Saskatoon, and Edmonton. The reception was warm.

Three new works were officially unveiled during the Winnipeg Christmas season: *Les Coryphées*, to Tchaikovsky, inspired by the paintings of Degas, *Kaleidoscope*, a colourful melange of European national dances (both of these had been previewed on the western tour), and the controversial *Dionysos*, Gweneth's idea of a bacchanalian orgy. Maenads and satyrs danced with the thyrsus, the symbol of fertility, and Robert Bruce's backdrop was dominated by a giant nude female form. The wife of the Lieutenant-Governor sat through the ballet's opening minutes, then stormed from the theatre. "I only hope," she cried as she departed, "that these girls don't understand what they're doing." "It was a real hornet's nest," says Betty gleefully. "I sometimes think we were terribly ahead of our time."

Paddy Stone left again at the turn of the year. He had flown to New York from Ottawa for auditions with Frederic Franklin, then ballet master of the Ballet Russe, and with George Balanchine, who was at that time working in musicals.

He had been well received, and the encouragement had given him itchy feet. How much more progress, after all, could be made in Winnipeg? In January of 1946 he went to New York, and by May had landed a job in a Broadway production of *Annie Get Your Gun*, with Ethel Merman. He was spotted during the run of the show by an agent for the Sadler's Wells Theatre Ballet in London, and was offered a 42-week contract. He left for London that fall, stopping off in Winnipeg for two "farewell performances." His work would not be seen on Winnipeg stages again for a decade.

With Stone gone, major recasting was necessary. David Adams, now 17, took over some roles, though Adams himself was to leave for London that summer, first to study at Sadler's Wells and then to dance with a variety of companies. And Arnold Spohr took over as Dionysos. "I became a real star due to absolute necessity," he says. "There was nobody else." Technically, he was less than excellent. He was another who had started too late. But he was a versatile dancer

Sheila Killough (left), Eileen Hyman, and Viola Busday in Les Coryphées.

Paddy Stone (centre) is Dionysos. Lillian Lewis, Margaret Hample, and Dale Clark (standing left to right) are maidens.

Pleasure Cruise. *(Harold K. White Studio)*

and an excellent partner, and he could always cover up. "He always *looked* so grand," says Betty, "and no one noticed what his feet were doing."

Betty (now known as Betty Hey-Farrally) had also announced her intention to retire from performance. And Frank Morriss, who dropped in to watch rehearsals, commented in his "Here, There and Hollywood" column in April, 1946: "I hope she changes her mind. Betty's gift for comedy has been one of the company's strong points." (In fact, she continued to dance selected roles until 1949.)

Morriss added: "I was extremely pleased and flattered to have the boat in the new ballet, *Pleasure Cruise*, christened S. S. Penelope after my little daughter. Thanks for the honour, ballet people, and thanks for a very interesting afternoon." (That kind of folksy friendliness characterized those years. When Morriss's abilities as a critic came under attack in the columns of the *Free Press*, Gweneth and Yeddeau wrote to defend him: "Many times Mr. Morriss has given us more than a rough idea of what he thought about our shows, but each panning has caused us to pull up our socks and vow that next time we'd make him eat his words. We honestly feel much indebted to F.A.M. for helping us raise our standard of production.")

Pleasure Cruise was first seen in May, 1946, and Morriss called it a "lightly rowdy frolic . . . a wow of a show." Maley, in *The Tribune*, agreed: "A

tremendous hit . . . escapist entertainment of the most rib-tickling sort."
Danced to music of Ibert, the ballet depicted the antics of a group of holiday-makers taking the ocean air on a cruise ship in the 1890s. To underline the effect of being on a ship at sea, designer Dennis Carter arranged to have another "ship" pass, far out on the horizon. The dancers were to lean out from the "deck," hands shading eyes, to watch its progress. The effect was achieved simply enough—Carter walked across the back of the set, behind the "ocean," holding the passing ship on a stick above his head, bobbing it along above the painted waves. At the third performance, Carter's assistant handled this task. Unfortunately, he tripped on a sandbag and the distant vessel seemed to sink abruptly. Eventually it popped up at centre-stage and bobbed and rippled across to its appointed exit—so fast that the scanners never had a chance to catch up with it.

In the summer of 1946, the long association between the company and the Banff Centre School of Fine Arts began. Gweneth and Vancouver teacher Mara McBirney were invited to Banff, Alberta, to advise on the make-up of the dance component in the school's theatre division. It was decided that a course in the

Betty Farrally (crouching left) and Gweneth Lloyd with students at the Banff Centre summer school in the late 1950s.

technique of the Royal Academy of Dancing would be introduced the following year by one of the Winnipeg Ballet's teachers and principal dancers, Joan Stirling. Jean McKenzie taught at Banff in 1948, and in 1949 Gweneth herself took over. First as teacher, later as head of the dance division, she was to spend the next 20 summers there.

And still Gweneth's ballets poured out. In March, 1947, Winnipeg saw the première performances of three new works: *Object Matrimony* (based on Jane Austen's *Pride and Prejudice*, to music of Schubert), *Arabesque* (a traditional *grand divertissement* built to display the technique of principals Lillian Lewis, Arnold Spohr, and Jean McKenzie), and *Concerto*, to Rachmaninov's second piano concerto.

"The deep surge of rhythm reveals the concerto as fluctuating patterns of swirling motion and colour," said the program note for the Rachmaninov work. "Sombre emotions sweep in purple vortices shot with threads of crimson and tinged with fierce violet and fleeting lilac." According to Viola Robertson (then Viola Busday, and a performer in the piece) it was "Greek movement in *pointe* shoes." Gweneth claims now that it is her favourite of all the ballets she

Arabesque I.

choreographed, but David Yeddeau says that was not always so. In fact, he says, it took him considerable persuasion before she would consent to make the ballet at all: "LP records were just beginning at that time, and I discovered a recording of the Rachmaninov—just my dish, romantic, emotional, all the corny things. I took it down to the beach, where Gweneth was holidaying, and I played it to her, and she said "Never" and I asked her to listen to it again, and Betty liked it, so we were two against one, and she gave in and did it."

The costumes and backdrop had an equally fortuitous origin. Since the costume budget was non-existent, it was decided to re-dye the costumes from an early ballet (*Kilowatt Magic*, thinks Yeddeau). "They were some ghastly green colour, so we had the colour taken out of them, but it didn't come out completely, so I told the dyer to use the colour that would take most—purple—and it came out in three shades, lilac, violet and deep. And we did one in red, for contrast." There was no money for a new backdrop, either, so Yeddeau took an old one and turned it around. "It had seams on the back and looked terrible, but I got it up on the paint-frame and started to paint it—a kind of twilight blue, to show off these costumes. It was wintertime, and I couldn't get anyone to help paint. And it was after midnight, because I couldn't get into the theatre until then. And at midnight they turned the heat off, so it was freezing—so cold I had to paint with gloves on. And after the first night Gweneth saw the painting I'd done and didn't like it, so the next night I thought I'd better paint it more her colour, so I put more water in. . . . Then I was getting madder and madder because I was freezing and nobody was helping me and I thought, what the hell, *I'm* doing the set, to hell with her, and I mixed the paint up again, and I was getting a marvellous streaky backdrop—and of course it was ghastly, it was dreadful, I was so ashamed of it . . . but you know, when we lit it a certain way, all in blue, the light created the most fantastic sense of perspective through all these damned changes of mood and temperament I'd gone through. It was such a success that she now claims it as her favourite ballet."

In March, 1947, the company was invited to take part in a UNESCO-sponsored international choreographic competition in Copenhagen to be held the following June. A campaign was launched to raise the $36,000 needed to finance the trip. All levels of government were steadfastly unhelpful. When a request for a $5,000 contribution came before the city council finance committee, Alderman S. E. Graham, with all the subtlety and insight that was to characterize the council's attitude to the ballet company for many years, commented: "With Europe in the condition it is today, I can't see spending

$36,000 to go over to Denmark and do a little dancing." The troupe tried to raise the funds privately, but by the end of May, just days away from their departure date, they had reached only two-thirds of their target amount, and Yeddeau announced that the trip had been cancelled. All the money that had been raised was handed back, and Yeddeau went to Toronto for the summer "to recuperate."

In Toronto, he met Boris Volkoff, whose company had also been unable to raise sufficient funds to go to Copenhagen. It was an encounter that was to have an enormous influence on grassroots North American dance. From it can be traced the development, nearly a decade later, of the entire U.S. regional dance festival movement. "It suddenly occurred to me," Yeddeau recalls, "that these people in Toronto were doing the same sort of thing we were doing in Winnipeg, but neither of us had any knowledge of each other. Why not get together and share this—and perhaps help to consolidate an audience for ballet? And why not invite other companies as well?"

There were not, as it turned out, many other companies to invite. Yeddeau wrote to what he recalls as "over one hundred" ballet schools across Canada, outlining the festival plans and asking if they had companies. He received three replies: one from Ruth Sorel, who taught Mary Wigman style and ran a company in Montreal; one from a Montreal man who said, yes, he had a company but it was so bad he wouldn't even allow it to appear in Montreal, let alone Winnipeg; and one from some people in Vancouver. Small pickings, perhaps, but enough for a start. Yeddeau set about organizing.

The First Canadian Ballet Festival was booked for the Playhouse Theatre, Winnipeg, for the weekend of April 29-May 1, 1948. Four companies—the Winnipeg Ballet, Ruth Sorel's modern dance group, the Boris Volkoff Canadian Ballet and Vancouver's Ballet Society—were scheduled to perform (with the Winnipeg hosts paying travel costs and arranging billets). Madge Tupper pulled strings and secured the presence of the Governor-General of Canada and his wife, Viscount and Viscountess Alexander of Tunis. Gweneth bought a new gown. Yeddeau had a new dinner jacket made.

But with only 72 hours to go before the scheduled Thursday-night opening, calamity struck. The swollen Red River, which had been threatening the city for days, rose and flooded the downtown area. One of the stricken buildings was the Playhouse. The only possible alternative location was the old Walker Theatre, which had by now been converted into an Odeon movie house. Manager Henry Morton was willing to make the Odeon available for two days—the Friday and

Saturday—but the $1,500 price was far in excess of the nominal rent they had expected to pay at the Playhouse.

Reluctantly, Yeddeau and Gweneth decided that the Vancouver group's participation would have to be cancelled so that the money committed for the 20 Vancouver performers' travel expenses could be freed. The Vancouver dancers were devastated. A 30-minute work titled *Masquerade Ball* had been prepared for the occasion, and hopes and excitement were high. "You've never seen such tears," said Kay Armstrong, the work's choreographer.

In Winnipeg, meanwhile, the troubles had barely begun. Ticketing for the performances became a major headache. The festival had already come close to a sell-out situation before the floods came. A total of 3,000 tickets had to be returned to the box office, renumbered and reissued. Police had to be called out to supervise the crowds, and since the 1,155-seat Odeon held 310 seats less than the Playhouse, several hundred disgruntled individuals had to settle for refunds. As the crowds milled at the box office, dancers and theatre staff were busy inside the Odeon cutting up calendars and sticking the numerals onto the backs of the numberless seats.

Setback followed setback. When Yeddeau and his technical crew moved into the theatre late that Thursday evening to prepare their equipment for the Friday opening, they discovered that the stage was unusable. The last live act to perform there had been a circus, and the elephants had wrecked the surface. Shortly before midnight, John Russell made panic calls for deliveries from lumber suppliers, and he and a stage crew spent all Thursday night laying a new beaverboard floor.

The visitors from the east arrived hours late due to the prairie floods, and when they reached the studios all turned to chaos. The heating system was not functioning, thanks to the flooding, so Boris Volkoff took it into his head to teach a warm-up class for the assembled companies. Photographers and reporters were doing what seemed like a constant round of interviews. A Sorel dancer, Leo Ciceri, suddenly disappeared in the direction of the University of Manitoba, where he had arranged to write his fourth-year arts exams for McGill University. And Ruth Sorel herself—"a tall, *soignée* lady, blonde, with a big black hat, and a bunch of dead flowers on her chest," according to Yeddeau—made imperious trouble over the fact that her company's name was printed one size smaller than the others on the newspaper advertisements (though she backed down when Yeddeau hinted menacingly that he could get her on the next train out of town if she really wanted to withdraw). Wide-eyed in the background, taking it all in,

Arnold Spohr (extreme left), Jean McKenzie (extreme right), with company in Chapter 13.

was little Marilyn Young, later to be a principal with the Winnipeg company. This weekend was to be her biggest moment yet: she was going to present a bouquet to the Governor-General's wife. She practised her presentation on anyone who stood still long enough to accept it.

There were performances by the Sorel and Volkoff companies on Friday evening and Saturday afternoon, but it was the Saturday evening performance that was the glittering gala affair. A box to the right of the stage had been prepared for the vice-regal party; its rim was draped with black velvet and studded with clusters of white narcissi and smilax, and above it hung a Union Jack. Sharing the box with Viscount and Viscountess Alexander were the Lieutenant-Governor of Manitoba and Mrs. McWilliams (who had obviously patched up her differences with the ballet for the occasion), and highly-placed visiting officials from India and Australia. Scattered around the theatre to mark the boxes of the various consular agents were the flags of the United States, France, Sweden, and Poland. Also present were the city's mayor, senior officers of the armed services and members of the general public who had paid as much as $2.50 for a ticket (in the loge section) or as little as $1 (the back of the balcony).

The program was tightly scheduled. The Winnipeg company was to open the presentation with Gweneth's *Chapter 13*, a New York cops-and-robbers melodrama first seen the previous fall, followed by Ruth Sorel's group doing *Three Miniatures*, the Winnipeg company again in *Etude*, and the evening was to close with the Volkoff company's presentation of the Polovetsian Dances from *Prince Igor*.

The guests were seated without a hitch (Marilyn Young presented her bouquet beautifully and received a handshake for her pains) and as the first piece began, Yeddeau, in his role as house manager, went out to the lobby to check that everything was running as it should. He was accosted there by a uniformed Mountie who asked him when "this thing" would be over. "About 11:00," said Yeddeau. "No," said the Mountie, "*this* thing" (he jerked his thumb in the direction of the auditorium) "that's on now. I need to know because I've got to bring the car round—they're leaving as soon as it's over." Yeddeau was horrified. How could he let them leave without seeing the *guest* companies

Marilyn Young presents her flowers to Lady Alexander at the First Canadian Ballet Festival.

perform? There was only one effective way of keeping the vice-regal party in place until the full performance was over, and he took it. He scuttled backstage, alerted Ruth Sorel to have her group ready to enter the moment the Winnipeg company came off the stage, and ran the entire evening without a break or an intermission.

The strain of the whole thing was too much for Arnold Spohr. He danced a major role in *Chapter 13* and the lead (with Jean McKenzie) in *Etude*. After his final exit from the Chopin ballet he collapsed in the wings, suffering from what was described at the time as a heart attack. It was the first of many occasions on which Spohr's health would give out while he was at the service of the company.

At a post-festival meeting the following morning, the heads of the three companies, together with Vancouver representative Beth Lockhart, set up a National Ballet Association, with Yeddeau as president, to organize the festival as an annual, non-competitive, national arts event.

The reviews of the occasion seem to mark the first recorded time that a writer talked about the Winnipeg Ballet in terms of its location—"wide and free as the spirit of the prairie, fresh as the wind that sweeps across it," wrote Constance Grey Swartz, of *The Vancouver Daily Province*. "Here is the breadth and virility of the Middle West, strong in technique, uninhibited in feeling."

In a seemingly-prescient summing-up in *The Winnipeg Tribune*, Randolph Patton examined some of the implications that this weekend coming-together held. He spoke of the potential of the festival—"to bring into being, in Canada in the course of years, something which will with vivid perfection express Canada as at times was Russia expressed by the Diaghilev company." He held out no special hope that this would be done by the choreographers who had been seen in Winnipeg at the weekend, and he pointed out that the Canadian audience had much to learn about ballet —"the audience is over-sophisticated with respect to entertainment values, pathetically at sea with respect to symbols. Much of the richness of ballet lies in its allusiveness." But he also saw the national potential for the art. And he pressed the festival organizers to follow through on what they had begun, establishing an annual ballet festival as their contribution to the cultural development of Canada—and eventually, he said, "a Canadian Ballet of full professional status, presenting the works of Canadian musicians, artists, and choreographers, might become a national institution, giving performances not only within Canada but also in other countries."

The Canadian Ballet Festival was to lead—sooner than anyone at that time realized—to the formation of a national ballet company of exactly the type he described.

Establishing herself as a "character" in the company in these years was Eva von Gencsy. A former resident of Budapest and Salzburg, she reached Winnipeg in 1948. Under the Displaced Persons Quota Act she volunteered to be a maid, and spent a year masquerading as a domestic servant for board member Clarence Shepard and his wife. Almost immediately on arriving in the city, however, Eva joined the company, and it was always Mrs. Shepard's good-natured complaint that she wasn't able to accept social invitations because she had to stay home and do the dishes while her "DP" went to rehearsal. On the occasions when Eva did stay in—to help out by handing round glasses at a cocktail party, for instance— she would put on her false eyelashes and be the star turn. She danced a wide variety of roles, and much later became director of Montreal's Les Ballets-Jazz, but in the opinion of many, her finest hours on stage were as Odile in Act Two of *Swan Lake* in the early 1950s.

Betty tells a curious story from these times, concerning the gentle ghost of Patricia Litchfield. One of the earliest principal dancers with the company, "our Pat" died in June of 1945, following a tonsillectomy. Some years later, Betty moved house in Winnipeg. Soon after she moved into her new home, "strange things began to happen. The dog went round barking and growling at things that weren't there. I was sitting in the living room once with David and Gweneth and I saw someone go up the stairs. I asked David to go and see who it was, but it was no one. A few days later someone told us we were living in Pat Litchfield's old house, and at this point we got rather silly and funny about it and would talk to her if we ever heard noises or anything —we'd say, 'Oh, come on, Pat, everything's fine, calm down, it's all right' because she'd always been a very nervous sort of girl. It became part of our lives. You could lie in my bedroom and hear footsteps walk from my door to the next door and back again. Once, when we had people staying with us, the little boy said to his mother, 'Would you close the cupboard door, mummy, I don't want to see the lady come out of it again.' Suddenly for no reason the electric fan in the kitchen would go on. Once we were having a party, waiting for one of the girls to arrive, and I saw somebody outside the door in a grey suit—two of the men saw it as well—but when they went to the door to let her in, it was nobody. That was our Pat. She was a nice ghost. Nobody was frightened of her, because it was just Pat."

The company's attitude to the classics of the ballet repertoire was always ambivalent at best. Gweneth, who arrived in Winnipeg with only vague memories of classical ballets she had seen, was in any case more of a modernist than a classicist (both in style and inclination) and even if she had had any special leanings in that direction the limitations of her company's technique would have quickly corrected them. At first, the pressure to do "famous" ballets was great, but Gweneth resisted it. In a place like Winnipeg, she counselled, they should be doing things of their own, in their own style. In David Adams's words, "we were a tits-and-teeth company—tremendous enthusiasm and vitality-plus on the stage. Everything tended to be rather high powered—and that suited us fine, because that was what we were best at doing." It was a trademark that rubbed off on everyone. When David Adams went to England in 1946, the English thought his style of dancing brash. But, ironically, it was Adams who gave the company its first real taste of pure classicism. After two years in England he came back laden with classical bits and pieces which he proceeded to mount on the company —Nijinsky's *Spectre de la Rose,* London's version of Petipa's *Swan Lake* (the *pas de trois* from act one, the *grand pas de deux* from act two, the black swan *pas de deux* from act three), and London's version of Petipa's *Sleeping Beauty* (Bluebird variations, the lilac fairy, the rose adagio and, eventually, the *grand pas de deux* from the finale).

The fall season of 1948 opened with a two-performance Winnipeg program featuring Adams as guest artist (his *Swan Lake* snippets with Jean McKenzie, *Spectre de la Rose* with company member Margaret Hample), and in late November the company undertook a tour of Eastern Canada (London, Toronto, Ottawa, Montreal). Adams was to stay with the company for eight months, performing as a guest dancer and choreographing his first ballet, a neo-classical piece to music of Brahms called *Ballet Composite*. While in Winnipeg he met visiting Vancouver teacher Mara McBirney, and in 1949 travelled to the West Coast to join her group and to make two works for her: *Theorem A,* and *l'Auberge des Rosiers*. He returned to the Winnipeg company in the 1950-51 season, and created two more ballets for his colleagues there before moving to Toronto to join Celia Franca's fledgling National Ballet company in the fall of 1951.

Throughout the fall of 1948, high-speed alterations were made on the music for *Chapter 13*. The original choice for the work had been a recording of Gershwin's Piano Concerto in F, but the company was threatened with legal action if they continued to use the Gershwin score. Rather than throw out what was already proving to be a successful ballet, Gweneth, Betty, and Yeddeau

Jean McKenzie and David Adams. (Phillips-Gutkin)

decided to commission another score. Robert Fleming, a 26-year-old Saskatchewan-born composer based in Ottawa, was already highly regarded as a composer of precise and practical orchestral scores for the National Film Board, and he agreed readily to prepare new music for the ballet. He never actually saw the piece while he was working on the music—the collaboration was entirely by correspondence and the score was not completed until four hours before the company was due to dance it at the Eaton Auditorium in Toronto that November. In the circumstances, however, that was not such a problem as it might sound. The score has been widely spoken of since as "the first original score commissioned for a Canadian ballet company," and so it was—but what Fleming had done was to sit down at his music paper with a copy of the Gershwin music and compose new themes, melodies and arrangements on a matching rhythmic structure. The company might never have heard Fleming's piece, but they knew the counts by heart.

In terms of public and critical acclaim, the Eastern tour was a triumph. Critic after critic spoke of the company's freshness, its spirit, its liveliness. In the Montreal *Gazette*, Herbert Whittaker called the company "Canada's most successful dance project to date." In terms of finances the tour was yet another disaster, but that was no deterrent to Gweneth and her stalwarts. They returned to Winnipeg and the following January mounted their most lavish home season in many years—two gala tenth-anniversary performances with a 32-piece orchestra (under Walter Kaufmann, conductor of the Winnipeg Symphony Orchestra) and the première performances of three new Lloyd ballets.

Principal among these was *Visages*, to a Kaufmann score; in it, a young girl and her lover (McKenzie and Spohr) were assailed by the spirits of Indecision, Jealousy, Lust, Fear, Greed, Hate, and eventually Tragedy (the program helpfully noted the costume colour of each). The other new ballets were *Arabesque II*, to Glazunov's *Scènes de Ballet*, a *ballet blanc* that had already been seen during the Eastern tour, and a new *Slavonic Dance*, also to music by Kaufmann.

At the beginning of March, 1949, the company travelled to Toronto for the Second Canadian Ballet Festival. The idea had snowballed; nine other companies took part. And now, the significance of David Yeddeau's original scheme for a cross-Canada gathering of dance companies becomes apparent. Anatole Chujoy, the founder and editor of *Dance News*, attended the Toronto festival, and returned to New York filled with enthusiasm for the get-together concept. From that time on, he was to press regularly for a similar arrangement in the

United States, and it is in large part due to his lobbying that the first Regional Ballet Festival was held in Atlanta in 1956.

Not altogether surprisingly, the Winnipeg Ballet emerged at the top of the heap. Three Lloyd ballets were seen — *Visages, Finishing School,* and *Allegory,* an abstract work to César Franck's *Symphonic Variations,* which drew whistles, bravos, and eight curtain calls. "The country owes an accolade to Winnipeg for its leadership in this field," wrote the Toronto *Globe and Mail* in an editorial. "Orchids to Winnipeg, we say, feeling sure that this must be the appropriate flower." The Winnipeggers blushed, curtsied, and ran off home.

1949-54 Downs and Ups

That first decade was innocent, penniless, uncaring. But now came uneasy, unsettled years, times of ferment. Financial calamity and growing success were to change the face of the company for good. It was the end of an era: the pioneering was over. Strangers were elbowing in and the family would never feel the same. Gweneth was to leave for Toronto within 18 months; Yeddeau was to leave even earlier. Ultimately, Betty was left to carry the founders' flag alone.

They were in money trouble. Not all the leftover debts from the 1948 festival had been cleared. The eastern tour had lost money. The orchestra, as usual, had been so expensive that the January shows had barely broken even. Lady Tupper's counsel was blunt. If they expected to raise any more money in the city, they were going to have to agree to make the company a non-profit cultural organization, with a properly-constituted board of directors. Nothing (stressed Lady Tupper) would change: Gweneth would remain director, Betty would remain ballet mistress, all would be as before . . . except that elected citizens would take over the responsibility for the smooth management of the company.

Gweneth and Betty were far from happy at the idea. They had poured all their energies and a good portion of their potential earnings, in free classes and coaching for the dancers, into building the ballet. Now they were being asked to   69

Eva von Gencsy as The Lady Known as Lou in The Shooting of Dan McGrew. *(Phillips-Gutkin)* give their baby away. But what else could they do? Without financial help they would probably have to disband. Without the backing of an official organization, they were not likely to get the financial help. Reluctantly, they told Madge Tupper yes, go ahead; organize it.

The stories about Madge Tupper have become legends. People speak in shocked delight of the way she bullied and pestered and pushed. She was an intense, tiny woman, but no one ever thought of her as small. "She was the original autocrat, always flaming and snorting at something," says Gweneth. "She was really terribly difficult. But she was a help—people helped from sheer fright." "If you stood up to her she was all right," says Betty, "but if you kowtowed down to her she was pretty terrifying." "She knew perfectly well what she was doing," says Yeddeau, "but most of them were so dumb and had so little sense of humour that they didn't appreciate her."

For Madge Tupper, ballet was a family affair. Her husband, a big, slow, gentle man, good-naturedly allowed himself to be pressed into service like everyone else; he handled the legal business. After he died in 1960, the only ring she ever wore was his signet. It is a measure of the woman's warmth and straightforwardness that her retarded daughter, Margot, always accompanied Madge Tupper to meetings. In a 1951 program the girl was listed as a member of the board of the ballet's women's committee.

In March of 1949 (the year Newfoundland entered Canadian Confederation), the Winnipeg Ballet was incorporated under the laws of Manitoba as a non-profit cultural organization. Dr. A. H. S. Gillson, president of the University of Manitoba, was named president, and there was a provisional board of directors of 21. Lady Tupper was named vice-president, David Yeddeau remained manager, Gweneth was director of ballet, Betty was ballet mistress, R. A. Kipp was treasurer and Sir Charles Tupper was honorary solicitor. Gweneth made all the usual public noises—"I feel this is the beginning of a new era . . . something for which we have worked and which we have had in mind as one of our goals during the last 10 years"—but there are still those who believe she knew, even as she allowed the board to take over, that she was soon to move on.

Under the new regime, the company embarked on a controlled series of performances designed to give maximum exposure at minimum cost. Between the board's inception in March of 1949 and its "first annual meeting" the following November, three sets of home-town programs were presented, and a major, month-long tour of nine Eastern Canadian cities was undertaken.

Olivia Wyatt (centre) and, clockwise from top right, Kit Copping, Sheila Mackinnon, Naomi Kimura, Rachel Browne, and Beverley Barkley in Romance.

However, only two new ballets were presented (David Adams's *Ballet Composite*, to Brahms, and Gweneth's *Romance*, a traditional romantic piece to more Glazunov), and the tour was done with two-piano accompaniment rather than a full orchestra. Accordingly, money was made.

At the November annual meeting, Gillson—re-elected for a second term—was able to announce that the ballet's debts had been paid off and there was a balance of about $4,000 in the bank. Immediately, Madge Tupper started to press for salaries for the dancers and more tours for the company. Paying the dancers was the only way the board could be sure of keeping them, she said. Without money, the dancers would slip away and "the company will gradually drift back to second or third place in the dominion, instead of remaining in front." Who, now, would allow that?

Eva von Gencsy (left) and friends in a scene from The Shooting of Dan McGrew.

New works in the spring of 1950 included Gweneth's *The Shooting of Dan McGrew* (based on the Robert Service poem and depicting "what *might* have happened the night the boys were whooping it up down at the Malemute saloon"—a garish popular entertainment that was to remain an audience favourite for years), and Arnold Spohr's first venture into choreography, *Ballet Premier*.

Spohr's steps forward are often hesitant, and this was no exception. Gweneth had been asking him for a year to try his hand at the craft, and he kept putting it off, putting it off, until one day he heard the Mendelssohn Piano Concerto no. 1 and decided he would make that the vehicle for his choreographic debut. Like many company members, he had taken a teacher's course from Gweneth which included lessons in how to choreograph—her way—and the ballet proved to be Russian in style, classical in technique, modern in idiom. Frank Morriss praised its fresh charm, its clarity, its variety, its sparkle. Guy Glover, a National Film Board producer and well-known dance adjudicator who had been hired to make a cross-country adjudication trip for the upcoming Third Canadian Ballet Festival, described it as "a dance work which is worthy to take its place in the repertory of any dance company alongside the creations of the

Arnold Spohr and Jean Stoneham in Ballet Premier. *(Phillips-Gutkin)*

half-dozen internationally recognized choreographers. It is to be hoped that not only the Winnipeg Ballet but other Canadian companies will be able to make use of his great talent before he has been snatched away to London, New York, or Paris."

Dan McGrew was Gweneth's last ballet before her departure for Toronto. On October 3, 1950, one day before the opening performance of the 1950-51 season, Gweneth boarded a train headed east. At the station to wave goodbye were two people: Betty . . . and Frank Morriss.

Now, nearly 30 years later, Gweneth's official story—and it makes a lot of sense—is that she left for purely financial reasons. She and Betty had brought up young Richard together, and he had reached the age where they thought he should be sent away to a boarding school to be educated "in the way we British people thought he should be educated." They were unable to finance that on their income from the school in Winnipeg, so it was decided that Gweneth would move to Toronto and open a branch of the school there, leaving Betty to look after the company. ("They didn't need me so often now for choreography because they were getting other people—which was quite right—it wouldn't be good to have the same choreographer all the time.")

It was probably not that simple. For one thing, Gweneth resented outsiders interfering in what had been for decades a private affair, and she found it difficult to work with the board—"they were always having her in tears about this, that or the other," Betty recalls. However, one board member from that time thinks: "What they needed and wanted was a sugar daddy who would pay their debts and expenses without question. Such angels are rare." According to this individual, Gweneth never intended to stay and cooperate with the board once it was set up. Rather, she already had her eye on the possibility of a job as head of the much-talked-about new national ballet organization in Toronto. According to another board member from that time, Gweneth actually left Winnipeg hoping to be given charge of the new company—"Well, they never said that, but that was always what was understood."

The National Ballet theory is on the surface a tempting one. Certainly, Gweneth was aware of the flattery she had been receiving in Eastern Canada, both on the tour and later at the festival. And she was equally aware of the consternation that the success of the Winnipeg company was causing in certain Toronto hearts.

A group of Torontonians out to establish a "national ballet" had in fact already approached her for advice on how to go about it. Modern-day National Ballet lore

Gweneth Lloyd circa *1950. (Phillips-Gutkin)*

makes no mention of Gweneth's contribution in this regard, but, according to Gweneth, it was *she* who told the Toronto group to go to England to find someone who knew how to set up a dance company. (They subsequently contacted Sadler's Wells director Ninette de Valois and de Valois recommended Celia Franca—the woman who was eventually to found the National Ballet of Canada.)

It seems most likely that Gweneth left for a combination of all three reasons—money, dissatisfaction, ambition. She never made any official announcement of her departure; she was to retain the title of director for several seasons, and she would return from time to time to mount new ballets. But that October day was the end of an era.

The fiercely independent Yeddeau, unwilling to knuckle under to anyone, had already gone to Toronto after a tiff with the board. He was to handle a limited amount of touring stage management for the company for a year or two, but otherwise his connection with the group had been severed for good.

Betty, however, stayed on. Early in 1949 she had married Ken Ripley, who had danced small parts with the company the previous year, but the marriage had lasted only a matter of months. Now, alone, Betty made the company her life. She held few of the board members in particularly high regard. The Richardsons, John Russell, Lady Tupper . . . those she could tolerate. "The rest of them didn't really know the first thing . . . but they had money." And it was money that was making the difference. At the annual meeting early in November, Lady Tupper was able to announce that the dancers were now being paid for a nine-month season, aggregating $500 monthly. That worked out to anything from $17 for a corps member to $25 for the company's top male dancer, Arnold Spohr—"and $15 of that," he recalls, "went to a therapist for a bad knee."

The Third Canadian Ballet Festival in November of 1950, was a triumph for the Winnipeg Ballet greater than any it had previously known. They danced nothing that had not been seen in Winnipeg—*Visages, Dan McGrew, Ballet Premier,* and some of the *Sleeping Beauty* snippets that David Adams had given them—but they became the toast of Montreal.

Spohr's *Ballet Premier* was acclaimed as the best ballet of the entire season. Sydney Johnson, of the Montreal *Star*, said *Dan McGrew* was "so cleverly contrived that it would be as much at home on a Sadler's Wells program as it would be on that of Les Ballets de Paris." And Howard Newman, from New

York's Theatre Guild (New *York!*) said "a more engaging and talented group of dancers is not to be found on this continent." Frank Morriss, who travelled to the festival with the company, was naturally overjoyed by the hometowners success. It was late November, the football season was at its peak, and he crowed: "If the Blue Bombers play football Saturday afternoon as well as the Winnipeg Ballet danced here Wednesday, Winnipeg's a cinch to have the Grey trophy." Winnipeg lost 13-0 to Toronto. Perhaps it was an omen.

Omen or not, in Montreal for the duration of the festival was one Celia Franca, from the Metropolitan Ballet, in London. She had been invited to Canada by the Toronto group to look at Canadian dance talent and to advise them on possible courses of action; Gweneth and David Adams (who had danced with Celia in London) went to the airport to pick her up. She watched everything, fell in love with the country's potential, and told *Canadian Press* she planned to return—"I am anxious to help in any way I can," she said. "Canada is ready for a national ballet company. Canadian ballet is a miracle of achievement in the face of terrible obstacles, but there is a danger that ballet in Canada may disintegrate. In each of the companies in the festival, I saw one or two dancers who are ready to turn professional . . . however, they cannot be expected to improve unless they are given the opportunity."

Guy Glover added fuel to the flames when he suggested, in his report on the festival, that the best dancers seen at Montreal should be gathered together to form a professional company—"a creditable Canadian Ballet which could contribute something of value both to the history of ballet and to the cultural development of this country."

These were fighting words to the folks back home. Thundered Morriss, in a *Free Press* editorial in March: "A new company is being formed to tour Canada and no doubt efforts will be made to take away Winnipeg's leading dancers. If such a thing should happen it will be a shame. The need exists for a Canadian ballet company, but meanwhile the Winnipeg Ballet has been such a civic asset that it should not be allowed to die . . . let's keep ballet in our midst." In May, on the occasion of the company's major spring season, another *Free Press* writer, K. Haig, termed the news that Toronto was about to set up a "national" ballet company "so unsportsmanlike that it verges on the impudent. Let Toronto improve its own ballet by all means. . . . But let us have done with the arrogance—and the complete and blatant untruth—of this 'national' business. . . . If and when the National Ballet comes, its roots will always and forever go back to Winnipeg."

In August, Celia Franca wrote to Betty announcing that she was about to undertake a cross-Canada tour for the National Ballet Guild of Canada, and asking for the loan of the school's studio in which to conduct her Winnipeg auditions. The horrified board sent back a letter stating clearly that the Winnipeg company considered itself the originator of professional ballet in Canada and asking in icy tones what exactly was meant by the *National* Ballet Guild. Mrs. Mulqueen, of the National Ballet Guild, replied with a charming letter offering all kinds of congratulations and flattery to the Winnipeg company, and explaining briefly that the guild aimed merely "to provide a professional field for Canadian dancers." Lady Tupper, meanwhile, was able to report that a Mrs. Hess, also of the National Ballet Guild, had told her that the organization was still in such a formative stage that no chairman had yet been appointed for its board.

But it was only a matter of time. In the fall of 1951 Celia Franca crossed Canada looking for dancers. David Adams was invited, and went. With him went his wife, Lois Smith, who had also spent a season dancing with the Winnipeg company. Lillian Lewis, Jean McKenzie, and Arnold Spohr—the company's top talents—were all invited to go to Toronto, but refused. Their commitment—personal and professional—was to the Winnipeg company. They belonged to its pioneer generation, and their loyalty had been forged in the fires of the founding decade. Spohr and Jean McKenzie are with the company still.

The company itself was progressing from strength to strength. The Sadler's Wells Ballet had made a return visit to North America at the beginning of the year, and Ninette de Valois—who crossed Canada on a lecture-tour as her company crossed the U.S. Midwest—recalls meeting a group of 40 women in Regina who had chartered an aircraft to take them to Winnipeg in March to see the ballet. De Valois was not scheduled to visit Winnipeg, but she dropped in anyway, because she had heard so much about the company. Betty remembers the visit clearly. The company had planned to run through a couple of the ballets with Spohr as the main performer, but he had hurt his knee, and had to send in a substitute in one of the works. When Spohr was introduced to de Valois, she made some polite comment about his knee. "Yes," he said, "it's like this"—and, according to Betty, "down came his grey tights, down, down, down, to the bottom, and madam said 'O-o-u-ugh'—you know—and we just stood there and had a long discussion of Arnold's knee, Arnold in his old dance belt and me pretending this is what happens all the time in our studio."

The March (1951) production was a gala benefit to boost company funds. It featured an 18-piece orchestra under Eric Wild, now the permanent musical director, and the first performances of two new works by David Adams—*Geschrei*, a satirical piece on the Charleston era, to music of Milhaud; and a *pas de deux* to music from Khachaturian's *Masquerade* suite. It was the first occasion on which no original work of Gweneth's had been featured.

Spohr's second ballet, *Intermède*, to the Cimarosa Concerto for Oboe and Strings, with sets and costumes by John Graham, was introduced in May. And in June, John Russell announced that the company would be receiving monthly honoraria ranging from $80 to $100 for the nine-month season for a total dancer-salary aggregate of $1,440 a month.

The big performance excitement that year was the company's fall appearance before Princess Elizabeth and the Duke of Edinburgh during their tour of Canada. This was one of Lady Tupper's greatest coups—topped only by her

Intermède. (Left to right) Sheila Killough, Lillian Lewis, Viola Busday, Victor Duret, Arnold Spohr, Bill McGrath, Sheilagh Henderson, Eva von Gencsy, Kay Bird. (Phillips-Gutkin)

Janie Adams presents a bouquet to Princess Elizabeth at the Command Performance in 1951.

wangling of the "royal" appelation two years later. Even before news of the royal tour of Canada had been made public, she had been lobbying among her influential friends to get a Command Performance by the company. The Lieutenant-Governor of Manitoba, McWilliams, whose wife was still no great friend of the ballet, opposed the proposal from the start, and firmly decreed that it was not to happen. He had reckoned, however, without Lady Tupper and her contacts. The noise she made in Winnipeg and Ottawa was heard (and heeded) as far away as London. By the time the smoke died down, the Royal Presence had been assured.

The ballet was to be the only theatrical entertainment offered to the royal couple on their visit to Winnipeg, and Sheila Killough, who danced in all the ballets that evening, wrote (or had written for her) an unaffected account of her feelings for the *Christian Science Monitor*. "I think we floated through our 'Classic Ballet' [*Ballet Premier*] but the next was a tragic emotional one danced with masques [*Visages*]; only when I bowed over the Princess's hand . . . did I feel suddenly self-conscious in a form-fitting stockingette costume." At the end of her article, she sent a personal message to Elizabeth. "You would laugh at our attempts to act at being a Princess! We wear a tiara and dress just like yours. Oh,

we know your jewels are real, but we have to pretend ours are, or we couldn't
really act the part. . . . We are sorry now that we gave you such a serious ballet.
How we wished you could have stayed for the next number. It was a comedy and
lots of fun. We feel sorry, too, that you did not have any young friends in the
Royal Box. We had a party after the performance and we wished that you could
have come. You could have hung up your tiara with ours and pinned a white
gardenia in your hair, and danced and danced with Philip the whole evening."

"Poor Elizabeth," says Gweneth, who had travelled back to Winnipeg for the
occasion. "She must have hated every minute of it. She's not faintly interested in
ballet." When all the excitement was over, the ballet added up its bills. The
evening had cost $8,790, more than $3,600 over budget, but there was still a
clear profit of $2,440 on the night. It was the company's biggest single-event
gain to date.

Variety continued to be the keynote of the repertoire. While she was back,
Gweneth mounted a new ballet—*Rondel,* to music of Vivaldi, all about three

A scene from Rondel. *(Phillips-Gutkin)*

Arnold Spohr and Eva von Gencsy in Swan Lake, Act Two. *(Phillips-Gutkin)*

Marina Katronis and Bill McGrath in Baba Lubov. *(Phillips-Gutkin)*

girls in love with the same troubadour in fourteenth-century Provence—and a production of Fokine's *Les Sylphides* was attempted. The Christmas performances featured *Baba Lubov,* a children's ballet based on Russian fairy tales, choreographed by Joy Camden, an English teacher and dancer who had been appointed assistant ballet mistress at the beginning of the season. In February of 1952, a new *Swan Lake, Act Two,* "after Petipa," was featured.

The company toured western Canada in the early part of 1952, reaching the Pacific coast for the first time, and in May went east again, first to Toronto, where it took top honours at the ballet festival, and then into Quebec and the Maritime provinces. Touring was becoming its livelihood, and in June New York impresario Sol Hurok declared an interest in booking it for a cross-U.S. trip. The board was not happy with the proposed terms, however, and entered negotiations with Columbia Artists Management, Hurok's main rival. Then, in September, they received a proposal for a *world* tour from Nicholas Koudriavtzeff, the Montreal impresario. It was a tempting proposition ("There should be no doubt in anyone's mind that every effort should be made to arrange this tour," wrote Russell in a private memorandum to the board) but there was one snag: the company would have to cover transportation costs of an estimated $25,000-$30,000.

Eventually, Lady Tupper's firm hand was needed to bring order to this touring tangle. She flew to New York at the end of November, 1952, and returned with a contract from Columbia to tour the U.S. for four to six weeks in the late winter of the 1953-54 season. It must have taken hard bargaining. Almost certainly she clinched it with a promise to make the company internationally saleable by arranging to have it designated 'royal,' because as soon as she was back from New York she announced to the press that the Columbia tour would probably be undertaken under the name of the *Royal* Winnipeg Ballet. "However," she added, in her supremely offhand way, "permission must first be obtained to *use* the title." She made it sound like a routine matter: in fact, there were only two other "royal" companies in the world, the Danes and the Swedes (Sadler's Wells was not to become the Royal Ballet until 1956). But, by leaning on her contacts in the Royal Household and in the retinue of Governor-General Vincent Massey in Ottawa, Madge Tupper pulled it off. "She had her pressure points in Ottawa," Kipp recalls, "and she knew how to use them."

One of the first persons she notified—a copy of the cable still exists—was William Judd, then of Columbia Artists Management, in New York. The company was on tour when it received the official word, and the news that it had become "royal" was announced from the stage in Montreal.

In the summer of 1952, the company moved from 4,000 feet of studios on two cramped floors on Main Street to 5,000 square feet of well-lit space on the top floor of the newly renovated Norlyn Building at 309 Hargrave Street, a few blocks away. At the time, it was an insignificant-enough event, one more small step in the company's gradual growth: no lightning flashed, no thunder roared. But the move was to prove of momentous significance in the company's future. It would bring the Winnipeg Ballet as close to defeat as it was ever going to come.

Gweneth Lloyd, now firmly established as a teacher in Toronto, was still titular Director in Winnipeg, and returned at regular intervals to advise Betty and the board on policy, and to set new ballets. In the fall of 1952, she created what many consider the crowning achievement of her choreographic career—*Shadow on the Prairie*. Commissioned by James Richardson and Sons, the work was made to original music (based on Scottish folk themes) by Robert Fleming, with sets by John Graham. It is popularly regarded as the first ballet ever made on a specifically Canadian theme, and it is true that it was a major Canadian work long before the demand for "Canadian content" in arts programming became fashionable. However, Gweneth herself was no newcomer to themes derived from her adopted country—she had used them as early as 1939, in the brief *Grain* and *Kilowatt Magic* ballets, and again in *The Shooting of Dan McGrew* in 1950. And while Canadianism was of course by no means Gweneth's only contribution to the company repertoire, these early Canadian works were particularly valuable in establishing the company's uniqueness as an ensemble deriving from and rooted in Canadian soil.

Shadow on the Prairie was hailed at its première as "a definite work of Canadian art" (Morriss) and "a Canadian work of major stature" (Maley). And it delighted audiences not only in Manitoba but right across Canada, both in live performance during a tour in 1953 and on film in a nationally released National Film Board production (the first ever to feature a full-length ballet). *Shadow on the Prairie* did what all successful popular art does: it identified and discussed common human problems in an accessible manner. However, it also disturbed certain hometown complacencies. The plot concerned a young Scottish immigrant and his agorophobic wife, who discovered the openness of the prairie too much to take after the sheltered glens of home. Neither kindly neighbours nor loving husband could calm her, and "in an agony of nostalgia and fear of the great snowy wastes [she] dies, tragically sheltered in death by the wooden walls of her marriage chest." Some members of the ballet board—perhaps conscious of the

Carlu Carter in the climactic moment of Shadow on the Prairie.

way Gweneth had left Winnipeg—took the plot to be a statement by Gweneth about the antagonism she herself felt for life on the prairies. In fact, Gweneth had discovered the story in a novel she had been reading about nineteenth-century life in the Dakotas, and had merely adapted the story to suit her own purposes.

During its first full-length cross-Canada tour, early in 1953, the company made a brief six-performance trip across the border to Duluth, Hibbing, and Virginia, Minnesota. This not only marked the first time a Canadian ballet ensemble had ever performed in the U.S.; it also brought the company its first taste of professional administration. A bright young manager-booker named Henry Guettel saw the company perform in Duluth, was impressed ("the most outstanding group I have every witnessed"), and wanted the job of running it. His application came at exactly the right time; the company was too big to be run any longer by a volunteer board, and he was taken on as of June 1 at $400 a month, rising to $500 after six months. The board was in a spending mood. Just a month earlier, the executive committee had raised the company size to 24 (from 18) and the year's salary bill to almost $43,000. Unfortunately, no one seemed to have paid much attention to where all this money was to come from. When Robert A. Kipp became president in September (succeeding Russell) the picture was once again grim. The main fall show featured the première of *Children of Men,* a new Arnold Spohr ballet dedicated to Lady Tupper. The presentation lost money, mainly because it was in direct competition with the Sadler's Wells Ballet, which came through with Margot Fonteyn dancing *Swan Lake* and took the town by storm.

By mid October the company was broke, and looking at an anticipated deficit of about $23,000 on the season's $131,000 budget. The upcoming Columbia tour would help; but, for that, sets would need refurbishing. To finance that, five board members—Kipp, Mrs. Richardson, Russell, Mrs. C. S. Riley, and Gordon Osler—each guaranteed $1,000 against an increased bank over-draft.

To raise money, someone suggested a personal appearance by movie star Joan Crawford, one of about 50 individuals whose names appeared in the company's souvenir book as honorary patrons. Miss Crawford was unavailable. Eventually they settled for a series of guest appearances at the January hometown shows by Alicia Markova, the English ballerina who had recently crowned a distinguished career by spending several seasons as prima ballerina with the London Festival Ballet, which grew from a company she and the English dancer Anton Dolin had created in the late 1940s. In Winnipeg, Markova might not be as big a name as Crawford, but at least she could dance. She agreed to do three performances, at $1,000 a show.

When she first arrived, in 25-below weather, she was "a bit impossible," according to Betty. "She didn't like her first dressing room, so we gave her another, and she didn't like the second one because the boys went to the toilet next door. . . ." But she was marvellous with the company. She took time to teach and coach the dancers, and when the costumes for *Les Sylphides* failed to meet with her approval, she dug into her own pocket—something of a first, according to several persons who knew her ways with money—and paid for new top layers. The show turned a profit of almost $2,000, and it was agreed that she would rejoin the company in February in Washington.

By now, Celia Franca had organized a small company in Toronto. Late in January, 1954, two-thirds of the way through the first performance of her company's week-long Toronto "season," the applause for a performance of Anthony Tudor's *Lilac Garden* just dying down, she stepped to the front of the Royal Alexandra Theatre stage. The ballet was in "a desperate financial situation," she said. It needed $50,000. Without it, the National Ballet would fold—a tragedy for Canadian culture. Would everyone please give what they could?

The Winnipeg people, with their company only days away from setting out on a major tour, were furious. On her own initiative, Gweneth immediately bought space in the Toronto newspapers (on the same page as the National's daily show ads) to state the "true facts" about the state and future of the art of ballet in Canada. She set out the impressive record of the RWB ("Canada's first professional ballet"), detailed the work opportunities that existed for dancers across the country, and concluded: "While it is regrettable that one company finds itself unable to remain solvent despite generous public support, it would be more regrettable that the hard-working young dancers should be misled and disillusioned regarding their opportunities in the future."

Winnipeg stood solidly behind her. "She had her own position to defend as the originator of professional ballet in Canada," Kipp told the press. "My personal opinion is that Miss Franca has made some very unfair statements in advertising her ballet company. But as president of the RWB, I say that each of our companies have their own problems and those problems won't be solved by us fighting each other." Hear, hear, said commentators across the country—"Canadian ballet won't have a leg to stand on unless the two legs can refrain from kicking each other," wrote one. Celia Franca just smiled. "It is not in my nature to reply to such charges," she said sweetly.

The tour of Eastern Canada and the U.S. was launched under twin clouds—money trouble and political controversy.

The board had of course not come close to erasing the $23,000 pre-tour deficit, and only days before the trip was due to start the ten-member finance committee (chaired by Bob Kipp) found it necessary to put up personal guarantees of almost $13,000. But no sooner had they raised the money that made the trip possible than Kipp cancelled the opening booking—a two-night stand in Sudbury, a nickel-mining town in northern Ontario.

The problem was politics. Initially, the Sudbury appearances were to have been sponsored by the local chapter of the Imperial Order Daughters of the Empire, but the financial load had proved too great and the responsibility had been assumed by the Sudbury chapter of the International Union of Mine, Mill and Smelter Workers. The union's political leanings were no secret—it had already been expelled from the Canadian Congress of Labour for having Communist leadership—but it was only a chance conversation on a train that alerted Kipp to the potential threat this link might pose to the company's U.S. appearances. McCarthyism was at its height. It was probably not unreasonable to expect that the company might be stopped at the border. A ban like that could be calamitous: the U.S. trip was budgeted to net the company more than $30,000.

And so, on the eve of the company's departure from Winnipeg, it was announced that the performances in Sudbury would have to be cancelled "due to sickness in the company." Eva von Gencsy and Jean Stoneham, the two female leads, would be unable to travel, said the announcement, due to "24-hour 'flu." The Mine Mill people, who had sold out both shows, were not convinced and made various counter proposals (stand-ins, program changes, a smaller company). The company refused them all.

The Sudbury shows were scheduled for January 29 and 30, a Friday and Saturday, but on the Thursday evening, Eva von Gencsy was reported dining out with friends, and one Friday newspaper report quoted her saying: "People told me I had the 'flu, so I had the 'flu. I never felt better than I do right now, though." In the Saturday papers, however, she was backtracking hard: "It was all a terrible mistake," she was saying. Her poor command of English was to blame, she said: "If I say I feel good, it is only because I am so happy to be going on tour." It was true, she said, that many members of the company had had 'flu. She herself had had it on Tuesday and had been told to go home. Yes, someone asked, but did she have it on *Thursday?* "There has been so much excitement with the tour. It is hard to say what day you have 'flu and what day you feel fine."

So their entry to the U.S. was assured. But as far as their ability to deliver the goods was concerned, they were still at the babes-in-the-woods stage. Putting on performances for the indulgent and not particularly well-informed folks back home was one thing. Setting out to impress the more knowledgeable audiences and critics of the major U.S. cities was quite another. The RWB arrived in Washington less than a month behind the Sadler's Wells company, ostensibly on the same terms. Markova's presence—she danced in three performances at the end of the week-long run—helped draw the crowds, but the company was received with a cool, somewhat condescending politeness by most of the Washington reviewers. Margaret Lloyd, in the *Christian Science Monitor*, called it "a winsome little company" and said Markova's appearances were "artistically . . . out of proportion to the company's present state of development." John

Haskins in the Washington *Times-Herald* said the company had "the virtues and the faults of youth." John Martin, in the New York *Times,* pointed out that the company was "still in the process of growing up" and added that "the boys, of course, are not that good." He concluded, however: "All in all, it is a most impressive little company, and a bright feather in the cultural cap of our neighbor to the north."

Plainly, everyone was making a special effort to be nice—which may have been a response to the company's projected youth and freshness. It is, curiously enough, a response that recurs and recurs in reviews through the years: the company's much-vaunted "prairie innocence" has always seemed to bring out critics' geniality.

Well, almost always. In Chicago that spring, Claudia Cassidy preferred not to mince matters. "Royal or no royal, this Winnipeg visitor is no ballet," she said. She called the engagement—which sold out the 4,200-seat opera house—"a callous booking made on the managerial hit and run theory that anything goes, at least the first time."

The company returned home with a tour loss of almost $13,000. This brought the season's loss, as of April 19, to $25,982.94. The finance committee and the board held a joint *post mortem.* Should the ballet continue? And if so, how was it to be maintained? Several individuals—Mrs. Richardson among them— thought this might be a good time to suspend operations for "reassessment and reorganization." But Betty registered strong opposition to that. If you took a year off, she said, you were finished; you lost dancers, and you started again from scratch. Someone else suggested the company should be reduced in size, but Betty, Lady Tupper, and several others opposed that, too. A smaller group would need entirely new choreography (expensive), it would no longer appeal to Columbia for touring purposes, and, anyway, it would never be able to present "first-class ballet."

Well, something had to happen. If they were to carry on, they were looking at an annual in-town deficit of $40,000, exclusive of touring, which it was felt should in future be self-supporting if it was undertaken at all. Lady Tupper agreed that the company couldn't go on without paying its debts, but thought that "Winnipeg is prepared to do more, if asked." Several other board members agreed this was a good time to go to the people, but no one was willing to take on the job of raising major funds. The discussion lasted two and a half hours. Many avenues were explored, but no one is on record as having suggested arson. In the light of what followed, it is just as well.

1954-58 Fire and After

Small coincidences led to the creation of the Royal Winnipeg Ballet; they now came close to destroying it. A piece of faulty wiring, the company's expansion to larger studios in 1952, the worst gale in Winnipeg for 35 years . . . they call it now, simply, The Fire. No one died; dreams died. Blessings that come disguised as calamity never seem like blessings at the time.

After, there was rancour and bitterness. The power, such as it was, was fought over. Artistic directors came and went. It was a turbulent period, but the board of directors sailed through, serene. Through close to half a decade of upheaval and change, the half-page advertisement taken in each year's souvenir-book by a local firm of architects and consulting engineers consisted entirely of the following quotation from François Guizot, the arch-conservative and staunch defender of the French status quo in the middle of the nineteenth century: "The study of art possesses this great and peculiar charm, that it is absolutely unconnected wtih the struggles and contests of ordinary life. By private interest and political questions, men are deeply divided and set at variance; but beyond and above all such party strife, they are attracted and united by a taste for the beautiful in art. It is a taste at once engrossing and unselfish, which may be indulged without effort and yet has the power of exciting the deepest emotion—a taste able to exercise and gratify both the nobler and the softer parts of our nature—the imagination and the judgment, love of emotion and power of reflection, the enthusiasm and the critical faculty, the senses and the reasons."

Ruthanna Boris in her ballet, Le Jazz Hot. *(Maurice Seymour)*

It was Winnipeg's worst fire: three million dollars-worth. It began late in the night of June 7, 1954, in wiring behind an electrical sign on the front of the Time building, a business block at 333 Portage. Hurricane winds, caused by the violent effect of masses of moist, cold air from the west meeting masses of moist, warm, central-U.S. air somewhere to the east of Denver, howled in off the prairie. At their 1 A.M. peak they were clocked at 72 miles an hour. The first fire alarm was given at 1:18 A.M. the second sounded 40 minutes later, the third at 5:53. But the firemen—95 dutymen, another 150 specials and every piece of equipment in the city—couldn't contain it.

Five major downtown business buildings went up in smoke. Ninety tenants were forced to evacuate apartments. More than 100 businesses were either destroyed or damaged. One of them contained the headquarters and studios of the Royal Winnipeg Ballet. Everything was lost—costumes, sets, original musical scores, the notebooks containing the details of Gweneth's original choreography—everything.

Betty first heard about the fire at six that morning. "A phone rang and a voice said, 'This is Billy Ainsley, the Winnipeg Ballet's on fire.' I said, 'Oh, come on, Billy, don't be so silly,' but he said, 'Yes it is, it really is,' so we got up and went down and got there just in time to see the whole of the ceiling, the floor, go through—you could see all the trunks which had the costumes in." She tells the story with a wry, exhausted resignation, mimicking the voice of the boy as she recounts his part in it. "Apparently it had started much earlier, and if the absolute nits had phoned or said anything . . . if they had said there was any likelihood that this was going to spread we could have got everything out and nothing would have been lost at all."

Gweneth was back in Toronto when it happened. "I was just crossing Yonge Street to the studio and I saw a billboard—Big Fire in Winnipeg. I didn't think much of it—then I thought, well, maybe I'd better buy, and it said about everything being burned. . . . I think that's the worst I've ever felt in my life. I had to go to a friend's house to lie down. I couldn't do anything."

When they added up their losses, the bill came to $36,000. Even after insurance, they were still $20,000 in the hole. They set up temporary head-quarters in a former liquor store and doggedly went to work. Calamity is supposed to bring out the sympathetic; the city's "ballet day," with collecting-boxes in the stores, raised $459.55. Young Thomas Chisholm, of 645 Oak Street, sent a dollar bill and 54 cents in change; with it came a note scrawled on a sheet from a child's scribbling-pad: "please take this money for new costumes." The Canadian Embassy staff in Brussels sent $30—"a little encouragement from Canadians abroad." It was slow going. Late in July, Kipp wrote to the dancers to apologize for not having sent out contracts for the coming season. "It is impossible for us to know, right now, how large a company we will have. . . . We will be unable to make any definite promises at least until late September." But the dancers had to eat. One by one they left Winnipeg. No one seemed to care, and Frank Morriss was enraged. He called the board "too timid in its approach" to the problem of raising funds. "Do we want the company or don't we?" he wrote. "Somebody should make up their mind, and fast!"

Behind the scenes, people *were* making up their minds. Board members supplemented the meagre public donations to wipe out the leftover deficit ($27,000) from the previous season, leaving the slate clean. And at the end of the year Faye N. McKenzie, Jean's father, launched a high-powered, well-organized, "do-or-fold-up" fund-raising campaign. The target was $50,000—to finance a company of 20 dancers, plus new costumes, music, and sets for six new ballets. The provincial government set the tone with a special grant of $5,000, and by March, the company was beginning to get back on its feet. Betty had found new premises for the school, on Smith Street, and the dancers who had remained in the city were back to their daily class routine. That month, at the persuasion of Kathleen Richardson, the Winnipeg Junior League pledged $5,000 to cover the costs of a new ballet—but *only*, they specified, if the $50,000 was raised and the company's future was assured.

The funding campaign was so successful that in less than six months it had gone $5,067.16 beyond its target. In June, 1955, Betty was appointed artistic director for the September-to-February period at a salary of $2,100 (Gweneth, retitled, became simply founding director). On the advice of New York *Herald Tribune* critic Walter Terry, Betty tried to get the young New York choreographer Robert Joffrey for the job of ballet master—he had already expressed an interest in doing some ballets for the company—but the board decided to hire Nenad Lhotka, a Yugoslavian dancer who had worked for the previous decade in ballet in Zagreb. Paddy Stone wrote offering a new ballet, and the hiring of dancers began. Arnold Spohr, who had spent the post-fire period consolidating his own career in a variety of areas of dance (ice shows, jazz, musicals, TV) had applied for the post of ballet master but had been advised by the board that they "did not deem it advisable for him to return to the company in view of his many outside interests" although they would be pleased to welcome him back as guest artist in a revival of *The Wise Virgins*. The reconstituted Royal Winnipeg Ballet met as a company of 22 dancers for the first time that September. Former company members Carlu Carter and Bill McGrath—who had been married that summer in Los Angeles—were principals.

The new season officially opened with a dry-run performance in Brandon on

November 11. The return of the company to Winnipeg was spread over three nights, beginning on November 14. Everyone was there—provincial and civic dignitaries, the proud board, Gweneth—and Betty did the rounds of the company before the curtain went up, distributing sprigs of white heather for luck. The repertoire mixed old and new: Gweneth's *Wise Virgins*, remounted under the title of *Parable*; various classical excerpts—the *Don Quixote pas de deux*, for example, and a *Swan Lake, Act One pas de trois*—with Petipa's choreography reproduced by Mary Skeaping, ballet mistress of the Sadler's Wells company; *The Devil in the Village*, a remounted and abridged version by Lhotka of a two and one-half-hour Czech narrative folk-ballet classic for which his father had written the music 20 years previously; and Stone's new work, *Clasico*, which was financed by a grant from Flora McCrea Eaton (who was in attendance with a large Eaton-family retinue for the work's first performance). It was all a great success. "All the work and all the sacrifice has been justified," said Morriss. "After its ordeal by fire, the company has emerged better than it was before." "The phoenix has risen from the ashes," said Lady Eaton in her gracious cable of congratulations.

The Junior League went to Betty for advice on choreographers to approach for their new commission, and she gave them three names. They chose Ruthanna Boris. It was another turning point; it changed the company's image, character, way of life.

Brooklyn-born Ruthanna Boris had come through Balanchine's School of American Ballet, danced with Ballet Caravan, the Metropolitan Opera Ballet and prima roles with the Ballet Russe de Monte Carlo. She started to choreograph with the New York City Ballet in 1951, and by the time she and her husband, former NYCB dancer Frank Hobi, reached Winnipeg, they had already been operating a small concert company of their own. She is a tiny woman with intense, dark eyes. Warmly outgoing, she can also be very imperious, and from the beginning there was no nonsense. One of the first things she did when she arrived in Winnipeg in January of 1956 for rehearsals for her new ballet was to tell two of the company members to diet. Her approach upset a lot of people. "There we were," says Kathleen Richardson, "toddling along, being crusaders on the prairies, and suddenly we were transformed into professionals." Betty took a wait-and-see approach. In person she "got on quite well" with the Hobis. Professionally, she was enough of a realist to recognize a potential challenge.

The work Ruthanna Boris prepared on the Junior League's money was

Left: Marina Katronis and Paddy McIntyre in the Don Quixote pas de deux; *right: Carla Carter in 1955. (Eric Skipsey, Phillips-Gutkin)*

Paddy McIntyre (standing centre) and Marina Katronis (right) in a scene from The Devil in the Village. *(Phillips-Gutkin)*

Frank Hobi and Ruthanna Boris.
(Marcus Blechman)

Pasticcio. The name is an Italian word for a stew, and the idea was that she would throw into it any choreographic idea that worked—"They wanted a big new thing to bring them into the twentieth century," she recalls. "I knew they'd be clean dancers because they were RAD trained, but I was afraid they'd be inhibited too. But at least they were Canadian, not English, so maybe . . ." *Pasticcio* was seen in February. On the same bill, Boris and Frank Hobi danced the grand adagio from *The Nutcracker*. Not to be outdone, Lhotka also danced on that program, taking the lead role in his *Devil in the Village*. Boris and Hobi went down very well indeed, and so did the new ballet. Highly impressed, the board invited them to return for the next season. Boris and Hobi said they would consider it.

In March, the company launched a new $30,000 fund drive, designed to raise sufficient money to cover the anticipated deficit for the coming season. Council alderman David Mulligan voiced what was no doubt still the opinion of many Winnipeggers when their appeal for $2,000 in city funds came up later that month. He called the ballet company "a bunch of galloping galoots" and questioned why it should be subsidized. "It's all right to say I'm not aesthetic," he said, "but how long is this going to go on? Which would do most good, the ballet or a school for retarded children?" "Judging by Alderman Mulligan's remarks," commented company publicist John Piasecki, "he must have received his cultural education in the front row of a burlesque theatre." And Kipp added: "Mr. Mulligan should do a little more studying of what the arts contribute to a community before he makes such untempered statements. . . . The ballet is the best and cheapest publicity our city has ever had." They got their $2,000.

Late in June, Kipp announced that Ruthanna Boris and Frank Hobi would return to the company in September on a six-month engagement as prima ballerina and principal dancer. Betty Farrally would remain as artistic director, he said, and Lhotka would retain his position as ballet master, but the Hobis would also help train and build the company. However, when Boris and Hobi arrived that fall—trailing a new music director, Robert Drumm, three new dancers (Alfa Liepa, Paul Sutherland and Lawrence Gradus) and a promise from Lincoln Kirstein that Winnipeg could have the entire New York City Ballet production of Boris' ballet *Kaleidoscope*—there was nothing for them to do. The cost of hiring them had forced the board to cut the company size to 16 and drastically curtail performance plans. The company's bookings amounted to nothing more than a few pencilled-in dates at the Playhouse.

Ruthanna Boris was not one to take that sort of thing lightly. "The Royal Winnipeg Ballet is going to give performances in Winnipeg this year if we have to dance in the middle of Portage Avenue," she declared. "Let's get out and do things."

The ballet was now in the curious position of being run by a triumvirate pulling in three different directions: Betty Farrally, with her solid background in the way things had always been; Lhotka, who was trying to bring to it some of the flavour of Zagreb and the Cecchetti technique; and the New York City Ballet-oriented Boris. Lhotka had never been regarded as anything less than a superb ballet master and his contribution to the upgrading of the company's performance standard had already been considerable, but he found the new situation untenable. Not much more than a week after the arrival of the Hobis, he resigned. Ruthanna was trying to boss things around too much. "Miss Boris is supposed to be the prima ballerina and choreographer," he said, "but I understand the board gave her powers beyond that." Questioned by the press, Kipp admitted that, yes, Boris's contract gave her "almost absolute power" in the company—greater even than Betty Farrally. Soon after this, Lhotka was pictured in the newspapers busy at a new job as a labourer in the CN freight yards.

Gweneth, commenting from Toronto, was particularly sniffy, as were several Winnipeggers, about the proposed new ballets for the coming season. All, it turned out, were to be creations of Miss Boris. Frank Morriss leaped into the fray. "Is the ballet, which has struggled through flood and fire to the stature of an internationally-known group, going to end up as the vehicle for the stellar talents of one ballerina?" he asked. "Let's hope that the Royal Winnipeg Ballet survives with the vitality that it has had in the past, rather than being the tail to the kite of the undoubtedly gifted Ruthanna Boris of New York." Ruthanna herself pooh-poohed all the noise and calamity. She had been asked to present terms on which she would come to Winnipeg. She had presented them. Betty had flown to New York to discuss them (particularly the question of the division of authority) and terms acceptable to all sides had been agreed. What was all the fuss about?

The situation worsened through the year. Ruthanna gave the company and the board no latitude. She demanded more work—why not establish the company on an annual basis with a performance a week? She demanded better work—"She went right back to basics," says Marilyn Young. "She thought we had attempted things technically that were beyond us so we never did more than one pirouette and everything was clean and very precise—a very kind of Balanchine influence. We learned a great deal from her."

Midway through November, Betty received a call from the immigration office. A dancer had arrived from England to join the company. Would Betty kindly come and collect her? Entirely unannounced, but with every intention of joining the Winnipeg Ballet, Sonia Taverner, a former member of the Sadler's Wells ensemble, had emigrated to Canada—complete with her mother, father and 13-year-old brother. It was soon evident that she would be an asset to the company, and since there was no money in the budget for unexpected additions to the company roster, an anonymous member of the board agreed to pay her salary for the balance of the season. Sonia Taverner was to become one of the company's brightest stars.

The 1956-57 season was no great box-office success. On the opening night there were 500 persons in the 1,465-seat Playhouse; on the second night, 350. New president Faye McKenzie blamed "adverse weather conditions" but Morriss's review suggested that "what was lacking was depth and variety. Every item in the repertoire [two new Boris ballets, *Comedians* and *Roundelay,* plus a revival of *Dan McGrew* and a showpiece *pas de deux* from *Raymonda* for Boris and Hobi] is a cream puff—the kind of ballet that deserves a closing spot after weightier items have been disposed of." It is also likely that Boris's move toward "modernism" was giving the conservative Winnipeg audience pause. Her work on technique, however, was plainly paying off. Everyone agreed that the company had never danced better.

A two-night program in January drew somewhat larger crowds to see revivals of *Pasticcio* and *Clasico* as well as Boris's new twenties spoof, *Le Jazz Hot,* and solos by the two stars—Boris in *The Dying Swan* and Hobi in *The Dance of the Sabra*—but Morriss commented: "The RWB continues to serve dessert." He was not to be won over until the final Winnipeg performances of that season—an

Jim Clouser (left), Marilyn Young, Ted Patterson, Marina Katronis, and Richard Rutherford in The Comedians. *(Campbell and Chipman)*

A scene from Roundelay *by Ruthanna Boris.*

all-Boris program featuring revivals of *Roundelay* and *Comedians,* plus *Cirque de Deux* (her first venture into choreography, dating from 1951) and the world première of *The Wanderling.* It was, said Morriss, "a triumphant occasion."

Throughout the season in Winnipeg, Betty had worked loyally, in the face of increasing friction within the company, to keep everything together and functioning, but the western tour that followed proved the breaking point. Hobi had been suffering from serious mental strain, and shortly before the tour electric shock treatment had been administered to counter his severe depression. On the tour his strain increased—he was handling lighting and staging as well as dancing—and Betty found the inevitable upheavals too much to take. When the company returned to Winnipeg, she gave the board a simple ultimatum: the Hobis, or her, but not both. It was not that much of a problem for the board. The Hobis had proposed terms for the coming season under which the company would be committed to a $70,000 budget, with more touring and higher salaries for the dancers. In view of the loss in past months, however, the board felt a little drawing-in of horns should take place. 1957-58, they said, would be a "Manitoba-first" season, and the budget for the year would be held at $40,000. Thus, no more Hobis. In any case, it is not clear now whether the Hobis would actually have returned even if there had been agreement to their plans. Ruthanna was unhappy with the psychiatric treatment her husband was receiving, and was anxious to get him back to New York. "We loved the company," she says, "but Frank's health came first."

In the eyes of most board members (Kathleen Richardson was perhaps the only dissenter) the Hobis' departure was a blessed relief. Ruthanna Boris's passage through the company in her brilliant and uncompromising short reign had left a trail of trampled toes. But the board's troubles had barely begun.

Betty took a holiday in Florida, returned to Winnipeg, promised the board she would present a concrete plan of action for the coming season (1957-58) by June 1, and then went to Penticton, British Columbia, to act as dance adjudicator at a music festival. Meanwhile, in Winnipeg, the financial situation worsened steadily. On May 9, Betty received a cable from John Russell stating that a board meeting was to be held that night to discuss the company's future. Betty replied to the effect that "as far as I'm concerned, you can stay as you are, or you get bigger, or you cut the whole thing off and finish, because you couldn't get any smaller." She doubted, she said, that many dancers would stay in Winnipeg if they were not able to tour, since touring was the only time they could save money. She says she added a request that the result of the board meeting be wired to her, since she didn't wish to return to the city if the company was planning to fold its operations or postpone them for a year.

Betty's reply was read to that evening's board meeting in the dining room of the Richardson mansion on Wellington Crescent. It is probably significant that neither John Russell nor Faye McKenzie, both staunch Farrally-Lloyd supporters, were present. After some deliberation, the board decided to form a small company that would work in Winnipeg only and do no travelling at all for the coming year. It was claimed at the time that Betty was contacted by telephone the following day and given these details, and that she immediately asked to be released from her work with the company. Betty, however, claimed she was fired—"The facts of the case are these," she said, in a prepared statement to the press: "On May 10 . . . at 8 A.M., Mr. Joseph Whitmore, vice-president, phoned and informed me that the board of directors had decided to engage someone else in my place." When she reaches this point in her telling of the story today, she chuckles, still, in sardonic disbelief: "Eight o'clock in the morning they phoned me when I was away and said thank you very much we're going to get [chuckle] someone else to run the company [chuckle]."

These were bitter times. Gweneth resigned noisily from her position as founding director, proclaiming that she didn't want to be associated with the "retrogressive" steps the company was being forced to take and complaining at the "appalling bad manners" that had been shown Betty. In an interview with *The Tribune*, she stated candidly that she thought the company should close down entirely "rather than go back to the beginning and start all over again." Betty stayed in British Columbia, and was joined there within the year by Gweneth. They bought a charming log house on a treed lakeside bank several miles south of Kelowna, and established a thriving dance-school business serving the region. Although they continued to operate their Winnipeg school until 1962, they didn't go back to Winnipeg in person until 1974, when they returned as guests of the company to share in celebrations of the thirty-fifth anniversary of the company's founding. The city of Winnipeg finally caught up with its obligations to the two women in the summer of 1977, when it presented Civic Achievement Medals to them both, and to David Yeddeau, in a small ceremony at the closing night of performances at the 1977 Dance in Canada Conference at the Manitoba Theatre Centre. Betty, recovering from an auto accident in which her pelvis was fractured in two places, stayed at home in Kelowna and let Gweneth pick up their engraved medals. Both their names had been misspelled.

By early summer of 1957 all the dancers but two had left town, and Morriss was wailing: "What is the ballet going to do without Betty Farrally? For the last few years, through fire, fighting, and the inner intrigues that beset dancing organizations, she was 'the company.' Undoubtedly the reason for the box office fiasco of last season was the feeling that her hand had been removed from the wheel. . . . Her service to the company has been far beyond the call of artistic duty. . . . What will the company do without Betty?"

The beleaguered board was working desperately to come up with answers. Nenad Lhotka, who by now was running his own school in Winnipeg, was approached. He said no. International advertising produced a short list of three possible candidates for the job, all of whom were brought to Winnipeg to be interviewed. Choreographer-teacher Benjamin Harkarvy, an energetic, shaven-headed 26-year-old out of the Fokine School in New York, was the eventual choice. Kathleen Richardson remembers him at his interview as "terribly reasonable, terribly sensible, terribly on the right track. . . . We were all very impressed." From there, almost immediately, things began to go downhill.

Harkarvy arrived in Winnipeg in the fall with six dancers, among them Richard Rutherford, Rachel Browne, Frederic Strobel, and Charles Czarny, and a music director, Richard Wernick. The future looked bright (The Canada Council had just made its first-ever dance grants, $20,000 to Winnipeg and $50,000 to the National Ballet) but the pressures were enormous. Harkarvy had to be director, choreographer, and ballet master (he was "a very fine teacher," according to Richard Rutherford) and on his shoulders lay the responsibility of making the season work.

Apart from one ballet by Ruthanna Boris (*Roundelay*) the entire repertoire was to be new—the first step in a two-year plan for the company's reorganization. Under this plan, the first year was to be devoted primarily to the building of the company and its repertoire ("maximum work and minimum performances," as Kathleen Richardson put it in her presidential report at the end of the season) and not until the second year was touring to begin.

The November performances included the world première of a new Harkarvy work, *The Twisted Heart,* based on the Pagliacci theme, to music of Wernick, plus Harkarvy's *La Primavera,* first seen that summer at the Jacob's Pillow Dance Festival. They were well received ("a smartness and freshness suggestive of the RWB's early years," said Maley) but dissent simmered within the performing ranks and there were growing problems between Harkarvy and the board. He remembers its members as very provincial. Few had any real breadth of view, and Kathleen Richardson, well, "I used to get so angry with her . . . I just felt she didn't understand anything I was saying." (In 1976, Harkarvy returned to Winnipeg, as a guest of the RWB, with his own company, the Pennsylvania Ballet. On hand to do the welcoming honours was Kathleen Richardson. They were perfectly polite and pleasant to each other. Time, as he says, is a great healer.) What angered him most was his growing belief that the board was quite content to have reduced the company to the status of a toy.

"People seemed very satisfied with it. There were no ambitions to bring the company back to the level it had reached before the fire."

In January of 1958, two more Harkarvy works were seen—the new *Fête Brillante*, to Mozart, plus his *Four Times Six*, originally made for a New York concert company—but the only critical success of the five-evening presentation was a revival of Arnold Spohr's *Intermède*.

Spohr himself was just back in town from a year in England. He had done the usual mad mix—a musical in Chelsea that lasted a week, some classes in kathakali technique (a classical Indian dance-drama) some jazz, and for a month he had partnered Alicia Markova in *Where the Rainbow Ends* at the London Coliseum. However he had returned to Winnipeg in the spring of 1957 to be with his sick mother, and had agreed to take over teaching duties for Gweneth and Betty at their Canadian School of Ballet.

Pressures on Harkarvy, meanwhile, intensified. He had a further full evening of ballet to prepare for the season-closing program in March, but he found himself in such conflict with the board that in the middle of February, less than a month before the performance dates, he resigned, effective immediately. Wernick resigned as well.

Harkarvy says today that he and the board clashed on two issues—the lack of touring, and the use of guest dancers (the board wanted them; Harkarvy wanted to develop company talent). Another problem mentioned at the time was Harkarvy's demand for what he considered an experienced business manager to handle tour bookings. John Graham, who was then chairman of the production committee, says costumes were the catalyst ("He wanted a set of costumes remade, and I said flatly that it couldn't be done") but Harkarvy doesn't remember that. In any case, he says, it wouldn't have been the kind of situation to make him leave. Some have speculated, with the benefit of hindsight, that Harkarvy was merely using Winnipeg as a stepping stone to higher things, and fled for greener fields in Holland as soon as the opportunity presented itself. (He became ballet master of the Netherlands Ballet that year, and established the Netherlands Dance Theatre in 1959.)

Anyway, it was messy. Members of the board were quoted in the press (anonymously, of course) as saying that Harkarvy's departure was "good riddance." Gweneth, contacted in Toronto, said pithily: "A happy release after a lingering illness." On the other hand, 12 members of the company—all but one of the remaining ensemble—signed a statement to the press declaring warm support for Harkarvy, and praising his teaching and company direction.

None of this solved the problem of the looming March shows. Who could they possibly turn to? Well, who else? Arnold Spohr.

1958-64 Arnold Tiptoes In

Yes, said Arnold Spohr, he would mount the March shows for them.

It would be idle to speculate, now, on what might have happened to the RWB had Arnold Spohr not been available when he was; all we know is that it would have been a different company.

Outside Winnipeg, the world was changing rapidly. The nuclear age was already under way. The space age was beginning. In January, 1958, the U.S. launched its first earth satellite. Three years later Yuri Gagarin became the first human traveller in orbit.

Spohr's accession to power at the RWB had none of the dramatic impact of these events, of course. It was to take him years to develop the flair and vision that was to characterize his contribution to the company's growth, years to find and gather around him the individuals who would help him make that growth a reality. He began as a convenient puppet of the board of directors, and his assumption of real leadership came, like his confidence, gradually.

Nevertheless, his return to the company would become recognized, in retrospect, as the beginning of a new era, and a new lease on life, for the RWB.

In three weeks during that spring of 1958, Arnold Spohr managed to mount what Kathleen Richardson was to describe as "the best show we'd seen for years."   *105*

Marilyn Young and David Shields are watched by the judges in Brian Macdonald's The Darkling. *(Campbell and Chipman)*

Overnight, he became the obvious candidate for the post of artistic director—
"Everyone said well, heavens, ask Arnold to stay," she says, and the following
day she and Jack Graham did.

It was lunchtime. Arnold was just finishing company class on the Playhouse
stage. They stood in the wings and Arnold listened attentively, in that serious
way that he has, as they offered him the company, and then he turned it down. He
didn't think he could handle it, he said, he really didn't. They persisted, leaning
on his pride, his sense of duty. Obligation to others has always been a weak spot
with Arnold Spohr, and he began to soften. By the time they left him, he had
agreed to think about it. Even so, he was torn by agonies of indecision for the next
two weeks. He phoned Betty and Gweneth for advice. Betty said he'd be mad to
take it on; there were too many problems. Other friends told him the same.
Gweneth told him to try it.

He finally agreed to do it out of loyalty (and pride) because there was no one
else. However, he made it clear he considered himself barely suited for the job.
And in some ways he was right. His years away from the company had allowed
him to enlarge his performing experience. He had expanded his technical skills
with classes in New York and London. He had gained confidence and expertise
as a teacher. But his practical experience as the head of a ballet company was
nil, and on the surface at least it would seem amazing that the board of a ballet
company at the RWB's stage of development would want to entrust its future to
an individual with such limited qualifications.

In a curious way, however, that inexperience might actually have weighed in
his favour. The board members had suffered several seasons of distress at the
hands of demanding professional directors from outside the company—
individuals who had insisted (as was their perfect right) to be given the power to
take the company in radically different directions from those established by its
founders. By the time Spohr arrived on the scene, the board had probably had
quite enough of firebrands and temperament. Spohr, with all his self-doubt and
inexperience, was tractable.

There were other, more important factors in his favour. Winnipeg bred, he
had an insider's understanding of the city and its people. Most of all, though, he
was an instrument of continuity, a bridge back. Spohr was a company original,
picking up the torch. He was steeped in the Lloyd-Farrally first principles—
principles on which the company had been founded, and principles on which it
had thrived: audience-building populism, variety, entertainment, and its own
distinctive blending of classical and modern dance styles. His great contribution over the next 20 years would be to oversee the company's international

expansion without losing sight of those precepts. There are persons today who believe that it is long past time for the RWB to abandon them and to embark on new and different courses—a change of size, a change of repertoire, a change of touring policy, a change of image. That is as may be. But 20 years ago those precepts (and Spohr) were the company's salvation.

Spohr may have hesitated at first, but once he had agreed to take on the job there was no stopping him. He recognized from the start a need to improve himself—not only in the business of dancers and dancing, but in his understanding of life, the human condition—and he brought a characteristic doggedness and determination to the task, looking, learning, and travelling the globe on a voyage of discovery that has never stopped.

Looking for dancers that summer, he went to the Banff Centre summer school of the arts and found a choreographer: Brian Macdonald. Macdonald was to have a major influence on the company. The ballets that developed the RWB's international reputation throughout the 1960s were almost all by him. He forged for the company the character it was to carry around the world.

Macdonald "fell in love with movement" in 1944, much the way that Spohr had done. As a 16-year-old freshman law student at McGill University, in Montreal, he attended a performance by a touring New York company, Lucia Chase's Ballet Theatre. It was not to become the American Ballet Theatre until 1957. He was entranced by the expressive ability of the moving body, and enrolled for ballet classes. Six-foot-two, bright red hair, he made the girls giggle. His dance classes were financed by a job as music and nightclub correspondent for a Montreal newspaper. One of the persons he was sent to interview was Celia Franca. He was excited by her plans and almost immediately he left the newspaper to join her newly-formed National Ballet. His dancing career ended two years later, in a smoky Montreal nightclub where he had taken a summer job as a dancer between National Ballet seasons. The act closed with a spectacular leap off stage, and one particularly crowded night a ringside patron stood up just as Macdonald was making the jump and they collided. The impact knocked Macdonald sideways, and he fell and broke his arm. It never healed properly.

So he became a choreographer, which was what he had wanted to be in the first place. He choreographed everything—a weekly TV variety show for Radio-Canada, ice shows, aquacades, Montreal Alouettes cheerleaders, a routine for stripper Lili St. Cyr, and endless student musicals at McGill University, one of which was the national hit, *My Fur Lady*. It was during the run of *My Fur Lady* that he met Spohr. At the time, it looked like a blessed matching. They were, in a sense, kindred spirits, close in age, close in types of experience. He agreed to come to Winnipeg to make a ballet for the company, and the work—*The Darkling*—was seen at the season's October opening.

The Darkling, an examination of the ways in which individuals' secret selves can disrupt a relationship, featured Marilyn Young and Michael Hrushowy in the lead roles, and received an enthusiastic welcome from a near-capacity audience at the Playhouse. Maley called it "the most provocative ballet yet produced by the RWB" and Macdonald was given an ovation.

But the real hero of the evening was Spohr. "He has brought the company back to the path it trod so successfully until it strayed into devious byways," said Morriss. "As director, Mr. Spohr is unmistakably at the helm of dancers who are working as an ensemble. The spirit, which was lacking, is there again."

It was a hard-working fall for the tiny company of 17. By the end of the year Spohr had added nine new or revived ballets to the repertoire—among them his own *E Minor*, to the Chopin Piano Concerto, *The Chinese Nightingale* by German-Canadian choreographer Heino Heiden, and *Grasslands* ("the joys and hardships of farm life on the great plains") by Robert Moulton, a promising young choreographer who was to dance briefly with the company the following year. Marilyn Young was so busy dancing that she and Grant Marshall (another University of Manitoba architect who had done some set-designing for the

Robert Moulton's Brave Song. *(Campbell and Chipman)*

David Shields and Marilyn Young in the Sleeping Beauty pas de deux. *(Campbell and Chipman)*

company) were forced to postpone their wedding for six months. By the end of the 1958-59 season, the company had completed 42 performances for a total audience of 33,500, compared with ten performances the previous season to a total audience of 5,768. And the budget almost balanced (a loss of $3,000 on a total expenditure of $120,000).

Arnold Spohr spent the summer of 1959 in London on a Canada Council grant, attending rehearsals and classes of the Royal Ballet and filling some of the gaps in his knowledge of the classics in private classes with Peter Wright, the English choreographer, teacher, and director. While in London, he hired a Royal Ballet soloist, David Shields, and brought him back to Winnipeg.

Shields arrived just in time for the company's second royal performance. Queen Elizabeth and Prince Philip were to return to Winnipeg on a whistle-stop tour of the Canadian West, and it was arranged that as part of their 11 hours in the city they would attend a performance by the ballet.

Winnipeg went into its usual spin. Alderman Slaw Rebchuk said it was "disgusting" that the Royal couple should have to see the ballet instead of enjoying the fresh air in the park. Alderman David Mulligan, of "galloping galoots" notoriety, sneered at the dancers as "jumping jacks."

It was a debacle from the beginning. In order to accommodate the thousands of Winnipeggers who, it was assumed, were just bursting to share an evening of culture with the royal couple, the 9,200-seat Winnipeg Arena, a massive, drafty ice palace, was taken over. A stage was erected. Seats were built over the ice area. A royal box was constructed. Mr. Andrew Currie was put in charge of providing the royal umbrella in case of rain.

As late as a week before the show, ticket sales were desperate. The performance committee voted to make "at least 400" tickets available to "veterans, old age pensioners, and wheelchair cases" (a practice known in the trade as papering the house) but the hospital couldn't find any veterans who wanted to go, though there *were* two members of the Canadian Paraplegics Association who were interested in free tickets if there were any to spare.

The Queen and Prince Philip arrived 25 minutes late and stayed for an hour. According to a *Canadian Press* story, "in the pale light reflecting from the stage [they] appeared disinterested [sic] much of the time. The Queen fumbled with her diamond necklace and adjusted her tiara and the Duke slouched in his chair in the hot, humid, smoky arena." The books closed on the evening with a deficit of almost $13,000.

The success of *The Darkling* won Brian Macdonald a contract to return in the fall of 1959 to do a comedy. He spent the summer in Vancouver, putting together a production called *Jubilee* for the International Festival, and while he was there his wife, Olivia Wyatt (a member of the RWB the previous season) was killed in a road accident. Choreographing the comedy for the RWB, he once told an interviewer, was the only thing that saved him from suicide. It was *Les Whoops-de-Doo*, a ballet that would become, for a while, a company trademark—dedicated to "the misalliance of classical ballet and the Western myth." It parodied the styles of various choreographers (Jerome Robbins, Agnes de Mille, and Gweneth Lloyd, among others) and its most popular moment seems to have been that at which Marilyn Young drifted through a corral on *pointe*, doing a parody of the rose adagio from *The Sleeping Beauty*, to the goggle-eyed amazement of the lounging cowboys. It was first performed in Flin Flon, Manitoba.

Les Whoops-de-Doo *in rehearsal. Top: Kit Copping (left), David Shields, Marina Katronis, and (extreme right) Beverley Barkley on Bill Martin-Viscount's knee. Bottom: Virginia Wakelyn and Robert Lee Jones. (Campbell and Chipman)*

Robert Johnston, who had been manager of Macdonald's *My Fur Lady* company, joined the RWB in the 1959-60 season, and one of his first proposals as general manager was the importation of a pair of Russian dancers to give cachet to the following season, the company's twenty-first. Letters were sent, Kathleen Richardson was summoned to the Soviet Embassy in Ottawa, and then, for a long time, there was silence. Affirmative word eventually arrived less than a month before the Christmas-period performances in which the guests were tentatively scheduled to appear. The dancers chosen (in Russia) were Olga Moiseyeva and Askold Makarov, from the Leningrad Kirov company, and the signing was a major coup: an exclusive for Winnipeg, and the first occasion under the then-new Soviet cultural regulations on which Soviet dancers had been permitted to leave the country.

Winnipeg did it with all the trimmings—mayor at the airport to greet them, plus half the ballet board and most of the company. The Russians found themselves part of triple celebrations: Christmas, New Year, and the company's twenty-first anniversary. Their opening performance (the leads in *Swan Lake, Act Two*, adapted by RWB ballet mistress Gwynne Ashton from Petipa's original, and the *Don Quixote pas de deux*) earned actual bravos from the Winnipeg audience—"as rare as lilacs in December," commented *Free Press*

Arnold Spohr (left) and visiting Russian dancers Olga Moiseyeva and Askold Makarov celebrate the company's twenty-first anniversary. (Campbell and Chipman)

writer Ken Winters. Richard Rutherford remembers that "they adapted to us very quickly: they realized how limited we were, compared with what they were used to, and I think they just took the attitude, we will do as much for them as we can." Back in the Soviet Union, the Russians said they had found some "extremely gifted dancers" in the Canadian company. "Unfortunately," they said, "the Winnipeg Ballet gives preference to modern trends and pure ballet is too often supplanted by fancy tricks."

In sum, the venture showed a net profit for the company of $2,800. However, everything else had lost money, and by early January, 1961, honorary treasurer J. G. Scott was reporting a bank overdraft of $38,000, and another $4,000 owing in bills.

The tight financial situation meant stringent spending controls in all areas, though this didn't stop the board from aiming high for new ballets. Agnes de Mille was approached and agreed to come the following year, and the clever and forceful Sol Kanee convinced George Balanchine to allow the company to have his *Pas de Dix* for the cost of getting it taught. Kanee, a prominent miller, a longtime director of the Bank of Canada, and an active civic worker, had been brought onto the RWB board by Kipp during Harkarvy's brief reign, and became a vice-president in 1958. Later he was to become president and eventually RWB chairman. "He was a very strong person, a dynamo," says Spohr. "He'd get in and get things done."

How he got the rights to *Pas de Dix* is a tale Kanee likes to tell against himself. He was introduced to Balanchine in New York, and the choreographer expressed a desire to help the company in any way he could. Kanee promptly asked for a ballet. Balanchine offered him *Concerto Barocco*, his famous and much-revived plotless ballet to Bach. Kanee, who knew virtually nothing about ballet, wasn't sure the RWB would have the talent or the forces to carry the work. Did Mr. B perhaps have something else? Balanchine offered him *Serenade*, the famous setting of Tchaikovsky that is now in the repertoire of companies in many countries. Kanee, ever pragmatic, asked how many dancers it needed. Twenty-eight, he was told. "Too many," said Kanee, beginning to wish he hadn't asked. "Do you have anything for, say, eight to ten?" Balanchine suggested *Pas de Dix*. "And how many dancers does *that* have?" asked the distraught Kanee.

Pas de Dix was for many years far beyond the company's technical capabilities but it became a popular staple of the repertoire. At a total price of $665 (transportation, hotel expenses, and the fee for Balanchine's ballet mistress, Una Kai, who travelled to Winnipeg to set the work on the company) it was a handsome bargain.

Total attendance for the 1960-61 season was 63,732, nearly double the total for the previous season. The board's continuing parsimony had kept the year's net loss down to just under $5,000, but, with an accumulated deficit running now at $25,000, the financial picture remained bleak. It was the same in Toronto and Montreal—Ludmilla Chiriaeff's company, Les Grands Ballets Canadiens, which had grown out of the Montreal ballet festival of 1956, and the National Ballet of Canada, were both struggling. The fledgling Canada Council was helping—in the 1960-61 season it gave $20,000 to Les Grands, $40,000 to Winnipeg, and $100,000 to the National—but demands for a more equitable distribution of these funds was growing. The Council's annual report that year suggested that "in order to determine what course of action is most likely to contribute to raising the standard of ballet in Canada as a whole, the Council may seek expert advice from outside the country during the next season." Spohr is convinced today that "the Council only wanted one company, and we were supposed to be out." He and his colleagues in Winnipeg were not about to sit back and let *that* happen.

Rimma Karelskaya and Boris Hohlov, two soloists from the Bolshoi company, joined the company at the end of 1961 for a series of Christmas shows plus a major-city western tour. They were well received on the tour, but in Winnipeg there were many empty seats—a product of the Winnipeg need-for-novelty syndrome, perhaps. Russians? They'd performed with the ballet the year before. Something different was needed. That "something different" came in the late winter—the new de Mille and Balanchine works.

Spohr distinctly remembers his first contact with de Mille soon after she had signed the contract for her new ballet, *The Bitter Weird*, to be made on music from *Brigadoon*. He was passing through New York, and he "thought we might be able to have a little visit, so she could get an idea of what she was getting into." He phoned her, and no doubt came on in his ebullient way, but "she was as cold as winter." It was no better when she turned up to begin rehearsals in Winnipeg in mid February. "She was absolutely closed toward me, like a wall—and after all, who am I, a kid from Winnipeg?—I had to prove myself." He did, in splendid fashion. She mounted *The Bitter Weird* in about a week, then went away, leaving the work—not without considerable reservations—in Spohr's hands. However, when she returned, she was "delighted and astonished" to find that the ballet had not disintegrated (as might have been expected in other places) but had in fact been refined and clarified. "We've been pals ever since," says Spohr.

This exposure to New York professionalism was just what the company needed. *Pas de Dix* was no easy dance to do ("you get to that marathon of a solo, then straight into the long *galop*, and then the coda—it's be-sick-in-the-wings time, finishing that," says former principal Sheila Mackinnon) and *The Bitter Weird* made greater interpretative demands on the dancers than had ever been made before, but these were the kind of challenges on which the company thrived. It was just as well. In the audience at the first Winnipeg performance of these ballets in March, 1962, were two individuals who held the power of life and death over the company. The Canada Council had gone ahead as hinted and hired two outsiders to look at the state of Canadian dance and make recommendations on future directions—Lincoln Kirstein, of the New York City Ballet,

Agnes de Mille with a portrait of Lizzie Borden. (Martha Swope)

and Richard Buckle, ballet critic of the London *Sunday Times*. Also asked for his opinion (and present in March) was Guy Glover from the National Film Board.

The March performances were gratifyingly successful. *The Bitter Weird*, with all that New York glitter and novelty, could hardly *not* have drawn crowds in Winnipeg, and the opening night at the Playhouse was a sell-out. But if it was the glamour that got them there, it was the dance and the performance that brought them to their feet when the ballet's final curtain came down. Wrote Winters, in the *Free Press*: "At some point during the eight bravo-studded curtain calls which left no doubt that the lady from the south had just put the world's frostiest audience into her pocket and melted its heart, trim, tiny Agnes de Mille walked onto the Playhouse stage to receive her due and her flowers. A professional to the hem of her simple triumphal gown, the choreographer wore her success like a spring flower; she shared her praise and showed her pleasure. Miss de Mille had reason to be pleased. The Winnipeg company's performance of *The Bitter Weird*, the Brigadoon-derived ballet she had retailored for its use, was absolutely stunning." He singled out Richard Rutherford as "brilliant" in his actor-dancer interpretation of the ballet's tragic lover—and so did many others, including de Mille, for whom he was always a special favourite.

The opinions and recommendations of the Canada Council trio were never made public, but the burden of their conclusions can be seen in the continued survival of all three companies, and in their extensive financial underpinning by the Council to this day.

It was becoming increasingly obvious that the company should have a school of its own. Without a school, there was no way of assuring a steady stream of fresh dance talent—it was still, after all, no easy task to attract potential company material to Winnipeg. There was also money to be made from the dance-school business; demand for instruction was so great that waiting-lists were necessary. Betty and Gweneth were the chief complication here. They still operated, by proxy, the Winnipeg branch of their Canadian School of Ballet, part of whose premises the company rented as its headquarters. And Gweneth had explained in a letter to the board when the company school proposal was first put forward at the beginning of 1961 that the income from their school, while "surprisingly small" (about $3,000 a year) was "absolutely essential to our livelihood." But by the spring of 1962 the board had found what it considered suitable alternative premises for itself, complete with sufficient space for a school of its own, and the

A little revelry before the wedding in Agnes de Mille's The Bitter Weird.

executive committee came to the conclusion that the RWB had "a moral obligation only" to the founders. How best to discharge that? They gave Gweneth a simple option. Either close down the Canadian School of Ballet and accept a position with the new school as curriculum advisor at a fee of $1,000 a year for five years, or accept an offer from the ballet to pay its portion of the rent for as long as it took her to find more suitable premises for her own school, up to a maximum period of a year. It was not much of a choice. She became curriculum advisor and closed down the school. The official school of the RWB was opened on September 30, 1962, by the Lieutenant-Governor of Manitoba, E. F. Willis. Head of the teaching staff was former leading dancer Jean McKenzie.

Despite the momentary successes, these were doldrum years. Arnold Spohr was still feeling his way. Planning was sporadic and uneven. Performance levels were low ("In a current Winnipeg Ballet cast nothing matches but the costumes," wrote Winters in January, 1963) and in the area of choreography there was no daring. Apart from the de Mille and Balanchine imports, there had been little of merit or durability in the half-dozen recent additions to the repertoire, and the company was coasting. Spohr was on the point of giving up completely:

Sheila Mackinnon and Winthrop Corey (foreground) and company in Aimez-vous Bach? *(Martha Swope)*

"We worked so hard all the time, but all our engagements kept falling through, because we really hadn't got on a footing yet—who wanted us?"

Throughout the winter and spring of 1963 the board dithered. All kinds of projects were announced—new ballets by Robert Moulton and Brian Macdonald (whose works were already known in Winnipeg) and British choreographers Walter Gore and Peter Darrell. A new full-length *Coppelia*. Christmas visits by two Royal Danish Ballet stars, Kirsten Simone and Henning Kronstam. But this wasn't planning, this was dilettantism. The company had lost $35,000 on the previous season alone, and here they were, anticipating a further loss of $14,000 for the coming year, and not enough money in the bank to cover the

payroll for more than a week and a half. Impossible, said treasurer Gordon H.
Pawling; cut back.

The warning came none too soon. In February, Pawling was prophesying an accumulated deficit of $104,000 by the season's end, and board members were being tapped for immediate donations of $250-$300 each to cover the payroll and keep the company solvent.

It needed Brian Macdonald to lift the company out of this rut, with a ballet titled *Aimez-vous Bach?* Originally choreographed for his summer students in Banff, it was introduced to the RWB repertoire in January of 1964 and had an

Brian Macdonald.

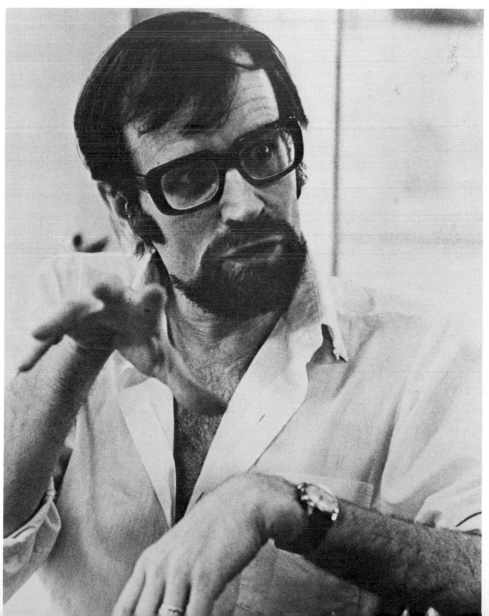

enormous popular and critical success. "Here is a work," said Winters, "which is modish, deft, cheeky, handsome, and utterly beguiling." It was also, in no small sense, the salvation of the company. In the audience that January was Ted Shawn, one of the pioneers of dance in North America, and the founder of the influential Jacob's Pillow Dance Festival, held each summer in Lee, Massachusetts. Both the other Canadian companies had appeared there, and Spohr had been pestering Shawn for years to come to Winnipeg to "audition" the RWB. Finally, he had consented. He signed the company for two weeks that summer after seeing only one performance. He loved the dancers, and the sense of enjoyment they projected. Most of all, though, he loved *Aimez-vous Bach?* It was better, he said, than Balanchine's *Pas de Dix*.

The company's relationship with Macdonald blossomed. In March, his

The company at Jacob's Pillow. Ted Shawn is second from left with Spohr beside him. (John Lindquist)

"spanking new spoof" *Pas d'Action* was introduced and at a small ceremony beside a crackling log fire at the riverside home of board member Vaughan Baird, a blizzard raging outside, Spohr announced that Macdonald had been appointed "choreographer to the RWB." It was the first time in Canadian ballet such an honour had been bestowed on a Canadian choreographer. To mark the occasion, he was given a pair of gold cufflinks engraved with the company emblem (the letters RWB garlanded by a circle of bowing ballerinas in long tutus). The title placed no special onus on the recipient. He was not required to live in the city or sign any special contracts, and in fact the following June, Macdonald left Canada to become director of the Royal Swedish Opera Ballet in Stockholm. But it represented a tangible claim on him, and one that would prove of increasing value to the RWB in the coming years.

At Jacob's Pillow the company found itself the summer's star turn. Shawn had billed the RWB "the glittering crown jewel of the 1964 season," and the dancers, rising obligingly to the occasion, dazzled. The reviews were like gifts. Walter Terry, in the New York *Herald Tribune,* called the company "one of the most engaging ballet groups functioning this side of the Atlantic." The *Christian Science Monitor* praised the "joy, vitality, and mastery that conquered the capacity audience with the first steps." And *Time* said: "There is nothing derivatively European or effete about the Royal Winnipeg, it has a personality all its own: Winnipeg is a ballet company notable for youth, boldness, and exuberance, for a *corps de ballet* of unusual wit, dramatic sense, and precision. Most importantly . . . the Royal Winnipeg's talented male contingent is one of the most reassuring masculine presences on the ballet stage today."

"Jacob's Pillow—that's where I saw daylight," says Spohr. "That's where we became famous."

1964-70 Up and Away

This was the Royal Winnipeg Ballet's golden age. It was like growing up; everything began to fall into place. "It's incredible what a couple of favourable reviews from New York critics can do," the company's new manager commented as the momentum of the Jacob's Pillow success swept the company through its silver anniversary season and into the major leagues of international dance. Suddenly everyone, everywhere seemed to want the RWB. And with the success, inevitably, came a new spirit. The deficits loomed just as large, but they no longer seemed so horrifying. The company felt a new confidence in what it could achieve. "You were out marching for your art and your city," says one who was there. "It was crazy, fun, thrilling." "What next?" an admirer gasped the morning after their London successes. "Next, the world," smiled Arnold Spohr.

His optimism reflected the new sense of possibility that was abroad in the world. This was the period when man was to walk on the moon, when hearts were to be transplanted: what was not possible? It was also a period of turmoil. John F. Kennedy had been assassinated in 1963. In 1964, Khruschev was deposed as head of the Soviet Communist party. Rhodesia declared independence from Britain late in 1965. Less than six months after that, Dr. Martin Luther King was killed in Memphis, Tennessee.

It was the time of hippies, of a generation that was by no means sure of how to come to grips with the social upheavals. It was the era of Haight-Ashbury. And Kent State.

The RWB reflected many of these concerns—the euphoria, the turmoil, the 123

David Moroni (left), Ana Maria de Gorriz, and Richard Rutherford with Russian interpreter in Moscow's Red Square, 1968.

emphasis on youth—in its repertoire. Its sensitivity to its times, and to the day-to-day hopes and concerns of its audience, was a significant factor in its snowballing success.

The summer of 1964 saw the arrival of two individuals who were to influence significantly the company's growth and character. J. R. (Jim) Cameron, an advertising man from the Cockfield-Brown agency, came in to do some special promotional writing. And J. S. (Sergei) Sawchyn moved over from a management job at Rainbow Stage, the city's summer theatre, to become general manager. Some years on, they would become an inspired management team, playing every angle to make the company sell, pumping every source to keep the company solvent. Much later, long after they had gone their separate ways, Cameron would be called back to rescue the RWB as it teetered on the brink of its greatest financial calamity. But in 1964, neither Cameron nor Sawchyn had any idea of what they were getting into at the ballet.

Cameron had been a ballet-goer in the 1940s and 1950s. He saw his first RWB show in 1947 while a double-major English and history student in the veterans' class at the University of Manitoba—a girl-friend was given tickets by Kathleen Richardson, otherwise he wouldn't have been able to afford the date—but his interest waned, and by 1964 he hadn't been near the ballet for years.

It wasn't even his decision to get involved again. Kathleen Richardson went to his boss and asked for the help of a qualified writer, someone who could make a convincing pitch, and the boss chose Cameron. The company needed help in preparing a crucially-important brief. Canada had been asked to send an opera company, an orchestra, a theatre ensemble, and a ballet company to the 1965 Commonwealth Arts Festival in London. The RWB board had already made a tentative pitch for this, but the grapevine was whispering that the choices were going to be entirely Eastern Canada, with the National Ballet as the dance component. It was Cameron's job to persuade Prime Minister Lester Pearson to designate the Winnipeggers as Canada's dance representative in London. He took the word "brief" literally, and wrote a single 78-word sentence, making a three-point argument in the company's favour—its portability, its popularity outside Canada, and the uniqueness of its repertoire (it was, he pointed out, the only Canadian company that danced things the English couldn't criticize on

their own terms). He backed up the note with a fat appendix of budgets, reviews,
repertoire notes—"and Celia Franca," as he likes to recall it, "never knew what
hit her."

Board member Vaughan Baird, the RWB solicitor, brought in Sawchyn.
Baird had watched him make a pitch for financial aid at a meeting of a local
council, and had been impressed by his style. Sawchyn wasn't sure at first that
he wanted the job—"I was aware of the success the company was enjoying, and it
seemed to me to be an arts commodity that could be moved. But I was thoroughly

*J Sergei Sawchyn during his reign as general manager. In the background is one
of six paintings of RWB dancers done in 1952 by Winnipeg artist Jack Markell.
(J. Coleman Fletcher)*

convinced that ballet people *were* galloping galoots in long underwear. And I was really afraid of the spectre of homosexuality—who wants to work with a bunch of faggots?"

"He had a lot of chutzpah when he first joined," one of his associates from that time recalls, "but he didn't have much finesse. He used to learn a new word every day, and use it in every sentence." Finesse or not, he had plenty of ideas (he called them "instincts") about where the company was going, and how it was to get there. Sawchyn was the first to recognize and exploit the company's marketability. He began to sell it like soap flakes, using mass-subscription sales gimmicks that are now in the marketing repertoire of every arts organization on the continent—free-trip sweepstakes prizes, door-to-door campaigns, direct-contact telephone "boiler-room" sessions. He sold it hard, aiming for excitement, and as far as Sawchyn was concerned there was nothing the RWB couldn't do. Wouldn't it be a great idea, he once wondered, if the company was to go to *Russia*? He began working on the project soon after he joined the company. Four years later, the Royal Winnipeg Ballet was dancing in Mosscow.

Another of his "instincts" was that it was about time the RWB was represented by Sol Hurok in the U.S.—"a company is known by the company it keeps," he says, "and at that time, being with Hurok said you were special." He drove hard for the things he wanted ("I was a forceful, not always likeable, sort of manager," he says, an opinion others share) and at the start of the 1964-65 season he was able to announce that the RWB had been booked by Hurok for an eight-week U.S. tour in the fall of 1965.

The 1964-65 season was a year-long recharging of batteries before the international exposure (London and New York) that lay ahead. Extensive tours took the ballet around Canada and the U.S. again. And each of the year's four sets of performances featured new ballets in a wide range of styles—*The Rehearsal,* another de Mille work, with the choreographer herself narrating a look at the mechanics of dance-making; *Tribute,* " a token payment of the debt we owe to our founders" by the young and ambitious Jim Clouser, who had risen from the ranks to the position of principal dancer and assistant to the director; the third act of Bournonville's *Napoli,* mounted by Kirsten Ralov, former star of the Royal Danish Ballet; and *Slaveni,* a narrative folk dance by Nenad Lhotka, who by now had formed a company of his own in Winnipeg. And as if to prove that success breeds success, the season's presentations played to the largest audience in years. In February, 1965, testing the wind of public opinion and finding it favourable, the company launched the most disciplined and intensive fund-raising campaign in its history, with a target of $259,000, spread over a three-year period. A new mood of confidence was abroad.

The visit to England in the late summer of 1965 opened inauspiciously. As the giant red-and-yellow neon signs advertising the RWB residence at the Piccadilly Theatre flashed on in Piccadilly Circus, company personnel turned up at London International Airport to collect the air-freighted sets and music, but found that a planeload of frozen peas had been delivered instead. The sets had been sent by mistake to Montreal, and the music was lost in Air Canada transit somewhere between Ottawa and London. Eventually, it arrived via an entirely unconnected airline, a day-and-a-half late, just in time for opening night.

The board had been flattered to accept the festival organizers' invitation to "open" the month-long event, but, as it happened, the company was competing for festival audiences with a royal gala by the Sydney Symphony Orchestra and a performance by a Nigerian drama company. In addition, the New York City Ballet had closed a triumphant London season less than a week before. The opening-night audience was small, and newly-elected president Sol Kanee, travelling with the company, complained that the festival organizers had made the RWB's visit "the best-kept secret in town." However, the company was received with flattery by the critics, and at the closing night in London they were forced to do an encore of the last movement of *Les Whoops-de-Doo*—the first ballet encore in London since the visit of the Bolshoi in 1957. Spohr, who had been "scared stiff" by the prospect of London, was beside himself. Besieged by autograph hunters after the closing show, he kept exclaiming: "I can't believe it—to have this kind of reception! It's marvellous, marvellous, marvellous!"

The company captivated everyone, as it so often has, by its freshness, enthusiasm, its "disarmingly exuberant youthful vitality" *(Daily Express)*. Where it scored less strongly was in the work it presented. "It is obvious," wrote John Percival in a long and thoughtful summing-up in *Dance and Dancers*, "that the company is to some extent confined by the need to cater for Canadian tastes, which on this showing were not, on the whole, notably sophisticated or subtle." Percival's colleague, Peter Williams, in a generally kindly piece, suggested Spohr should aim now to build a repertory that was "vital yet sophisticated, while still retaining that natural fresh air."

That advice was echoed less than two months later by New York *Times* critic Clive Barnes when he saw the company at the Hunter College Playhouse, in

Manhattan, and at Brooklyn College. "Undeniably," wrote Barnes, "this company . . . excels in a certain brash vigor that is always welcome." But he went on, "all the time, one has a feeling that the Royal Winnipeg Ballet is aimed straight at the heart of people who don't like ballet; and all the time one has the feeling that it has missed. . . . The company's qualities of vitality and freshness are evident. But if this company intends to make its mark in anything other than a purely local fashion, it will require a far firmer sense of artistic purpose. With good choreography, themes that mean something here and now, and a determination not to underrate either the taste or intelligence of its presumably unsophisticated audiences, the Royal Winnipeg Ballet could easily develop into a very worthwhile company."

Informed honesty of this kind was what Spohr and the company had badly been needing. It was advice they were to act on.

Richard Rutherford remembers the 1965-66 Hurok tour—the company's first—as "the most marvellous tour I ever went on. It was fall when we left Winnipeg—still warm, the leaves just beginning to turn. And as we went all the way down the east coast of the U.S., all through Florida, across the Gulf of Mexico, and up through California, the weather stayed nice."

Within the company, however, there were occasional storms. In November of 1965, the board was alarmed to read newspaper reports that Jim Clouser was apparently planning to leave Winnipeg at the beginning of 1966 to become artistic director of a new ballet company in Vancouver. The alarm was understandable. In his six years with the company Clouser had become a valuable asset, and Spohr had already talked of "developing" him as a choreographer in the way Macdonald had been developed. But itchiness of feet on Clouser's part would have been understandable too. He knew he could go no higher within the company, short of deposing Spohr, and he was ambitious. He had made five original ballets, of varying quality, and just prior to the England trip, Walter Terry had devoted an entire page of the New York *Herald Tribune* weekend section to a paean of praise for this "quadruple-threat man" (choreographer, composer, performer, teacher). Clouser in fact denied the newspaper reports, claiming he had only given Ballet B.C. permission to use his name as advisor, and the board formally exercised its contract option to keep him within the fold. But in 1967 he took what was described as a "leave of absence" from the RWB, and never returned. "Now that the company has reached a high degree of success," he told Frank Morriss in a 1968 interview, "I would find it confining to just sit there maintaining it. So I look elsewhere for a challenge."

Christine Hennessy (left), David Moroni, and Sheila Mackinnon in While the Spider Slept.

Two more Macdonald works entered the repertoire later that season. The January performances of 1966 included the Winnipeg première of *While the Spider Slept*, a dramatic work first made for the Royal Swedish Ballet in 1965. It was inspired by lines from a poem on the death of John F. Kennedy, and Winters called it the triumph of the season, "a very subtle and serious work of conscience and of art." And at the Stratford Festival the following August, the company introduced its big effort for the Canadian centennial—the world's first full-length ballet on a Canadian theme, *Rose Latulippe*. Macdonald had wanted to do a ballet on the old French-Canadian legend of the girl who danced with the devil to her doom ever since it had first been suggested to him by an early teacher. It was introduced with all appropriate ballyhoo, but the public and critical reception was, at best, lukewarm. Says Spohr: "It served a purpose—it was the first full-length Canadian ballet. Just a little too long, it needed to be weeded, though the choreography was good. The music [by Harry Freedman] and the style didn't jibe. The music was contemporary and the style was period. That's what I thought the problem was."

Brian Macdonald's Rose Latulippe. *(Douglas Spillane)*

The ballet's failure was a particular blow to company member David Moroni. Apart from a lead role in *The Still Point*, a work by U.S.-born, Germany-based choreographer Todd Bolender that had entered the company's repertoire earlier in the year, Moroni had been strictly a member of the corps since his arrival in Winnipeg from Ottawa in 1964, and *Rose* was his big chance. Dancing has always been a very serious business to Moroni, and he has few funny stories to tell. As a youngster, he felt—like so many others before and after him—that he would be the next Nijinsky, and when Macdonald threw him into a big part in *Rose* "I poured my guts into the ballet. I was so sorry that it didn't work any better than it did. Richard [Rutherford] and I got ourselves really just so worked up about the whole thing, and we were shocked when we discovered that it wasn't working."

The next two years were years of serious consolidation. Touring activity intensified. Kanee and Sawchyn brought the budget under control. And by

November, 1966, the major fund-raising campaign stood at more than
$200,000—within sight of its goal.

New ballets in this period included an ample variety of the showpiece *pas de deux* that had by now become an obligatory part of any RWB evening: two by Jim Clouser (*Out of Lesbos* and *Sylvia Variations*), the Bolshoi version of the *Giselle* peasant *pas de deux*, taught by guest company member Leo Ahonen, a Finnish choreographer-dancer who had studied in Russia; Ahonen's own *Daydream*; and *Spring Waters*, the famous brief splash of virtuosity by the Bolshoi Ballet's ballet master, Asaf Messerer. Large-scale additions to the repertoire included Macdonald's *Songs Without Words* (to the Schubert Octet); *Moncayo 1*, a Latin number by former company member Gloria Contreras; *Les Patineurs* ("a gift to the RWB from Sir Frederick Ashton," said the program); Clouser's *Riel* (commissioned by the women's committee to celebrate Manitoba's centennial);

Patti Ross (left), William Starrett, and Kimberley Graves in Les Patineurs *by Frederick Ashton (Peter Garrick)*

Agnes de Mille's *The Golden Age* ("a revelation of decadence and exploitation in the opera houses of the 1860s"); Jose Ferran's Spanish-flavoured *Pastiche*; and Anton Dolin's reconstruction of the historic *Pas de Quatre*, in which four of the nineteenth century's most famous ballerinas appeared together.

Throughout this period the configuration and the look of the company was changing and settling. The remarkably versatile Christine Hennessy entered as a principal in 1966. Within two years she would win a medal for "best female interpretation" in Paris. (She was looked over for suitability for the RWB by, of all people, Agnes de Mille, who had intended to mount a ballet on the special talents of the recently-departed Sonia Taverner, and wanted to be sure that her replacement would be suitable.) Hennessy, Richard Rutherford, and the effervescent, red-haired Sheila Mackinnon were joined on the roster of principals the following year by the Argentinian Eugene Slavin, a former principal with the revived Ballet Russe de Monte Carlo in New York, and by the quiet, intense David Moroni. After a single season as a principal, Slavin was promoted to the position of RWB ballet master, alongside Gwynne Ashton. Meanwhile, Slavin's wife, the blonde, Haiti-born Alexandra Nadal, rose to principal rank.

Principal dancer Sheila Mackinnon in Pastiche.

David Moroni (left foreground), Richard Rutherford, and Christine Hennessy in Agnes de Mille's The Goldon Age.

Hennessy, Mackinnon, Nadal, Rutherford, and Moroni would form the nucleus of performance power that would drive the company to its European triumphs.

In 1968, it all peaked; four major new works by internationally-famed choreographers (offered, with a stroke of genius, on a single bill) and staggering, unexpected successes in France, Czechoslovakia, and the U.S.S.R.

The four choreographers were all American—Todd Bolender, whose earlier ballet *The Still Point* was already in the RWB repertoire and who returned now to mount his *Donizettiana*; Anna Sokolow, who came to mount her sixties youth-generation ballet, *Opus '65*, first seen on the Joffrey Ballet three years earlier; the popular John Butler, whose *Sebastian* (later to enter the RWB repertoire) and *After Eden* had not long previously appeared; and the 23-year-old Eliot Feld, who had caused much excitement in New York the previous year with his ballets *Harbinger* and *At Midnight*.

Todd Bolender (left), Anna Sokolow, John Butler, and Eliot Feld in rehearsal. (J. Coleman Fletcher)

The Bolender and Sokolow works were Canadian premières. The Butler and Feld works were world firsts, created expressly for the Winnipeg company. Butler's was *Labyrinth*, an exploration of the plight of the lone individual in a hostile world, to music by Canadian composer Harry Somers. Feld's was *Meadow Lark*, a delightful eighteenth-century *fête champêtre* for six couples.

All four works were first seen at the opening of Winnipeg's lavish new $7.5 million, 2,263-seat Centennial Concert Hall that October. The program attracted international attention, and several critics flew in from New York for the première. Walter Terry went into ecstasies in the *Saturday Review* about *Meadow Lark* and declared the company "superb." Doris Hering devoted several pages of *Dance Magazine* to a glowing appraisal of the company and its new material. And Clive Barnes effectively cast the company's image for years to come: "Some companies have a style; the Royal Winnipeggers have a manner," he said. "There is a buoyancy to the company, a kind of prairie freshness, warm

e Hennessy (left), David Moroni, and Dianne Bell in John Butler's Labyrinth.

Richard Rutherford in Meadow Lark, *choreographed by Eliot Feld.*

and friendly and informal." In a weekend piece soon after, he added: "It looks as if a new wind is blowing across the prairie. I hope so, for it is with such artistic ventures . . . that Winnipeg shows that it has more to offer the world than a lot of wheat and the Royal Canadian Mounted Police."

His hopes might have been prophecies. Before the year was out, the RWB had become the darling of Europe.

Competing with companies from the U.S., Argentina, Austria, and France at the sixth Paris International Festival of Dance that November, the RWB took two of five prizes: the award for best company and, for Christine Hennessy, the gold medal for best female interpretation. Yet, the RWB was so little regarded before its arrival in Paris that several French critics stayed away from the opening performance, and one of the company members complained (to *Time* magazine) that "a lot of people seem to think that we're just a bunch of hicks." Overnight, however, everything changed. The opening program featured *Pas d'Action, Aimez-vous, The Still Point* and *Opus '65*, and while the two Macdonald works delighted the French, it was Christine Hennessy who drove them wild. In *Pas d'Action* she stood on *pointe* for 32 bars—as Richard Rutherford recalls it, "she just hit a balance in an *arabesque* and stayed there. The rest of us did our steps and waited for four bars, and then she was supposed to repeat the step, but she didn't, she stayed in the *arabesque*, so we went marching around for another four, and waited again for her to do her turn, but she didn't—she stayed, and eventually we had to knock her off *pointe* to go on with the choreography because there was nothing else to do." The next morning, Hennessy woke to discover herself acclaimed by *Paris-Aurore* as "a new idol."

Opus '65 drew a different response. Half the audience was hissing and booing, and the other half was cheering, with both sides trying to outdo each other. It was suggested later that the work's rebellious-modern-youth theme was too close to home for the young French, who had been involved in bloody riots the previous May, and the piece was dropped from all further tour programs.

Overall, however, the reaction was rapturous. "We were successful in Paris," says Spohr now, "because we could entertain." "We just went and did our things as we had always done," says Rutherford, "and they loved it; we got gold medals for it."

In Leningrad, however, where ballet is identified with the classical spectacle and purity of the Kirov, no one knew what to make of the cheeky RWB. The critics called the program "an evening of *divertissements*," and the capacity audiences at the 3,800-seat October Hall sat on their hands. The satirical

Christine Hennessy and David Moroni in a scene from Todd Bolender's Donizettiana.

cleverness of *Pas d'Action* sailed right past them (the authorities had refused to print Macdonald's lengthy and witty program note, which didn't help). As Sheila Mackinnon told an interviewer later: "We had been expecting maybe some gloom, but we just didn't believe that *silence*." The reception in Odessa was better, but it wasn't until Moscow that Soviet audiences really warmed to the company.

In attendance at the Moscow opening at the Operetta Theatre, along with

diplomatic-service dignitaries and officials from the Soviet Ministries of Culture
and Foreign Affairs, was a galaxy of past and present Soviet dance stars,
including Maya Plisetskaya (who stood in the aisle to lead a standing ovation for
Pas d'Action) and Rimma Karelskaya (with presents for her old friends in the
company—a spoon from her home, a bottle of wine). The Winnipeg dancers
were at their most effervescent and sparkling, Christine Hennessy continued to
do her tricks (Olga Lepeshinskaya said that in her early days "a dancer was
admired if she could stand on *pointe* while one ate a loaf of bread, but one could
eat a whole meal while Hennessy stood on hers"), and word about what one
newspaper called "Canada's Bolshoi Ballet" spread like prairie fire through the
city.

The crowd for the first night was so large that militia were called out. Tickets
were selling on the black market at the equivalent of $30 for a $3 seat. At the
evening's end the audience called the company back for more than 20 curtain
calls, throwing flowers and personal notes to their favourites.

The company jeers at the audience from the edge of the stage in Anna Sokolow's
Opus '65.

Curtain calls for The Bitter Weird *in Moscow, 1968.*

"Their method of applauding is to rush down to the orchestra pit and stand there and applaud," says Richard Rutherford. "And the artist continues to acknowledge the applause until there is no one left in the theatre. They don't just get up *en masse* and leave—they go away little by little when they themselves are satisfied. . . . On the last night in Moscow, David Moroni, Christine Hennessy, Sheila Mackinnon, and myself were still on stage stooping and scraping and carrying on when the rest of the company had taken off their make-up, changed and were on the bus waiting to go back to the hotel."

Canadian ambassador Robert Ford reported to Ottawa after the visit that "I can say without hesitation that during my many years in the U.S.S.R. I have never seen a foreign ballet company greeted with such enthusiasm and critical acclaim. This tour has done more to project a favourable image of Canada than any other effort we have ever made here."

From Moscow the company went to Czechoslovakia for performances in Košice, Bratislava, Brno and Prague. Tickets in Prague had disappeared within two hours of going on sale. On December 22, just in time for Christmas and the Winnipeg New Year shows, the weary but triumphant company flew home.

The most momentous season in the company's history closed on March 30, 1969, with a testimonial dinner organized by the board in honour of Spohr. Local boy had finally made good.

But there was no rest. The tireless experiments in repertory mixing and matching continued (Paddy Stone's *Variations on Strike Up the Band*, to rousing Gershwin; Agnes de Mille's classic Lizzie Borden drama-dance, *Fall River Legend*; Macdonald's social commentary, *Five Over Thirteen*). And in February, Jim Cameron came onto the company's paid strength as assistant to Sawchyn, responsible for season-ticket sales, fund-raising and publicity. Sawchyn had

Ana Maria de Gorriz (left), Louise Naughton, Teresa Bacall, Shirley New, and Veronica Graver in Variations on Strike Up the Band.

Christine Hennessy in a scene from Agnes de Mille's Fall River Legend.

Members of the company in Five Over Thirteen *by Brian Macdonald.*

already beefed subscriptions from a low of 137 to about 3,000. In the next two years, he and Cameron were to come close to tripling that. At one point, only the New York City Ballet had more subscribers than the RWB. They did it by unabashed hard sell, aimed directly at the youth generation's peace-love-happiness movement.

An eager collaborator in this was Brian Macdonald. Once again, his ballets

Annette av Paul and David Moroni in The Shining People of Leonard Cohen. *(Colette Masson)*

for the RWB were to set a style, pinpoint an era, catch a trend. There were two of them: *The Shining People of Leonard Cohen*, a ballet done to readings of poetry by Cohen, one of the idols of the hip young; and *A Ballet High*, performed in company with the rock band, Lighthouse, and billed as "the world's first rock ballet" (it was not: Robert Joffrey's *Astarte*, in 1967, has that dubious distinction).

The Cohen ballet had been in the works for some months when the company was unexpectedly booked to return to Paris for a month in the summer of 1970, substituting at the last minute for the Harkness Ballet, which had been called home to New York and disbanded midway through a European tour. Work on it was hurriedly advanced. Composer Harry Freedman put together an electronic background tape in three weeks, and when the first design for Ted Bieler's ingenious bed-sculpture set failed to operate properly, Bieler flew to Paris to join the company and build another in the ateliers of the Théâtre de La Ville. Despite the fact that the ballet was performed to readings of love poetry in English, the French audience took it to their hearts. "Far from Canada that night," said Macdonald later, "our poetry, music, sculpture, and dancing communicated very personal convictions about love."

Meanwhile, work proceeded apace on the creation of *Ballet High*, though without the actual presence of Lighthouse. As things eventuated, the company and the band had only three days to work together and to get to know each other before the ballet opened at the National Arts Centre in Ottawa that fall. Both works involved Sawchyn and Macdonald in what Sawchyn terms "imagineering"—a joint creativity in which Sawchyn seems to have been the facilitator or producer for Macdonald's flights of fancy, evolving ways to make the various bits of on-stage equipment work. "It was a beautiful time," says Sawchyn. "We did a lot of joyous things."

On the surface, then, the future for the partnership between Macdonald and the RWB could hardly have looked more promising. In fact, this was the point at which they separated for good. Partially, it was a case of ambition thwarted. Macdonald had already been in artistic charge of two companies (the Royal Swedish Opera Ballet and the Harkness) and was to go on to head two more (Israel's Batsheva and Les Grands Ballets Canadiens). In 1970 he wanted the backing of the RWB board in a bid to become artistic director of a company of his own based at the National Arts Centre in Ottawa. The RWB board saw no advantage in that for Winnipeg. Another company would simply mean federal dance funds would have to be spread that much more thinly. They refused their

Alexandra Nadal in A Ballet High, *with Lighthouse in the background.*

support. Another factor in Macdonald's departure was the gradual breakdown that had been occurring in the rapport between Macdonald and the members of the company. According to Sawchyn and others, Macdonald "needs to control people." "He was becoming very difficult and the dancers weren't responding to him any more," Spohr told an interviewer some years later. "I suggested that he might do better to leave. But I will always be willing to work with him again." The relationship has never resumed, though Macdonald's *Pas d'Action* was successfully revived in the spring of 1978.

1970-77 Entràcte

Now there was anticlimax, and how could there not be? The golden age had swept the company over peaks no one before had dreamed of scaling; now it was running free on a high plateau. Inevitably, attitudes changed. A phase of growth was over; it was a period of adjustment just as it was in the world at large. Muscles were flexed and tested, new faces came, old faces went—Spohr called it an identity crisis. And from the crisis came new character, as three new choreographers became increasingly important to the company—John Neumeier, then Norbert Vesak, and after him, Oscar Araiz, each of them leaving a recognizable mark.

The links with earlier days loosened, changed. Madge Tupper died in March of 1971. Spohr helped carry her coffin, and so did Frank Morriss, who wrote an affectionate obituary for the woman who had done so much for the company in its earlier years. Not long after, Morriss died as well.

Richard Rutherford and David Moroni retired from the performing roster in the fall of 1970. Rutherford, 35, became an associate director of the company, along with ballet mistress Gwynne Ashton, and Moroni, also in his early thirties, was appointed principal of the new and much-needed professional training program in the school. The promotions were intended to relieve some of the intense pressure on Spohr that had developed out of the company's successes. *147*

Salvatore Aiello in Sebastian *by John Butler. (Peter Garrick)*

He was making noises to the board about not being able to carry the load alone much longer, and in fact he collapsed from overwork the following March. Plainly, the appointments were also groomings for possible accession to the company throne if Spohr were ever to retire. Rutherford was ready for the move; he had had a good run (30 roles created on him in 13 years with the company, many of them as its male principal) and he knew time was running out. The company turned his farewell appearance into a gala affair. Dancers from the National Ballet and Les Grands Ballets came to Winnipeg to dance in his honour, and Agnes de Mille, who was by now becoming known in the business as the RWB's fairy godmother, was on hand to make the speeches. For both Moroni and Rutherford, that night was officially their last performance. In fact, both were to return.

Spohr had now come fully into his own as the ballet's chief motive force. At the close of the 1969-70 season, he was given a trio of major awards and decorations within the period of a month—Doctor of Laws degree, *honoris causa,* from the University of Manitoba; the Canada Council's $15,000 Molson Prize; and the Order of Canada. Sawchyn claims responsibility for "creating" Spohr—"I put his name on the posters, I made him important. It was a fantastic thing to see his attitude change. Eventually I began to feel that I'd created a Frankenstein monster." In fact, Spohr had now, perhaps for the first time, reached a point in his life where he could feel fully confident in his decisions. And it was now that his ceaseless questing for new choreographic talent was to pay off in the discovery of Norbert Vesak and John Neumeier.

Vesak, born in Port Moody, British Columbia, and trained in dance in B.C. and Washington State, was initially a recommendation by Betty Farrally, who shared teaching duties with Spohr at Banff each summer. She had seen Vesak's Vancouver-based contemporary-dance company, and suggested he be brought to Banff to teach. He did a ballet for the festival ballet that summer—much as Macdonald had done so many years previously—and Spohr liked what he saw. When the Manitoba Indian Brotherhood approached the company with a proposal to commission a ballet to mark the centenary of the signing of historic land treaties, the production committee pushed first for an Indian ballet. "I said not on your life," says Spohr. "I don't want any more step hop hop beep beep things—we had a *Brave Song* like that and the results weren't too brave." Vesak suggested making a ballet out of *The Ecstasy of Rita Joe,* a play by British Columbia playwright George Ryga, dealing with the tragic end of an Indian girl who is trapped between her own culture and the white man's. It had been a major success at the Vancouver Playhouse in the late 1960s, and Vesak, who was familiar with it from having done the stagework, said he thought it would be possible to get Chief Dan George (who had appeared in the original play) to participate in some way in the ballet. It has been suggested that the availability of Chief Dan—who had been nominated for an Academy Award that year—was the clincher in Spohr's decision to commission the ballet from Vesak. But Spohr says that was not really the case. Having Chief Dan would make great box office, "but I was already enthused—when he came along that was just a fantastic bonus."

The Neumeier contact arose out of the network of scouting friends Spohr had built in the world of international dance. Olga Maynard of *Dance Magazine* had seen the work of the Milwaukee-born choreographer in Germany, where he was at that time director for the municipal theatres in Frankfurt. She mentioned him to Spohr and Sawchyn in casual conversation in Toronto, and Sawchyn recalls going directly to the telephone and calling him in Germany. Neumeier eventually agreed to come to Winnipeg to mount his *Rondo*, which was at that time the central section of a triptych called *Unsichtbare Grenzen* (Invisible Frontiers). This was not regarded as any special deal at the time. Spohr imported outside

Left: Norbert Vesak; right: John Neumeier.

choreographers regularly—that spring, for instance, John Clifford of the New York City Ballet mounted his *Concert Fantasy* on the company. *Rondo* was duly given its first performance (July, 1971, Ottawa) on a bill that also included the world premières of Vesak's *The Ecstasy of Rita Joe* and Walter Gore's *The Last Rose of Summer*. *Rita Joe* was the ballyhooed production number, and the costliest RWB production to date. Its trendy social-conscience theme and its splendid theatricality earned it an ovation—17 or 19 curtain calls, depending on your information source. But the surprise of the evening was the success of the thoughtful, low-key *Rondo*. *Rita Joe* was to sell the company more tickets than anything that had gone before, but *Rondo* was to prove one of its greatest artistic successes.

Ana Maria de Gorriz (left), Alexandra Nadal, Maria Lang, Winthrop Corey, and Salvatore Aiello, with Craig Sterling prostrate, in Rondo. *(Colette Masson)*

Ana Maria de Gorriz as Rita Joe and Salvatore Aiello as Jaimie Paul in Norbert Vesak's The Ecstasy of Rita Joe.

At the beginning of 1972 the company went to Australia, where its most popular program was one the promoters originally didn't want—*Shining People, Meadow Lark,* and *Rita Joe. Rita Joe,* the company was told, wouldn't stand a chance in Australia. Who cared about the plight of an oppressed Indian girl in the skid row streets of a small Canadian city? In fact, the ballet's downtrodden-minorities theme has made it an audience favourite, not only in Australia but in South America as well. Australia took the company to its heart (someone in Brisbane even reviewed the RWB press kit—and loved *that*) and the company reciprocated. "We spent real time in each city," says Linda Lee Thomas, who was then principal pianist, "and everyone fell in love. The Aussies are charming people . . . it was summer . . . we were there for three months. . . . On the plane coming home, we were all crushed. Everyone wanted to go back."

For all the popular success of the tour, however, the artistic strength of the company was at its lowest ebb for years. People weren't producing, there were promising professional-program graduates waiting in the wings, and 11 dancers were let go. However, Spohr has rarely been able to bring himself to look people

Closing night in Melbourne, Australia, 1972. (Peter Garrick)

squarely in the eye and tell them they are fired, so the task fell to Rutherford. "It was horrible," he says. "He [Spohr] sat on the other side of the room but I had to say the reason why we're not renewing your contract is because such and such. . . . When we got to the end of all that—the tears and what have you—I said to Arnold, now that I've helped you fire half your company I want to tell you that I would like to leave too." And he did. He took a year's leave of absence and went back to visit friends he had made in Australia.

This was the start of the "identity crisis." Gwynne Ashton left. Musical director Carlos Rausch, who had joined the company in 1965, was replaced by Neal Kayan. And at the end of the 1971-72 season, general manager Sawchyn's sometimes-stormy eight-year relationship with the company came to an end. He had put the Royal Winnipeg Ballet firmly on the world map, built the hometown subscription audience, made the company one of North America's most widely toured dance attractions. But he had grown out of the job, he was tired of the massive administrative workload, and he wanted to expand his activities as a producer.

There was, too, the Arnold factor. On the surface of things, Spohr and Sawchyn parted on the most cordial terms—Spohr wrote him the kind of testimonial that wins lesser men medals. But they were no longer able to get on the way they both had. Both had changed profoundly in the eight years they had spent together. Both had become too good at what they were doing to be comfortable in each other's presence. Sawchyn ran off to join the circus—it had been a consuming passion since childhood. Later, he set up a touring agency of his own. His proudest achievement since that time has been the single-handed selection and importation to Canada in 1977 of the Moscow Circus, one of the most successful entertainment events in Canada's history.

Robert Dubberley, formerly assistant general manager of Toronto's St. Lawrence Centre for the Arts, took over from Sawchyn in April of 1972 and Cameron quit and moved to Niagara Falls, doing public relations first for Madame Tussaud's wax museum and later for the Skylon. The cycle of change gathered momentum. Christine Hennessy, who had become a mother in January, resigned from the company and left with her husband, principal dancer Winthrop Corey ("Wink was trained as a classical dancer," Spohr told an interviewer, "and we couldn't offer him the roles which really fulfilled his potential") . . . Frank Bourman, a dancer and teacher with wide experience in the U.S. was appointed ballet master . . . and Vernon Lusby, a former assistant

Craig Sterling and Louise Naughton in Eternal Idol *by Michael Smuin.*

to Agnes de Mille and the man who had mounted her *Fall River Legend* on the company in 1969, returned as a permanent associate director.

By the fall of 1972, the company's artistic-staff roster was not only filled, it was becoming topheavy. It was at this point that Richard Rutherford decided to return from his year's leave of absence, seven months early. He received by no means the open-arms welcome he had been expecting. No one had seriously thought he would come back, and his position was no longer vacant. Still, the company had made a verbal commitment to rehire him once his leave was up, and he hung around without pay throughout much of the 1972-73 season, watching the new works being mounted, attending all the performances; he even took a lighting course in Montreal to improve his value. He was officially reappointed in June, 1973. "They had already filled up the space," he says, "but they had to create something for me to do, so they gave me that funny title of production coordinator, which meant nothing."

Six new works were added to the repertoire in the 1972-73 season—two by Neumeier, one by Vesak, two by Michael Smuin, then of American Ballet Theatre, and one by British choreographer Jack Carter.

The first big triumph in a season of triumphs was unveiled that Christmas—Neumeier's new full-evening *Nutcracker*, an entirely fresh reworking of the traditional Christmas treat . . . so fresh, indeed, that it was no longer a Christmas story at all. The dancers worked alongside Neumeier as he refined and fixed his conceptions and characters, and "all of us," says Harriet Cavalli, who was rehearsal pianist at the time, "felt something special was happening. John is one of those rare human beings whom everyone either develops great respect for or falls in love with." Many members of the company did both, and Neumeier reciprocated. His choreographic career has been punctuated by discoveries of "special" dancers uniquely able to provide the kind of interpretation he seeks. Marina Eglevsky, who had joined the company with her husband, Salvatore Aiello, in the summer of 1971, proved to be one of these. Neumeier

The party scene from act one of John Neumeier's Nutcracker.

Marina Eglevsky (left) in Twilight. *(Peter Garrick)*

wanted her for his own company, and at the end of the season, she and Aiello (plus several other RWB dancers) quit the RWB to join him in Germany, where he now headed the Hamburg State Opera Ballet.

Moves like that are part of the RWB pattern. It is a problem that Spohr has become philosophical about; indeed, he sees it as a compliment to the company and good fortune for the dancers. "Who am I to say you must stay in Winnipeg?" he once snapped at a sceptical interviewer. "What kind of presumption is *that*? Everyone must pursue his art the best way he thinks possible."

Shortly before Neumeier's arrival for *Nutcracker* that December, Norbert Vesak spent three weeks working with the company on his next ballet, *What to Do till the Messiah Comes. Messiah* was meant to appeal to the same peace-love-happiness movement that Macdonald had earlier wooed so successfully. Its title was borrowed from Bernard Gunther's touch-therapy book of the same name, and its theme, as Vesak described it, was that "till the Messiah comes, man should try to make the world a better and happier place in which to live." It became the hit of the repertoire, and the 20-city, 60-performance cross-Canada trip that followed was so successful that the board authorized Dubberley to book a week at the City Center Theatre in New York for the spring of 1974.

Neumeier was appointed official choreographer to the company—the first since Macdonald—in the spring of 1973. His appointment was celebrated by the addition to the repertoire of his 1972 work, *Dämmern*, a quiet, introspective piece known at the RWB as *Twilight*. The following year, *The Game* was added.

Trish Wilson in What to Do till the Messiah Comes *by Norbert Vesak.*

The Game *by John Neumeier.*

This ballet—a treatment of life as a game of pinball—was placed with *Rondo* and *Twilight* to form an all-Neumeier evening under the overall title of *Pictures*.

These new works of Vesak and Neumeier gave the company a bolder and altogether more modern appearance. But Spohr, ever canny, knew it was important to maintain the diversity of his repertoire. The classic-lovers in the audience were well catered to (Benjamin Harkarvy's *Grand Pas Espagnol,* for instance, "a look back with affection" at the nineteenth century Russian-Spanish style, plus guest appearances by Margot Fonteyn and the late Heinz Bosl, and the entire National Ballet of Canada, doing *Swan Lake* and *Giselle,* on the RWB's subscription series). And, for spice as well as novelty, he introduced in the fall of 1973 Agnes de Mille's enduring dance-drama, *Rodeo.* Although the

Bonnie Wyckoff as the Cowgirl in Agnes de Mille's Rodeo.

1942 cowboy classic reached Winnipeg a little late for the company's prairie-fresh era, it was to become yet another signature-ballet for the RWB. Rodeo also served to introduce Winnipeg to the remarkable talents of Bonnie Wyckoff. She was taken on as a soloist in 1973-74, became a principal the following year, and went on to become one of the company's strongest and most versatile dancers.

But if the company was flourishing artistically it was in worse financial trouble than it had ever been. The 1973-74 season, originally budgeted for a small surplus, had lost more than $200,000, thanks to cost overruns and smaller-than-expected attendance figures. By the spring of 1974, with carried-over deficits of previous years, the company was $287,425 in the hole. Several firms in the city had cut off RWB credit. It was a desperate situation, but the board had seen it coming. Dubberley had left at the end of the year, and Jim Cameron had been summoned to do a rescue act.

He went at the budget for the forthcoming season with an axe, and he and Sol Kanee, by now board chairman, erased the deficit chiefly with $250,000 of the province of Manitoba's money—in the form of an immediate grant of $100,000, and a further grant of $150,000 to be paid in ten yearly instalments. In order that the $150,000 could be used immediately, an anonymous well-wisher (in all likelihood a board member—Kanee or Kathleen Richardson) arranged an interest-free loan repayable over the same ten-year period (itself, of course, a substantial gift in unexacted interest).

The dancers themselves were in South America during the worst of the financial storm. The biggest successes of the tour were the two works of Norbert Vesak—*Rita Joe* and *Messiah*. Ironically, however, it was in South America that Spohr was to happen on a new choreographic discovery destined to outshine even Vesak in importance to the RWB—the Argentinian Oscar Araiz. The first contact with Araiz occurred in Buenos Aires at the start of the tour. "It was a little old dusty theatre, half empty," Spohr remembers, "and suddenly this strong choreography and message came on, and I sat up and took note." (One of the ballets they saw that night was *Family Scenes*, later to become a staple of the RWB repertoire.) "Then, when we went to Sao Paulo, we were invited to see another company's rehearsals and there they did Oscar's *Adagietto*, and there again, I thought, wow!" Spohr and his aides met Araiz himself in Rio de Janeiro, and negotiations to bring him to Winnipeg were opened immediately.

By the time Spohr "found" him, Araiz had in fact already been acclaimed as

Argentina's most promising young choreographer, had achieved notoriety through what the Argentinian president had considered "objectionable" erotic overtones in his version of Stravinsky's *Le Sacre du Printemps (Rite of Spring)*, and had seen his work presented by companies in Holland and Germany. Nevertheless, Spohr was by several years the first North American director to give Araiz wide exposure—though as soon as Robert Joffrey saw the RWB's mounting of *Rite*, he invited Araiz to New York to mount something for him. (This caused Spohr a lot of heartache. He had badly wanted to introduce Araiz to New York himself. Ironically, the work that Araiz did for Joffrey—his *Romeo and Juliet*, which Spohr had hoped to get for Winnipeg—was roundly condemned by New York's critics.)

On its trip through South and Central America the company played to some of the most enthusiastic audiences and critics of its career. In Brasilia, 8,000 persons were at the city sports arena for what was termed "Brasilia's outstanding

The Ecstasy of Rita Joe—*in Brasilia "only one low and tentative whistle greeted the appearance of the bed."*

cultural event of the year." In a lengthy cable to Ottawa, the Canadian embassy noted that a reception at the ambassador's residence after the performance was attended by the vice-president of the republic, the president's daughter, and at least half of Brazil's cabinet. The RWB, said the note, "provided unique occasion to cement personal relationships with individuals who are running country and focus attention on Canada in unprecedented way."

The diplomats' emphasis on the RWB's ambassadorial role was an echo of the response in Moscow. It was heard again when the company reached Cuba, where, despite an almost total lack of pre-show publicity, the four performances were so successful that, as Spohr tells it, "there was fighting, and police had to be called in, people fighting for tickets. . . . We had a standing ovation every night . . . 200 boys from about 16 to 24 waited just to see us walk to our bus and wave to us—every night. It was a brilliant success, equal to the one we had when we won the medals in Paris, and the resounding success we had in Moscow, Odessa, and Czechoslovakia."

Queues form outside the Mella Theatre in Havana, Cuba, 1974. (Peter Garrick)

Sheri Cook (left), Roger Shim, David Hough, Ana Maria de Gorriz, and Harry Williams in Kurt Jooss's The Green Table.

In the fall of 1974, Winnipeg had its first taste of Araiz—his *Adagietto*, to the fourth movement of Mahler's Fifty Symphony. It was only 10 minutes long, but it almost stole the show from the show's guest superstars—none other than Mikhail Baryshnikov, who had defected to the West through Canada from the Kirov company the previous June, and Gelsey Kirkland, from the New York City Ballet, making their world première appearance as a duo. In November, Kurt Jooss's classic anti-war ballet, *The Green Table*—which Spohr had been after for years—was introduced. Both the duo booking and the Jooss addition were products of Cameron cunning. In the case of the guest dancers, he persuaded Baryshnikov's agent in New York that a Canadian appearance would be good for the dancer's image "so it didn't look as if he'd used Canada as a railroad station."

In the case of the Jooss, it was a matter of flattery—"We can only afford one new ballet [which was, as it happened, close enough to being true] and it has to be yours."

In the spring of 1975, Norbert Vesak—who was soon to be listed alongside Neumeier as an official choreographer to the company—offered to make a ballet for Richard Rutherford. Rutherford, who hadn't been on a stage since 1970 apart from one brief spell as a substitute in Australia, was intrigued. After his return from Australia he had found himself in limbo. His upward mobility within the company was limited. Lusby, as associate director, was now logically next in line, and Rutherford was no longer being groomed for leadership. However, his actual duties as "production coordinator" involved him in various organizational roles, and for much of the 1974-75 season he had also assumed the task of company manager on the road—carrying it out so efficiently that the board had taken the unusual step of sending him a letter of commendation and thanks.

But none of this gave him an artistic outlet, and he saw the new ballet as a fresh challenge. "Sure," he told Vesak, "choreograph me a part I don't have to dance and maybe I'll muster up the energy." He recalls it now as "an ego trip" and says he should never have done it at all. "I was 40, and I was going to appear on the stage practically nude. It was a big challenge. . . . But once I was in it and over with it I thought, you will never do that again. It wasn't worth it."

In Quest of the Sun, inspired by Peter Shaffer's play, *The Royal Hunt of the Sun*, dealt with the conquest of the Inca sun-king Atahuallpa (Rutherford) by a rabble band of Spanish adventurers. It was an expensive flop—just what the company could least afford. What began as an all-male ballet using only ten dancers finally needed 51 costumes. Its set (by New York designer Ming Cho Lee) included a 30-foot crucifix and a giant suspended sun. It came in at $21,000 over budget for costumes, $9,000 over budget for its creators' travel expenses. "It didn't contribute anything to the art form, either," says Rutherford.

On the visible surface everything stayed busy and bright. In the summer of 1975 the company appeared at the Israel Festival. The visit took place under the cloud of Middle East conflict. The sonic boom of Israeli fighter jets woke the dancers each morning. At the ancient Roman theatre in Caesarea, they performed behind barbed-wire fencing and could hear the throbbing of gunboats patrolling off shore. When Prime Minister Itzhak Rabin attended the performance in

Oscar Araiz demonstrates a movement for Betsy Carson (left) and Sally Ann Mulcahy during rehearsal. (Peter Garrick)

Jerusalem, curtain-time was delayed while each member of the audience was searched. In an atmosphere like that, the audiences wanted entertainment from their entertainment. *The Green Table*, which had been specially requested by the Israeli authorities, was a failure from the beginning—too close to home. Even *Rita Joe*, which was substituted, was too sombre. By the end, the company was giving its audiences programs composed almost entirely of froth and inconsequence (the greatest success of the tour was Paddy Stone's new ballet, *The Hands*, as trivial a piece of television variety-show entertainment as anything in the repertoire) and the audiences, delighted, were responding with their highest accolade, a slow and steady rhythmic applause: what the company members came to call "the Israeli clap."

Oscar Araiz spent the early fall of 1975 in Winnipeg, teaching the company his *Rite of Spring* and *Family Scenes*. (Outside the dance studio, Araiz is very shy, hates interviews, and finds it difficult to talk about his work. When he does

Harry Williams (left), Ronn Tice, Rodney Andreychuk, Eric Horenstein, Michael O'Gorman, David Herriott, and Baxter Branstetter in Rite of Spring. *(Jack Mitchell)*

talk, it is in a mixture of French, Spanish and what someone once called "tenacious" English. But inside the studio, he blossoms. From the start, his relationship with the RWB dancers was very close. Bonnie Wyckoff calls him "a luminous man, very childlike and innocent. Everyone trusts him and believes what he has to say. Everything about him is genuine. He draws out of people an incredible adoration; he has that power of convincing people with a word."

Aiello and Marina Eglevsky returned that fall, after two years with Neumeier
in Germany, to boost the company's principal-dancer strength to eight, out of 26
dancers, the highest it had been for years. (However, by the beginning of the
next season five of these principals had gone—Ana Maria de Gorriz, who had
been with the RWB through much of its mature growth, had retired, and Terry
Thomas, Anthony Williams, Craig Sterling, and Louise Naughton had left to
pursue new dancing careers in the U.S. To supplement the three remaining
principals—Wyckoff, Aiello, Eglevsky—Spohr brought in an Australian couple, Gailene Stock and Gary Norman. They had just spent a year with the
National Ballet of Canada, and they brought a touch of technical class to the
RWB. It was unfortunate that they only stayed in Winnipeg a single season
before returning home.)

At the end of 1975 the current balletic *causes célèbres*, the Soviet emigrés
Valery and Galina Panov, came in for six performances and $15,000, dancing
the same flashy rubbish they danced around the world in their brief turn in the
international spotlight. They were given a standing ovation.

Behind the scenes, however, the identity crisis was by no means complete.
Cameron's hard-nosed-businessman style was upsetting a lot of people. Jean
McKenzie thought his quiet efficiency "a good contrast with the hysteria," but
she was in a minority. Cameron's problem was that he didn't fit the company
pattern. Running the books is a job; being a dancer has to be a vocation. He
didn't play the games. As a businessman he saw the dancers as commodities.
"They can't stand my attitude," he says. "There is an instinct in ballet to dress
things up. My instinct is to go for essentials. They only need a person like me
when the going gets tough." Well, the going *was* tough—the deficit for the
season topped $100,000. Making the best of a bad job, the company launched
itself on a campaign to "earn ourselves out of debt," turned down a prestigious
invitation to dance at the Queen's Silver Jubilee celebrations because the
Canadian government couldn't be persuaded to come through with the necessary $125,000, and settled down to a hard-working North America-only year. If
all went well, the company would complete the season with a net surplus of about
$30,000. In fact they did even better. The end-of-season surplus for 1976-77
was about $43,000, on an overall budget of just over $2 million. By the time that
was declared, however, Cameron had gone.

But it was not just Cameron. By the start of the 1976-77 season, there was a brave
new look to the ranks of the artistic staff. Frank Bourman, who had arrived as

ballet master in 1972, had leapfrogged to the top of the list and now was associate artistic director/ballet master. And there were now no less than three other associate directors—Vernon Lusby, Richard Rutherford (who also continued to carry the title of production coordinator), and David Moroni (who also bore the title of principal, advanced student program). Spohr had been in charge of the company for close to 20 years, and was plainly tiring. His health fluctuated. Some even thought he was losing interest. Sooner or later someone was going to have to succeed him, and there was a variety of eager candidates—not all of whom were featured on the artistic-staff list. It was a dangerous and explosive situation; something was going to have to give.

Cameron was the first to announce his departure—mid-January 1977, effective immediately. His conflict with Spohr and the dancers had reached an impractical peak, though there is no hard evidence to support the allegation (made in my presence several times) that Spohr and the dancers signed a petition to have Cameron removed. "I persuaded the board to let me go," says Cameron, "because if there's going to be an argument between Spohr and me, they can't choose me—they're running a ballet company, not a set of books." Kanee, who had been instrumental in persuading Cameron to return to the company early in 1974, quit the board in protest. Cameron still nurses a genuine affection for the company, and he would probably go back, if asked, rather than see it drown. "I have a romantic notion that more should have been done to support Mozart and Keats," he once told me. "It follows that I am tempted to think there is some value in the result of my work . . . for dancers."

Richard Rutherford was next. He had reached a fork in the road. He was 41; he had spent half his life with the RWB, and yet what, apart from some moments of glorious memory, did he have to show for it? And what security did he have for the future? He was disillusioned, marking time. Whatever he did seemed to be taken for granted, swallowed up in the general artistic endeavour that was always, ultimately, credited to Arnold Spohr, director.

An objective outsider would probably say he ought never to have returned to the company after his leave of absence in Australia. But it is a curious fact of RWB life that people have often had to leave the company twice before the tie has been properly severed. Rutherford was one of these.

By the spring of 1977, however, he had come to realize that it was time to look elsewhere. At the end of the season he left the company, moved to Ottawa and went into the plant-nursery business. Late in 1977 he joined the staff of the Canada Council dance office, with special responsibility for administering awards to individuals aiming to improve themselves in the dance art—and found himself, as he told me early in 1978, "more closely connected to the dance world than ever before."

Another who left at the end of the 1976-77 season was Frank Bourman. Officially it was only a leave of absence, taken under doctor's advice as a means of easing the strain of a workload that had already caused Bourman's hospitalization three times. In fact, his chief reason for leaving was the board's unwillingness to confirm him as permanent director of the company in the event of Spohr's departure from the position. Spohr had personally promised him this, he says, for three successive years, but no one else knew. When he attempted to have it made official, however, the board demurred. According to Kathleen Richardson, they were certainly prepared to commit the company to an offer of the *acting* directorship, but were unwilling to tie the hands of any future board further than that. "After making the commitment that I had," says Bourman, "I expected them to do the same." His return to the company, he said, would depend to a large extent on what transpired in his absence.

What transpired in his absence was another major power struggle that was not to be resolved until the following spring.

1977-78 On the Rise Again

When chaos threatens, the Royal Winnipeg Ballet seethes like any other discontented family. It is a tight and tiny gathering of flamboyant temperaments, and minor disputes have a tendency to magnify into major clashes. But by the fall of 1977 there were more than internal differences to keep the company occupied. Ticket sales were falling. Audiences at home were becoming disenchanted with the company's programming. Performance standards were erratic. Finances were unstable.

It was long past time for change. After the buoyant successes of the late 1960s, the company had somehow lost its power to excite—or to be excited. The intermittent successes of Australia and South America had been exceptions in a generally unexceptional year-to-year existence. The daring had gone, and the company was on a plateau—"In fact," one board member confided to me, "I'll be grateful if it isn't going the other way."

Something had to happen. That something was New York.

By the fall of 1977, the identity crisis within the company was peaking.

In terms of programming, the shift in emphasis that had effectively begun with *Rondo* and *Twilight*—a shift that was moving the company slowly away from the flash-and-glitter look of earlier years toward a more "mature" appearance—was now swinging more and more in the direction of Araiz. By the middle of the 1970s *171*

Family Scenes, *choreographed by Oscar Araiz.*

Sheri Cook and members of the company in Magnificat. *(Peter Garrick)*

Spohr had effectively lost the services of Neumeier as the young choreographer's European career began to blossom, and he had begun to stockpile Araiz's work. In 1976 the Argentinian's name was added to the list (now totalling three) of official choreographers to the company. And for the start of the season that year Spohr bought two more Araiz pieces—his 1969 *Magnificat*, and a wholly new

Bonnie Wyckoff and Gary Norman in Mahler 4: Eternity Is Now.

made-in-Winnipeg work, *Mahler 4: Eternity is Now*. The following season he added a further three—*The Unicorn, the Gorgon and the Manticore*, a 13-year-old "Renaissance fable" to music of Menotti; *Festival*, a lively curtain-raiser to music of Flavio Venturini; and *Women*, to music of Grace Slick.

This emphasis on the imaginative modern ballets of Araiz was developing an entirely new on-stage identity for the company, an appearance of seriousness that by no means endeared itself to the Winnipeg audiences, or to many board members. Subscription sales began to fall away (by the beginning of the 1977-78 season they were down to just over 5,000, little more than half what they were in the early 1970s) and pressure began to mount inside and outside the company for a more equitable classical-modern balance.

In terms of internal organization, there were major changes. Edward A. Reger, who had been Cameron's assistant since May, 1975, had taken over as general manager. A former student at the RWB school, Reger came to the company from a post as acting general manager of the San Francisco Ballet. He is a young former Yale law student with a great deal of charm and an easy social manner, and he knows what dancing is all about because he went through the process: he is a dancer's manager in a way that Cameron never was, and Spohr (who recommended him in the first place) was delighted by his appointment.

On the artistic staff, the old days of topheavy administration were gone, but new fights were breaking out. David Moroni, while retaining his position as principal of the professional program, had become associate artistic director, which placed him, logically, next in line should anything ever happen to Spohr. But there were new and eager faces only a rung or two below him on the ladder of RWB power.

Margaret Slota (left), Marina Eglevsky, Sheri Cook, Bonnie Wyckoff, and Eva Christiansen in Women. *(Jack Mitchell)*

Salvatore Aiello was one who was making his presence felt. He had been the company's strongest male dancer for several seasons, with a particular talent for the dramatic—in the title role in John Butler's *Sebastian*, for instance, as the Young Chieftain in *Rite of Spring* and in a role that was created specially for him, that of Jaimie Paul in Vesak's *Rita Joe*. Now, in his early thirties, he was eager to develop other interests—one of the reasons he returned from Germany, he says, was because he wanted to expand his activities into other areas of company work. Aiello is a New Yorker of Italian parentage, with a background in musical comedy, and he was developing definite ideas on the kind of theatricality a company like the RWB should be projecting. He was also itching for a chance to try them out. He had already begun to choreograph (his work *Solas*, a solo for Marina Eglevsky to music of Villa-Lobos, had entered the company repertoire in October, 1976, at the same time as Araiz's *Magnificat* and *Mahler*) and he had been assuming more and more day-to-day scheduling and artistic-administrative work on Spohr's behalf. In the fall of 1977 he was promoted (along with Bill Lark, another company member) to the position of *régisseur*, which carries responsibility for "cleaning" and setting repertoire ballets and making sure the company performs them to the best of its ability.

Hilary Cartwright, meanwhile, had joined the staff as company teacher. As the ballet mistress of the Royal Ballet's second company, she had been imported by Moroni in 1976 to do some teaching at the RWB school. Spohr had spotted her and brought her back for the company for the 1977-78 season. The first time she saw the RWB run through some of its supposedly-classical repertoire she was horrified, and let Spohr know it. As teacher and as coach, she challenged the dancers to constant self-improvement. Nevertheless, she held out great hopes for the company. The material was all there, she said; it merely needed polishing.

Aiello and Cartwright formed a natural alliance, impatient to get things done. Spohr, meanwhile, was slowing down. He no longer went on all the tours, and he talked more and more openly about stepping aside and handing over control to someone else.

In February, 1978, he said it in public, in a telephone interview with a journalist whose call he says now should never have been put through. As he explained it then, he would assume the title of artistic adviser, and pass responsibility for overall direction to three other members of the company. He did not name his successors in the interview, but it was plain that he was referring to Aiello, Cartwright, and Moroni.

The announcement took the RWB board by surprise. "There are quite a number of ifs and buts," president John Condra was quoted as saying, "so it's in the preliminary stage."

It certainly was. Other important questions were demanding priority treatment. One concerned the company's financial situation. The company had closed the previous season with its accumulated deficit down to $137,000, but there were strong indications that this debt would increase substantially in the current year. And a fundraising campaign that aimed to raise $250,000 to cover an anticipated 1977-78 income gap was already falling badly short of target.

The other priority was the company's looming New York "debut" in March of 1978. The engagement—one week at the City Center 55th Street Theater—had been announced the previous August, and the company had been preparing nervously for the experience ever since. It was a psychological barrier as much as a financial one. While several of the more influential U.S. critics had reviewed the company either in Winnipeg or on tour, the RWB, in all its 40 seasons, had never played in a major Manhattan house (its Hunter College appearance in 1965, officially its first appearance in New York, was considered not to count).

Spohr, of course, had wanted to go to New York for years. It would give the company a chance, finally, to have its value properly affirmed in open competition. But the board had always hesitated. Some individuals had questioned the company's readiness as a performing ensemble. More, however, had questioned the monetary aspect. Manhattan theatres had been booked on several occasions, but each time the engagements had been postponed because of the extreme financial risk. The risk existed still. Even with the most optimistic estimates of ticket sales, the company would still face a net loss, on a single week in New York, of more than $100,000. This time, however, the financial problem was overcome by a guarantee from an anonymous member of the board (in all likelihood Kathleen Richardson) who agreed to assume any losses sustained on the New York engagement. Plainly, in the eyes of this board member and many others, it was time for the company to take the plunge.

Was the company really ready? Personally, after seeing the state it was in during eight performances of *Nutcracker* in Vancouver in November, 1977, I was doubtful. The company was looking ragged. Its principal-dancer strength was at its lowest ebb for several years (a fact that was somewhat disguised, on paper at least, by the company's new method of listing dancers alphabetically rather than by grade) and serious flaws existed in the overall performance strength. The men were uneven in presentation and technical achievement, and while the women were more assured technically (with Bonnie Wyckoff, Marina Eglevsky, and Evelyn Hart, a recent graduate of Moroni's program, particularly striking in solo work) the company as a whole seemed to need more polish, more finish, more cohesion. It simply wasn't projecting its best.

I expressed my doubts in a column in *The Vancouver Sun* and on CBC radio's "Arts National." I should have known better. The company's whole history is one of coming through under stress, and this was no exception. Spohr, Aiello, and Cartwright each brought their particular talents for improvement to the company: Spohr gave the work motivation and meaning, Aiello gave it projection and integrity, Cartwright gave it technical sparkle. The nervousness intensified right to the opening-night curtain-rise, but they came through. "The company is quite simply one of the finest ensembles of young dancers in the world today," said Barton Wimble in the New York *Daily News*. "There are no weak links. . . . Arnold Spohr's 20 years at the helm has paid off in an institution that embodies all the traits missing from the huge and heavy Edwardian machine that is the Canadian National Ballet: spirit, beauty of dancing, commitment to an idea that is original." Wherever Lady Tupper was at that moment, she must have been smiling.

Anna Kisselgoff, in the New York *Times,* picked up on the same idea. "With its accent on youth, drama, and the contemporary," she said, "the Royal Winnipeg Ballet has taken a very different road from the National Ballet of Canada . . . since it went full-blast into the full-length classics business, the Toronto company has definitely grown closer to its original model, Britain's Royal Ballet. The Winnipeg troupe once reportedly used American Ballet Theatre as its own model. In spirit, however, it seems closer to the Joffrey Ballet."

Clive Barnes, who had by now switched to a position as dance and drama critic of the New York *Post*, made a similar point. "In a sense," he said, "the American companies it resembles most are the Joffrey Ballet and the Pennsylvania Ballet—although the repertoire does not have the scope of the Joffrey nor do the dancers appear to have the Balanchinian style of the Pennsylvanians."

This lack of classical technique worried Kisselgoff. "From the ballets presented here," she wrote, "it seems that the Winnipeg company is not a troupe that aims for pure classicism, and in the male department it is quite weak in this regard. Yet more often than not its dancers are called upon to produce dancing of

The 1978 cast of What to Do till the Messiah Comes. *Joost Pelt (standing left) supports Bonnie Wyckoff (top) and Betsy Carson. In background are Bill Lark (left), Susan Bennet, Valerie Ford, Harry Williams, David Herriott, Eva Christiansen, and Eric Horenstein. (Jack Mitchell)*

a different sort—classically based but spread over a fusion of styles and idioms."

In New York, the chief exemplar of this fusion was Oscar Araiz. Spohr had chosen to build the New York repertoire almost entirely on Araiz choreography—five works, none of them seen before in the city—plus two Canadian pieces: Vesak's *Messiah* and Brian Macdonald's *Pas d'Action*. The opening program—*The Unicorn, the Gorgon and the Manticore* and *Mahler 4*—was described as "original but slightly disastrous" by Barnes. He was not at all enamoured of Araiz's work ("imaginative but not unduly talented") and later in the run he commented: "Araiz is not a man without talent, but he does seem to be a man without direction. And the Winnipeg Ballet made a mistake in placing too much confidence on him for their Broadway debut." Barnes complained in particular about Araiz's "inability to hear a beat without hitting it on the head." "He is always so much on the beat musically, with never a sense of rubato, and there is occasionally [a] strangely mechanical air to his choreography."

Kisselgoff was more impressed. "That he is a major talent is not in question. That he is a special talent with limited appeal is open to debate. Unlike most ballet choreographers, he is not concerned so much with steps or gestures as with spatial compositions. Over and over, he achieves his impact through groupings that are inventive and unexpected, and through the cumulative structure of one group after another." She called him "cerebral, theatrical . . . a ballet choreographer working like a modern-dance choreographer." She thought *Mahler* a "flawed" work, *The Unicorn* a "happy" one, and she considered *Family Scenes* "Araiz at his best. It is a whopper of a dramatic ballet,

Oscar Araiz's The Unicorn, the Gorgon and the Manticore. *Bill Lark (centre) is the Poet; the Unicorn is Roger Shim; the Gorgon, Marina Eglevsky; and Bonnie Wyckoff (lying foreground) is the Manticore. (Peter Garrick)*

all the more impressive because it treats familiar material in a totally personal style."

The general New York response was one of warmth. Even Barnes, for all his reservations, concluded: "It is, after all, a company that dares, and also, a company of quite exceptional dancers." He singled out Aiello and Marina Eglevsky for special praise: "They have a rapt fascination with each other . . . which is totally charming. The more I see of Miss Eglevsky, the more I like. The ballerina . . . is superb." Other reviewers paid special attention to Bonnie Wyckoff: "The ingénue to top all ingénues," said Kisselgoff, "tender and delicate, with the lightest and most amazing of floating bourrées across the floor."

Audience numbers increased steadily through the week, and most members of the company feel they could have made a major box-office success of it if the booking had been extended for a second week. "We succeeded because of our integrity, and audiences responded to that," says Spohr. "No imported stars, just us, and our verve and integrity, everyone supporting everyone else and accepting their own responsibilities. The kids really danced splendidly."

The experience left the company jubilant and revitalized. "It really worked," said Aiello. "It proves that we are a major company, not just a provincial organization full of prairie freshness. The company has finally lost its virginity." Back in Winnipeg, he and Cartwright both talked excitedly about their hopes for the company's future—a gradual increase in size, a broadening of the repertoire, new touring policies, new fundraising schemes. Both indicated strongly to me that they would leave the company if they and Moroni were not jointly given effective control.

Their optimism and ambition alarmed the board, which was by now glumly anticipating a season-end deficit of $250,000 (excluding the New York losses). Far from expansion of size and activity, the best the board could hope for in 1978-79 was a season of financial consolidation and retrenchment, based primarily on popular revivals. Board members were also by no means convinced that a triumvirate of artistic directors would work, or that the individuals concerned would be the right ones for the job. "There is no doubt that [Spohr] is unique, and it should be his company," Condra told me at the height of these uncertainties. "If he wants to go we'd need at least a year to replace him, and if he did we'd need a completely new set-up."

The discussion of succession was, in the end, rendered redundant by Spohr himself. New York had been a turning point for him. It had given him a new lease on life, new energies for the job. In mid April it was announced that he would, after all, be staying on, "primarily responsible for the artistic direction of the company." It was a matter of continuity, he told me. "The magnitude of the position is great. Someone in this position has to have the germ. Some members of the board say you have to let other people take the company their way, but you need the continuity. I'm continuing the Gweneth and Betty tradition. You need an understanding of the germ, the standards, the principles, that make this company. You need to retain its sense of humility."

Not everyone agreed with him. In the eyes of some it was this "humility" and attachment to first principles that had kept the company below its potential achievement in its pre-New York years. There was a strong faction within the company that believed the time had come for boldness and change of the kind Aiello and Cartwright proposed.

At the same time, there was a healthy regard for practicality. The first task, as everyone recognized, was to keep the company afloat. When the money situation had eased, it might be time to reconsider the future.

Spohr's retention of control was due to last for anything from one to three seasons, perhaps even more. Happily, however, neither Aiello nor Cartwright quit. Instead, they agreed to become associate artistic directors, along with Moroni. Responsibilities for each of the three were clearly laid down: Moroni retained the title of principal, advanced student program (which he claimed he was only interested in protecting in the first place), Cartwright was ballet mistress, and Aiello assumed the former Rutherford title of production coordinator.

The extent to which these promotions would allow a hand in the company's artistic direction was unclear. As far as day-to-day operations were concerned, the new titles merely formalized the work-sharing situation as it already existed. However, they did imply a recognition on the board's part of the contributions these individuals were making—and it gave them, too, the opportunity to step back with dignity from their positions of threatened resignation.

By the summer of 1978, an equilibrium, of a kind, had been achieved. There was, too, a new contentment—reflected most significantly, perhaps, in the fact that only three dancers left the company at the end of the 1977-78 season, a negligible turnover by normal RWB standards.

It was not a matter of false euphoria. No one doubted that there were struggles to come. But there had been struggles before—forty years of them. The company was ready, lean and bright-eyed as if from a long fever, for whatever was next.

2 The Company

The Board

The board of directors is responsible for everything. They're the head of the family tree. We look up to them.

ARNOLD SPOHR

There is one thing you mustn't do—interfere with a man's dream.

ATHOL FUGARD, in Sizwe Bansi Is Dead.

Kathleen Richardson is a big, gracious woman with a broad and gentle face that creases quickly into laughter. She has a lively and sometimes cutting sense of humour, and a sharp ear for the ridiculous; conversations with her are punctuated by sudden raucous chuckles. She seems genuinely fond of the dance (she likes to quote Lincoln Kirstein defining ballet as "a non-terminal disease") and her connections with the company date back almost to the arrival of Gweneth and Betty in the city. She was one of their earliest pupils. She took part in Gweneth's compulsory Greek-dance classes at River Bend school, and on Saturday afternoons she would be driven to the studio on Portage Avenue for tap classes. As early as 1953, when the company was in financial troubles, both Kathleen and her brother James (no doubt urged on by their mother) gave $100 each to help the company out (their mother, always a significant contributor to the company's survival, gave $1,000).

Kathleen Richardson joined the ballet board on April Fool's Day, 1955,   *185* succeeding her mother who stepped down at about that time to become head of the Winnipeg Foundation. She has remained a director ever since. In September of 1957 she became president of the board, and held the position for three years, through some of the noisiest and most turbulent upheavals in the company's history. Many persons involved with the RWB consider her the most significant individual connected with the company, not only through her family's financial involvements with the ballet, but through her constant participation in the decision-making processes of the board's production committee, which she has never left since joining it in the late 1950s.

Typically, she talks down her importance to the company, and laughs when she thinks of the time she has spent in its service; she sometimes wonders, she says, if it is only inertia that keeps her there. "I have tried to get out, you know. Sometimes I withdraw for periods of time—I think, oh, goodness, here am I, the oldest buffalo on the plains, they need a fresh face. And then some terrible thing occurs and they come to me and say you must help, you're the only one who can talk to Arnold . . . and I think [she laughs] perhaps I am." Spohr himself talks about her with affection. "She's the greatest philanthropist going, and such a humanitarian—so humble and sweet and good. And she has great kindness. If she thinks she's been a little rude to you, she'll worry about having upset you, and she'll come to apologize. She's just unbelievable." A former Winnipeg newspaperman puts it more succinctly. "For a rich lady," he says, "she's somebody."

John W. (Jack) Graham has been associated with the RWB, one way or another, for most of its 40 years. He was one of the early volunteers (the Ancient and Honourable Guild of Stagecraftsmen) from John Russell's department of architecture at the University of Manitoba in the 1940s. He began by painting backdrops, and did his first set design in 1951—an abstract linear piece for Arnold Spohr's ballet, *Intermède*. Other ballets he designed were Gweneth Lloyd's *Shadow on the Prairie* and Agnes de Mille's *The Bitter Weird*. In the latter part of the 1950s he became a member of the company's production committee, then its chairman, and eventually he made his way onto the board. He has stayed involved ever since, for a variety of reasons: the pleasure of working in the theatre, a long-standing affection for Gweneth and Betty, and the satisfaction that comes from contributing to the growth of an international-class ballet company. He is now associate dean of architecture at the university, a sandy-haired, wispy-bearded man with a thin face and lively eyes. His

Kathleen Richardson with Edward Reger (left), Robert Steen, mayor of Winnipeg, and Arnold Spohr in New York on the occasion of the company's March, 1978, appearance. (Jack Vartoogian)

conversation is measured, his statements considered; his is the voice of caution and moderation. It is heard often, and well respected, in company planning sessions in the board room.

Kathleen Richardson and Jack Graham, the company's two longest-serving volunteer affiliates, are both vigorous defenders of the curious, perhaps unique, system of artistic control that has evolved at the RWB, a system that sees effective power in all major artistic decisions vested in a small group of unpaid members of the Winnipeg community, the "production committee" of the board of directors.

In the absence of any form of private (or, at the time of the company's founding, public) patronage, the RWB was launched, like so many other North American ventures in the arts, on the goodwill, generosity and foresight of interested members of the community it aimed to serve. These volunteers served the company in many ways. In the early days, they acted as ushers at performances, stuck up posters, put up tent-cards in restaurants, sold tickets at the box office, pestered their friends to come to the shows. They raised money, pulled the city-at-large behind the project, put it (and kept it) on its financial feet, and provided advice on efficient business management—all prime duty for a volunteer arts board. "It was a kind of crusade," says Kathleen Richardson, "and if the company ever thinks of the board as anything other than a set of ogres, it's because we have this background of having mucked in."

The "ogres" image does persist. Along with the volunteer workers, the board has also attracted, over the years, its share of hangers-on and glory-seekers, and their attitudes have not always endeared them to the dancers: "They always think we're hysterical and temperamental," said one former leading dancer, "and I also get the feeling that [they think] we're second-class citizens: machines that you wind up and put on the stage and they do their thing." Bob Kipp admits: "It is sometimes difficult for board members to understand the dedication of people who give their lives 24 hours a day to the organization. But we tried very hard to smooth ruffled feathers. The most difficult problem has always been setting up a true line of communication between the board and the artistic people."

The company has always suffered too from the city's consciousness of its size, its sense of inferiority. "This is a world-class attraction," says former manager, Jim Cameron, "but people here are suspicious—they don't believe their kids can go to London and succeed." Spohr says he is convinced that the city is loyal—"if they found us in trouble they'd be with us"—but he complains, too, about the way the city takes the company for granted. "When we go to our political people for grants we are ridiculed and put down as if we were the scum of the earth . . . and yet they have the audacity to put in every ad, 'Home of the RWB.' Why don't they put 'Home of the Winnipeg Jets' or 'Home of the ice-skating team' or what the hell ever?"

Ken Winters, who served as a performing-arts critic for the Winnipeg *Free*

Press in the early 1960s, suggests the company initially developed "a rather precious, rather special audience—it had a nucleus of pansy lawyers and professors, a certain kind of highbrow girlwatcher who wanted to go see Jean McKenzie and Marilyn Young because they were exquisite. But, in the face of everything, the ballet went on putting on a season every year, very attractive, very highly rehearsed, and once the businessmen broke down their prejudices and went once, they went again and again."

The connection with the University of Manitoba has always been strong. "There is perhaps no civilized country in the world where dependence on the universities in the cultural field is so great as in Canada," said the Massey Commission report in 1957, and certainly, in Winnipeg, the company's development would have been far slower than it was had it not been for the participation, from the earliest days, of the professional academics. They were individuals with a natural (and a vested) interest in improving the artistic climate of their city. John Russell, who initiated the connection, later became a charter member of the Canada Council. His school of architecture provided a steady flow of excellent cheap help through the years, and John Graham has maintained the tradition. But it was by no means just the architects. There were musicians, artists and even administrators—the first president of the board, in 1949, A. H. S. Gillson, was also president of the university at the time, and the first treasurer, W. J. Condo, was also the university treasurer. In the circumstances, it is hardly surprising that the company dedicated its 1977 winter home-town performances to the university, in honour of its 100th anniversary and in recognition of its continuing support.

The fundraising effectiveness of the various RWB boards has fluctuated over the years, but the personal generosity of board members has been exemplary. Again and again, they have shown their belief in the company's enduring values by pumping in money to get it through immediate troubles; it has been a stealthy transfusion, but a life-giving one. However—and this is a problem that is by no means unique to the RWB—the act of supporting an art form seems inevitably to become confused with the ability to be creative in it, and very early in the professional history of the Winnipeg company, its board began to assume a role in the area of artistic choice. Having enabled it to continue to exist, the directors now felt at liberty to have some say in its future; the response is, after all, human enough, and by no means limited to our own society or times. In practice, the majority of arts boards, with more or less reluctance, will agree to leave an artistic director to his own devices within a set budgetary limit. In Winnipeg, however, the board has never been willing to hand over final artistic control to a single appointed individual. Rather, responsibility for major production decisions (repertoire, hiring, touring) is vested in a carefully-selected committee of eight to 10 members, drawn principally from the board itself, plus the general manager and Spohr.

"I know that in theory boards shouldn't do this," says Graham. "It is probably unique in board operations—but it is organically part of this company, and it would be very difficult to change. In fact, I think change would be wrong. We all manage to contribute something to the growth of the company—and in that sense it is a direct continuation of the way things were originally."

Sergei Sawchyn, another former general manager, has no time for boards in general—"They should be people who come in once a year to look at the bottom line, make broad general policy decisions and leave the day-to-day operations to the operating officers—what the hell does a stockbroker know about dance?" But he is warm in his praise of the RWB's production-committee system. He says he found it "good and workable," admired the members' involvement, and felt the "trade-off of opinion" between people like Graham, Sol Kanee (another longtime stalwart) and Kathleen Richardson was valuable for the company's planning.

Nevertheless, the system's operation has caused considerable friction over the years. It was a major factor in the departure of company founder Gweneth Lloyd, shortly after the creation of the original board. It caused the messy resignation-firing of her partner, Betty Farrally. It drove away David Yeddeau, who had managed the company through most of its first decade. It was the chief factor in the resignation of Benjamin Harkarvy in 1958. And while Harkarvy stresses today that he feels no bitterness toward the board or its members, he says the experience helped him realize something that was later confirmed for him when he became joint artistic director of the Harkness Ballet, a company founded by U.S. philanthropist Rebekah Harkness in 1964—"when the money is in the hands of someone who essentially has no understanding of the art or no training for it, there are inevitably going to be clashes with the people who have spent their lives training for that art."

The current incumbent, Arnold Spohr, seems less deterred by the system's drawbacks, probably because he knows that nowadays he is so well established he can always get his way. For years, however, Spohr's title was simply director ("It was terrible, the first two years working with the board—it was like putting up my hand to see if I could go to the washroom") and at one time the title of artistic director was conferred on the man who was in charge of sets and costumes. Eventually, as Spohr became trusted, clear lines of responsibility were established. According to Kathleen Richardson, Spohr's word today on company membership is final. In the matter of programming, however, the pattern is different. The board sets a policy for the company, allocates a budget, and Spohr is told he has a certain number of dollars for new productions. "What he does with that money is up to the production committee, working with Arnold," she says. In fact, it appears that final decisions are generally his ("Arnold gets really anything he wants, for heaven's sake") with the committee merely questioning and confirming—"and it works very well, because once it is set then Arnold knows that there's all his production committee prepared to say, well, *certainly* that's what we're going to do." Spohr himself makes it clear that "I have the last word if I really want it, but it's wonderful to hear others, and sometimes they say, sorry, this can't be, or they don't like this, and then, all right, we don't. We feed each other on what to do for rep, what music is good or isn't good, and then we make good decisions. It's better that way. I love it." However, it seems likely that the board-Spohr relationship only stays this harmonious because certain individuals (like Kathleen Richardson and Jack Graham) are sufficiently in tune with Spohr's persona to steer him clear of those who aren't. As Kathleen Richardson herself puts it: "Some of the best people on the board, from the point of view of raising money or being just plainly sensible and giving good judgment on what the company should be doing are people who couldn't stand Arnold, nor he them, and so you just try and see that they don't have too much to do with each other."

Arnold Spohr

" 'I cannot' is a phrase you must forget. When one wants to, one always can."

ELENA VALERIANOVNA PANAIEVA,
Diaghilev's stepmother

Arnold Spohr never asked for the job of running the Royal Winnipeg Ballet. He took it on as a favour, and sometimes he wonders whether he might have turned the job down had he known what he was getting into. He has threatened "a million times" to resign. In 1978 he announced publicly that he was stepping aside, then reconsidered. He protests, still, that the only reason he has remained at his post is because he considers himself a man of his word. But no one seriously expects him ever to give it up. He may eventually shunt himself sideways into a "consultative" position of some kind, as he suggested in 1978, but he has too much of himself at stake to let go entirely. For 20 years the ballet has been his life, and now he has no other.

Everyone underrates him. For his first 18 years in the job, the company didn't even give him a secretary. When Sergei Sawchyn became general manager in 1954, he had Spohr down as "just an effervescent, overblown ballet master"— an impression no doubt reinforced by the board members who took Sawchyn aside and quietly assured him that they, not Spohr, made the decisions around

Left: Spohr in the mid 1950s; right: with Eva von Gencsy in Gweneth Lloyd's The Shooting of Dan McGrew. *(Eric Skipsey; Phillips-Gutkin)*

there. For that matter, Spohr underrates himself. He hesitates and vacillates and heeds the advice of other individuals far too much. Yet it is Spohr, and Spohr alone, who is the presiding genius behind the achievements of the Royal Winnipeg Ballet. There have been others on the board and in the administrative and artistic staffs who have made significant and sometimes crucial contributions. None has ever come close to matching Spohr in influence or effect. He fuels the company's workings with a unique and peculiar mixture of love and excitement and energy and enthusiasm, and he guides its fortunes with an intuitive understanding of what the public will buy.

Physically, Arnold Spohr is fine-featured, slender (a reviewer in his dancing days once said he had "legs and profile in the Barrymore tradition") and 6 ft. 3 in. tall (he comes from a family of tall persons: he has a brother who used to be a

Mountie in Calgary, two tall sisters, and another brother who lives in Winnipeg
and is even taller than he is. "Together in their fur hats," Agnes de Mille once
wrote, "they make something of a portent in Winnipeg's snowy streets.")

His eyes can seem manic. When he is disturbed or excited, they widen and
gleam behind his spectacles. He talks an aggressive mile a minute, and first
encounters can be daunting. He sounds so effusive, so profuse, so extrav-
agant—words, images, ideas tumble from him in what seems like a haphazard
stream; there are days when he talks so fast flecks of foam appear at the corner of
his mouth. Some people, hearing without listening, look on him as a wild-eyed
burbler of no account, a whimsical innocent at large in a naughty world. That is
Spohr; somehow he must have missed the class where they taught the marshall-
ing of ideas into disciplined formation. But under the torrent there is always a
thrust, a thread. You laugh, listening, as you think of the number of persons he
must deceive into unguardedness.

He was born in Rhein, Saskatchewan, half an hour after midnight on
December 26, one year in the middle of the 1920s. He has always been
pleasantly coy about exactly which year, and it would be cruel, now, to go to the
records and check. His father was a pioneer Lutheran minister from Cassel,
Germany. The virtuoso violinist Louis (or Ludwig) Spohr died in Cassel in 1859,
two blocks from a house in which members of Arnold's father's family still live.
Spohr and his relatives have never bothered to investigate the possibility of
actual blood contact with the famous musician ("Some people do, to be proud,
but we don't look back—if these are our roots, fabulous, they already feed us,
and that's enough") but he likes to mention the possible connection. It gives a
subtle emphasis to his artistic leanings.

His mother was born in Latvia; when she was nine her family emigrated to
Canada and settled in the Latvian community of Libau, Manitoba. It was there
that she met and married the itinerant pioneer minister; for several years they
travelled the prairie, preaching Lutheranism to the farm folk, supplementing
his meagre salary with occasional gifts of food and bounty from the fields. Arnold
was the sixth child; two years after he was born the family settled in Waldersee,
Manitoba, and it is from Waldersee that his first firm memories stem.

"We lived in a white farm house—there was no town, just our house, a post
office-store, and a little white church on the other side of a little ravine. My
mother played the organ. We had a farmyard at the back, with a red barn and a
couple of cows, chickens, pigs, geese—I remember I always used to chase the
geese because I liked to see them fly," (he gestures) "maybe that's why I became

a ballet dancer. In the little red shed my mother had the axe and her log, and that's where she cut the chickens' heads off when we had chicken for Sunday. She was the only one that would do it; my dad was too chicken for that, excuse my pun. My dad was very sensitive." But very strict, too? "Mm, you'd better believe it, too much so. . . . "

Beside the house was his mother's vegetable garden—"She never took anything for granted; she was always pointing out beautiful things—flowers, clouds, grass, people . . . she was a great Christian. She got what she needed from the church. She gave to God of herself and always had time for everybody."

He went to school when he was five, a three-mile walk across the prairie to a little white schoolhouse, everyone together, learning how to spell. But within a year, his father was given $60 a month to take charge of St. John's Lutheran Church in the lively and cosmopolitan North End of Winnipeg, and it was there, at 579 Anderson Avenue, that Arnold Spohr was raised.

"My family was poor and I had to learn to fight, but that sort of life teaches you what is of value. I was brought up to respect other people, and to have humility. We had difficult times at home, but I found that peace came with giving, because when you are doing things with and for other people you have no time for your own problems, no time to become involved with your ego." It is from these times that Spohr's regard for fair apportionment in all things must stem. Everyone must have a share that belongs to him alone, and, equally, everyone must contribute to the general good from his own resources: the principle recurs and recurs in his conversation, and carries in all circumstances.

Both parents were interested in classical music, and they set him to piano studies from the age of 12. He became an associate of the Royal Conservatory of Toronto in 1947; his teacher was so convinced of his potential as a concert pianist that he gave him a year's free tuition. But whenever Spohr had to perform in public he found himself beset by a crisis of nerves: "All the black keys would turn to white and vice versa, and who needs to go through all that nonsense?"

His lanky body made him a natural for sports. At Ralph Brown Elementary he won ribbons, at St. John's Technical he went out for track and played basketball, though he never went on the school team. "They asked me to, but I always felt I wasn't good enough. I was always very insecure." Even so, there is a doggedness about him that refuses to let him go back on a commitment he has made. After grade 12, for example, he enrolled at the Winnipeg Normal School for a teacher training course. It involved practical in-class work which terrified him (the performance problem again) but he felt it was something that had to be done and completed—"and actually, if you face something you're scared silly of, you know, you come out stronger, because you find there's nothing to fear. . . . I had seen people quitting things, and what happened with their lives was that once they started quitting they were quitters always . . . a little like the kids today, none of them finish anything, so they never get a follow-through or develop their own character. I feel a lot of accomplishment and success really comes not from talent—talent isn't really needed in everything—but from hard work, bloody hard work. Application, concentration, thought thought thought, a little rest, persistence—and nearly everything is possible."

This solid Teutonic belief in the virtue of work permeates his life. After a series of exhaustion collapses, he finally insisted that a three-months-a-year rest period be written into all his future contracts—and promptly added a rider allowing the company to call him for two hours every day "for consultation." There is an earnestness of purpose that keeps him constantly applied and infinitely open to possibility. "You must never close doors," he says. "A lot of people in the artistic field do that, and the flow that generates an artistic life is stopped. It's through being open that you absorb and learn and thus progress— life is a continuous state of learning, and you don't close doors until the lid is over you."

When he first took over the task of running the company, he was convinced that he was totally inadequate for the job. So he set about learning—not just about dance, not just about the theatre . . . about everything. Life. For two months a year for four years he roamed the world, just looking. "It helped me grow up completely, because it gave me an understanding of people." The trips were financed in part by loans on his London Life insurance policy, in part by Canada Council grants. Everywhere he went, he hired guides—a significant metaphor for his future, perhaps—"so I would see and not waste time." The trips were plainly undertaken in a sense of innocent and rejoicing curiosity, and his delight in recounting his experiences is at times almost childlike. "I remember sitting in the top gallery of the Teatro Colón in Buenos Aires—I didn't have much money—and seeing a Berlioz opera. Who ever thought that later we would appear there and I'd be a director? I was a little nothing. . . . I'll never forget going into the Sphinx in Egypt: you walk up some boards a quarter of a mile or so, bent over, and one little rock or something was projecting and it scratched my back . . . and Abu Simbel—all that dye stuff which I touched and which they'll

In Africa during the summer of 1966.

never get back . . . on safari in Africa—seeing the lions and the leopards eating their prey, all bloody, but it never bothered you because it was so true. All you had to do with the animals was leave them be. It's people that's difficult. You don't know where the hell you are." In Kenya, he remembers, he had a seven-foot Masai warrior to look after him; even so he was so terrified of snakes he put his suitcase in front of the door. He toured the world—India, South America, Africa, Europe, Japan, Russia, the Far East—and everywhere he went he made copious notes, books and books of them. He put them in boxes in his attic, and hasn't consulted them since.

He is tireless, still, in his desire to know and grow. If there is dance happening in a town he is visiting, he is sure to be there, because "you never know, suddenly you might see something."

He seeks out great teachers ("If you learn from the top people you move up") and one year, after a decade of searching, he "discovered" Vera Volkova. There is no teacher Spohr has ever admired more; her influence on his teaching style, and on the RWB in general, is still felt. Born in St. Petersburg in 1904, she left Russia in the 1920s and lived in China and England (where she taught Margot Fonteyn) before taking up residence in Copenhagen as ballet mistress and artistic adviser to the Royal Danish Ballet. Until her death in 1975 she was the leading Western authority on the style of the Leningrad teacher Agrippina Vaganova, who had blended elements of various Russian ballet techniques to produce an unusually pure and expressive style. Galina Ulanova was another of Vaganova's pupils; today the purity and clarity of her teaching is visible in the dancing of the Kirov Ballet and of the former Kirov dancers who now make their homes in the West—Rudolf Nureyev, Mikhail Baryshnikov, Natalia Makarova.

What attracted Spohr and many other European and North American dancers to Volkova's classes was her ability not only to train bodies but also to liberate the expressiveness of the individual within them. She was famed for her verbal precision, for the clarity of the imagery she employed to motivate her dancers and to explain their movements to them—an attribute for which Spohr was also to become celebrated. He began making annual "pilgrimages" to watch Volkova at work in the late 1960s. He continued to make these trips for eight successive

Vera Volkova. (Rygmor Mydtskov Steen Rønne)

summers, assiduously compiling a collection of 10 large notebooks filled with details of her teaching—"the RWB bible," he calls them now (they too are in boxes in his attic). His associates (Moroni in particular, who possesses even more Volkova records than Spohr) echoed his veneration of this remarkable teacher. Eventually, Spohr was able to persuade her to spend several summers in Canada, teaching either the company in Winnipeg or the students in Banff. "The marvellous thing about Vera," says Spohr, "was that she always wanted to learn. She always had this curiosity, like a child. And she always had time for everyone—from the big star to the corps member who will never make it. They were all people of the theatre, and she loved every one of them."

There are certain constants around which Spohr's personal beliefs and his artistic policy revolve: professionalism, knowledge, integrity, dedication to the work, and an ever-present consciousness of his audience. The audience, after all, is why the company is there in the first place, and he never lets his dancers forget it. They must go out on the stage and enjoy themselves; that is their duty. "Communication is what theatre has always been about for me. If we can communicate we can succeed. I aim for the truth. If something is alive and has something to say, I have learned from around the world, a message will break through . . . if I can relate to you, you can relate back. If I can't relate to you, that's where I'm going to have a problem."

His friends cross a wide range: dancers, of course, directors, choreographers, critics, a number of musical figures—Liberace, Harry Belafonte, Van Cliburn. After Ted Shawn's invitation to the company to perform at Jacob's Pillow in 1964, the two became close friends. But that inbred humility won't ever let Spohr force himself. When his company performed for the Queen in 1959, he never did meet her because everyone else elbowed him out of the way. To get near her would have meant pushing. He won't do that.

It is the same sense of unworthiness that makes him so chronically insecure. He doubts himself constantly. He was the first person to give major North American exposure to the work of Oscar Araiz, but he needed to see Robert Joffrey snap up Araiz for himself ("Joffrey's got a terrific eye—he knows what's good or not") before he could feel properly confident about his choice. Unfortunately, this insecurity makes him tentative, and that tentativeness reflects on the company. He needs someone strong to support his artistic decisions, someone to help him say yes and no. Before the 1978 trip to New York, he was going dizzy trying to put together a repertoire for the visit—not because he didn't have sufficient worthwhile material, but because he didn't have the strength of his own convictions about what to take. He consulted everyone; his staff, his senior dancers, even New York critic Clive Barnes— "and in the end, it's really up to the kids, and the kids usually go ahead and deliver anyhow."

And there, of course, the circle closes. The kids deliver, in the end, thanks to him. "It is Spohr," says Bonnie Wyckoff, "who finds the way, however obscure, to draw out each dancer's special quality, apply it to dance, and put it on the stage. He seems to get us to do *more* than we thought we could do, fulfilling our potential much more readily than a director who can only think of his own ends, however lofty. He challenges our resourcefulness. He is also quite capable of inhibiting dancers, destroying their self-confidence, even driving them out of the company, so those who are not strong and resilient enough to take a certain amount in stride, suffer. But his intentions are never destructive and only weak individuals will succumb and break down under his pressure. What makes this company so strongly individual is the fact that most of us thrive on this stimulation from the sheer challenge of matching wits with him."

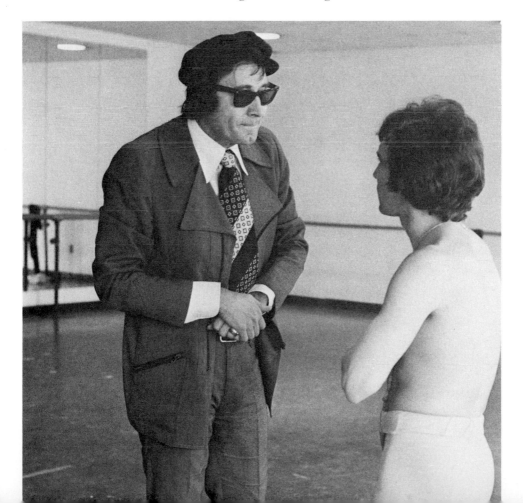

The late Nathan Cohen once called Spohr's approach to his dancers "a fascinating mixture of protective paternalism and unyielding discipline." The protective paternalism has possibly been his greatest downfall. He's too nice. He hates hurting people; the members of the company are his family, his life. He cares for them genuinely, shares their sorrows and happinesses, wipes their tears and caters their weddings. For years, in fact, he strove to be all things to all people, but he came to realize, perhaps none too soon, that "people can bleed you dry—without really wanting to—because there's so many helpless people. People realize there's this strength and they come to you for assistance. I had to realize that I must be myself and do as best I can for everybody, and that is all." Even so, he is too sensitive to be properly ruthless, which is one of the reasons for the sluggishness of the company's progress. Ruthlessness is a direct contradiction of his life-beliefs; and, anyway, he finds it hard to be disliked. When he did one of his periodic house-cleanings, firing 11 dancers, Richard Rutherford was required to do the actual dirty work. "It's human beings you're dealing with," says Spohr. "People maybe don't do that elsewhere—a dancer is an employee period, and at the end of the year you get your cards. I'd love to do that, but I can't." People have from time to time tended to take advantage of that, letting themselves get lazy because they know he won't be able to pluck up courage to fire them. But then his eyes begin to glint. Long experience has developed in him a habit of knowing when to clear the air and he finds a way to wave goodbye anyway. "I'll put up with so much baby stuff for so long, then I will charmingly say *au revoir* in a nice way where they think it's lovely and I've helped them."

Walter Terry has described him as "one of the greatest ballet directors I have ever watched at work," and it is in Spohr's qualities as a coach that the secret of the company's performing success is locked. In the normal process of dance-creation, once a new ballet has been mounted on a company by a choreographer it is passed into the care of a company member (a *régisseur*) who is then responsible for maintaining the choreographer's intentions in performance. In practice, works tend to deteriorate, often in subtle ways, as dancers and musicians make modifications that will let the dances fit more comfortably in day-to-day use. At the RWB, Spohr has reversed that process; choreographers set their works, go away, and return to find them (in Agnes de Mille's words) refined and clarified. "No matter what anybody does or how well I put something together, " says Sheila Mackinnon, formerly a principal dancer and now a

régisseur, "'it has to have the Spohr touch." That touch, again, is tied in large measure to his dogged application. Whenever a choreographer is in town, Spohr is at every rehearsal, listening, watching the eyes, the hands, the face, catching the flavour and the style so he can help his dancers reproduce it accurately when the choreographer has gone. He will go without sleep to be there. After, it is not the *steps* he remembers (he has to rely on films, notations, and the memories of his company members and *régisseurs* for that) but the shape, the mood, the feel. It is as if he looks at a piece of dance, and its essence sinks into his pores—and then, on the studio floor, he simply squeezes it back out in "motivation" classes, working with the dancers to help them find the why of their roles.

How he effects that motivation is one of the celebrated mysteries of the RWB. Says Bonnie Wyckoff: "He will be jumping around the room with his big flat feet, hair and glasses flying, spewing out the most outrageous things, crazy ideas, images, wild, funny references to anything that might be remotely related to the movement, pushing people here or there, laughing and gesticulating madly. *Inevitably* he will hit on some obscure image that will strike your fancy and click just exactly the right feeling for *you*. He is hell-bent on finding your own individual motivation that will spark *your* response and allow you to feel abandoned and completely yourself in a ballet, rather than moulded, shaped, drilled, and polished into place like a robot." One member of the board says primly of these sessions: "You listen to him and you think he's an idiot. You think he would be able to explain what it is he wants better than he does, but apparently not." It doesn't worry the company. Spohr inspires enormous affection in the people he works with. "For all his problems, for all his obvious

visual neuroses, there's just something about him," says Bonnie Wyckoff. "You shut off the intellectual approach and your heart just opens up to him." Kathleen Richardson agrees. "There is only one Arnold," she says, "and we are lucky to have him."

His announcement in the spring of 1978 that he was going to step aside took everyone by surprise. Some saw it as a catastrophe; others saw in it hope for a fresh future for the company under a new regime.

There are those who have long believed that the way must be paved for change. Some members of the board question the wisdom of retaining the same person in the same position for 20 years. "Arnold's getting older," said one person close to the company, "and he's less able to stand these awful pressures. Someday he's just going to explode, fly out in a million pieces."

Other persons believe it is Spohr, still, who makes the company what it is, and they press to assure him full support in his 20-year-old ambition to establish the RWB as a top international company "like American Ballet Theatre, but our *own*, not a carbon copy of anything: our own dancers, our own product, and our own trademark in the world." (His pinning of his dreams on ABT, the massive U.S. company whose turbulent but undeniably successful career has been built

on the principle of box-office success through the expedient of selling stellar performing talent paired with a repertoire spanning ballet's ages, is itself a telling factor in his make-up. Some would say the example of ABT provides shaky principles on which to found a ballet company, but Spohr stands by them firmly, and always has.)

He once told me there had only been three shows in all his years with RWB that had truly satisfied him. "The trouble was," he said, "we started with the cart before the horse. The exuberance, joyousness, all those words that people used, we started with that . . . but the style, the technique, is coming, and a very good one, and soon, I can tell you, I won't have to apologize."

The successes in New York suggested he might at last be getting there—and within weeks of the company's return to Winnipeg he had changed his mind about leaving. The decision caused as much controversy as the original announcement that he was planning to step aside.

He has always been aware of the fighting that has gone on over his succession. "I'm amazed everybody wants to be a director," he says. "You'd better be prepared for that, otherwise they gobble you alive. I've always been away ahead of the kids in everything. They gobble me alive, but, chum, there's more of me that I've still got put away. I'm way ahead of them for gobbling . . . . Running a company *is* hard, and you gotta know, and you see what a lot of people don't do is they don't go round and get themselves ready for a job. They come in and then when they're insecure or inadequate everybody's wrong, never them. They cover up and lie, and you've got to fill all the holes like the holes in the dam in Amsterdam."

He is candidly aware of his own limitations, and of his own strengths. He sees his role at the RWB as nothing more than a facilitator. He had a career as a dancer, and that was nice, and he did a bit of choreography, and that was nice too, but he knows he is not a creative artist himself. What he *can* do, though, is "see creativity realized." He makes it possible, he hopes, for something to happen that leaves you in awe. "The moments which leave you dumbfounded, and going home not able to speak . . . these are the things that keep me. All of us here, I think, are constantly striving for that magic moment when the spirit, soul or whatever reaches that private special world. . . . In dance there should be a *happening*. If this is achieved then I have realized a goal."

The Dancers

"*My ideal dancer is Erik Bruhn. Or Mikhail Baryshnikov. Brilliant, intelligent, they can do anything. They've got brain—that's what I'm looking for—and they're musical. That's all I want. Everything. That's my aim, my fantasy.*"

ARNOLD SPOHR

Nobody is born a dancer; you have to want it more than anything.

MIKHAIL BARYSHNIKOV

The end of Sheila Mackinnon's dancing career began the day she slipped as she pushed off for a jump and came down from three feet in the air on one knee: torn tendons, ruined cartilage behind the patella, three operations. She went back to dancing, but then the other knee began to go: osteo-arthritis, from all those knee-drops and knee-pirouettes, "and I thought, I can't . . . it's one thing to have three scars on one knee, but to have to aim for *both* knees all scarred up . . ." Sheila Mackinnon, lively, intelligent, redhead, is one of the old school. She was a star in the company's glamorous golden age and now she is a company *régisseur*. She thinks, quite seriously, no joking, that dancers dance because they're slightly crazy. "I don't think it's because we're sadistic or masochistic, it's just that we're mentally retarded. We don't know any better. I don't think it's devotion—it's because you *have* to. I couldn't have, I *wouldn't* have done

209

A scene from Rite of Spring *by Oscar Araiz. Betsy Carson is supported by Baxter Branstetter (left) and Ronn Tice, with Joost Pelt. (Jack Mitchell)*

anything else. I wouldn't have developed as a human being. From the time I was a small child, dancing to me was life itself."

Richard Rutherford has melting eyes, and a slim handsomeness. He looks the way we would all like to look at his age—10 years younger. He talks in measured, elegant, beautifully modulated tones, as if he might once upon a time have gone away somewhere to learn how to do it properly; there are few contractions in his speech. He has a quick, trusting smile.

He joined the RWB in 1957 with Benjamin Harkarvy, spent half his life with the company, reached disillusionment, and gave it up. In his best years everyone talked about Richard Rutherford—his vitality, his comic spirit, his exuberance, the evident delight he took in dancing. He was the company's brightest male star. His strength rested in his naïveté, his unquestioning innocence. It is tempting to use him as an image for the company—the innocent beginnings, the rise, the excitement, the stardom, the gradual coming-on of knowingness. Like Sheila Mackinnon, Richard Rutherford was a child, in that sense, most of his dancing life. He never questioned, never wondered what there might be in it for him; he danced as if his life depended on it. In those days, the late 1950s and early 1960s, that kind of innocence suffused the entire company. There were so few of them they all danced four ballets a night, but no one thought it strange or demanding—the curtain went up and there they were, a little more tired, maybe, but dancing, giving. "We didn't care whether it was good, bad or indifferent. All we knew was that we were going to get out on stage and do it for a public."

For Richard Rutherford, dance was a hiding-place, the way it has been for so many. He was always a shy, retiring person; at receptions for the company, he never spoke unless spoken to. But on stage he could be anything—a murderer, a villain, a clown—because when the curtain came down he didn't have to pay the consequences. His father only saw him dance once, "and he said he had never seen that person in his life."

David Moroni, handsome as a movie star, came to the company from Ottawa at the invitation of company member James Clouser in 1964. He, too, grew through the best years to the rank of principal. He, too, has that same, unquestioning loyalty, self-giving. He thought his first pay-cheque was a joke—"paying me for what I like to do best? I felt very strange." He resigned from performing in 1970 to take over the direction of the professional training programme in the company's school, and it is largely thanks to his efforts that the company is beginning now to build a source of dancers of its own.

David Moroni as Drosselmeier in Nutcracker.

Forced to compromise, Spohr and his associates would go to New York and take whatever dancers they could get—"buy them off the shelf," as Jim Cameron once rather indelicately put it—then work patiently to turn them into performers that could respectably be put on the stage. And each year, with the same unfailing regularity, the newly improved talent would be snatched away by more attractive companies. The RWB became accepted as a convenient stepping stone, and that incensed the intensely loyal Moroni. "What really offended me was the group of people who turned up at one audition with no performing experience whatsoever, yet expected to be taken on as soloists. That hurt. I was determined to show we are not Indiansville up here."

So he set up the professional training program, operated on a scholarhip basis as part of the already-existing company school, which Jean McKenzie had built from a beginning enrollment of 350 to about 900 pupils. From the start, the two programs were run as separate entities, though they interlock financially, and in theory should provide the possibility for a student to progress from classes as a tot right through to full company membership. This has not yet happened, though by the 1977-78 season more than 80 per cent of the company membership had been through Moroni's hands—a fact that gave special poignance to his brief return to the stage that season to dance the key role of the ballet master in Neumeier's *Nutcracker*.

The advantages of the program are obvious. The sense of loyalty is greater, and the students can be trained specifically for the RWB style. Already, Moroni has set up a small touring group from the program, offering public performances of items from the company repertoire, coached by Spohr, getting to know the way the company's system works. He is particularly concerned that the company's strength in the classical area should be increased—he sees classical technique as a point of departure for the extremely mixed techniques that the RWB's eclectic repertoire demands, and from the start he aimed to produce dancers with a sound basic technical command. It has been a struggle, he admits. If Winnipeg holds no particular attractions for working dancers from out-of-town, it holds even less for beginning dance students. "For the first two years I had to literally make do with whatever happened to wander in." But the word slowly spread. Today, the program is over-subscribed.

Eventually, Moroni would like to see the school established on a full-time residential basis, though he doesn't see that happening in the current national economic climate, nor in what he perceives as the current climate of conservatism in RWB board thought. And he would like to help raise the standard of work

in the company to the point where audiences would know they could rely on
seeing a good performance, whatever the work, because "every artist in the
company would be someone very special." But he is realist enough to know that
none of that is going to happen overnight. "I'm willing," he says, "to take the next
15 years to get where I want to go." His willingness to be considered part of the
company's proposed ruling triumvirate during the 1978 power-struggle upheavals was motivated, he says, directly by the interests of the school, whose
continued existence he felt might be threatened by any change in company
control that he was not a part of.

Spohr is enthusiastic about Moroni's program. (The two men are, in many
ways kindred spirits—the same insecurity, the same sense of wonder, the same
noble, loyal ambitions for the company they have devoted their lives to, the same
doggedness.) Spohr would like, in fact, to see the entire company composed of
RWB-trained dancers, and he has a habit of taking youngsters from the program
into the company before they are properly ready. On one occasion he actually
used a pair of recent school graduates as *pas de deux* "stars," which caused a
brief scandal within the company.

The problem with building the company from the school, of course, is that
star-quality dancers are rarely created fast. So far, the company's principal-
dancer ranks have almost always been filled by imports, and in recent seasons
there has been a woeful shortage of those. No replacements were brought in for
the Australians, Gailene Stock and Gary Norman, when they left the company at
the end of the 1976-77 season, which meant the star-dancer burden the
following year was carried almost exclusively by the three surviving imported
principals, Bonnie Wyckoff, Marina Eglevsky and Salvatore Aiello. The first
generation of school graduates was just beginning to make its way up through the
company, and several of these young dancers were given principal-dancer
responsibilities—among them Roger Shim, Evelyn Hart, Sheri Cook and David
Peregrine. However, for all the flashes of talent that these dancers showed, and
for all their implicit promise for the future (Evelyn Hart, for instance, could
prove to be the school's first big international success story—she has a clean,
elegant line, a natural ease and expressiveness, and she is an exciting dancer to
watch) they only hinted at the quality of dancing that RWB audiences might
legitimately expect. The problem was further complicated when all three of the
senior principals went absent from the company performing roster for a Western
tour in the late spring of 1978—Bonnie Wyckoff to guest for three months with
the Joffrey Ballet, Marina Eglevsky to guest with the New York company

Marina Eglevsky (foreground) with Eric Horenstein and Evelyn Hart in a scene from Nutcracker. *(Jack Mitchell)*

founded by her father (the Eglevsky Ballet), and Aiello to choreograph for the Manitoba Theatre Centre and then to concentrate on overseeing the Canadian portion of the tour.

By the 1976-77 and 1977-78 seasons, however, one besetting problem—that of dancer turnover—seemed to be lessening. It had plagued the company for years. Outside a small core of stalwarts, few dancers ever stayed long enough to absorb and project the style that Spohr is so concerned to develop, and one longtime RWB-watcher was convinced it was the company itself that drove them away—"it seems to suck everthing out of them, all those different styles, all those ballets, all that travelling." But Richard Rutherford thinks Moroni's program could lead to a revival of the company's early spirit, which changed noticeably after the rising, pioneer years. With the first flush of excitement over, new dancers had less to inspire them. Dancing became a job. Today, he says, there is the beginning of a new spirit, "a wonderful enthusiasm," in dancers who were hardly born when he joined the company.

Spohr is not so sure. He likes the general atmosphere at the RWB—"in other companies, you get claws out. Here we have claws, but the nails are cut. Basically, the people here are considerate and well-mannered for the other person, and I think that comes through in the dance." But, he says he finds today's dancers won't take proper responsibility for themselves. They complain to him, for instance, that no one compliments them on their success on this or that tour—"and I say, you got terrrific reviews, standing ovations here there and everywhere, what more do you want? You're dancing for communication with the public. There is your reward. Schnook. So eventually, if I get enough of that, I haven't got time. I've got to move on to a person who has enough brain. Brain is what makes it. Bonnie Wyckoff, for instance. She's so with it. She's got what it takes."

Bonnie Wyckoff is built like a boy-child. Her body is businesslike, a tool, an implement of communication; with the lively moulding of her hands, the alert turning of her head, the resilient firmness of her back, she can dominate the stage. Off stage, though, the focus is in her pale face. She is a transcendental meditationist, has been for years, and there is a quiet, centred serenity to her. She has no misgivings about the character of the RWB. "Here, more than in any other company I can think of, it is understood that there is a huge team effort, give and take, and an equal contribution of creativity from both director and dancers, and a healthy communication between us. I will be the first to admit that dancers in general are hard to get along with—egotistical, defensive, weird,

and terribly insecure. But I challenge anyone to find a company of dancers as open, loving, easy-going, and accepting as this group."

The dancers of the RWB are often scathing in private in their opinions of works they are asked to perform. They are candidly aware that they dance a disproportionate amount of hack work as audience-pleasing fill. But private opinion never intrudes on public performance. "Dancers have a funny way of making everything work for themselves," says David Moroni. "Even with ballets you don't like, you find something that will motivate you and make you keep on doing it. You have to, otherwise you lose your mind." In the same way, a dancer will spend his or her entire career—half a childhood and adulthood—working to perfect a single step. In the mastery of technique lies the clarity of communication. Bonnie Wyckoff describes that communication as a creative flow, dancers passing out energy, audiences seeing their own lives reflected. Spohr calls it, more simply, truth. However we name it, it is what we are all, dancers and audiences, there for.

Bonnie Wyckoff in Oscar Araiz's Mahler 4: Eternity Is Now.

On the Road

If you asked an American, right up to three or four years ago, to name a Canadian ballet company, they'd talk about the Royal Something Ballet. It's a well-known, well-travelled commodity. Mind you, if they were the world's greatest, they wouldn't be the world's most travelled.

DAVID Y. H. LUI
Impresario

The Royal Winnipeg Ballet has played, in its time, in close to 400 cities in 24 countries on four continents. Its portability is its livelihood, which is one reason why it has never been expanded in size: 26 or 27 dancers, the artistic staff, a skeleton orchestra, and one cello will fit exactly (tightly, but exactly) into a single bus. Everything else—sets, props, costumes, shoes, lighting system— goes into a 48-foot tractor-trailer, and the five-man technical crew, with different duties and time schedules, travels independently in its own 26-foot camper-motorhome (they wear out one a year). As a touring machine, the RWB is as sophisticated as they come. Its crew (largely comprised of former carnival men) is proud of its professionalism. In 1968, with the expenses of a tour to Russia looming, technical director John Stammers, general manager Sergei Sawchyn, and members of the technical crew perfected a lightweight packing and wardrobe system. It replaced the traditional theatrical wardrobe trunks,   *219*

Richard Rutherford, Ana Maria de Gorriz, and David Moroni in Paris in June, 1970. (Colette Masson)

some of them weighing up to two hundred pounds, with equally sturdy containers weighing only 26½ pounds each. The innovations reduced airfreight costs by over 50 per cent, and the system—they called it Tourlite—has since become a modestly lucrative sales-and-rental sideline operation for the company.

The company's value as a compact, mobile, inter-continental performance unit (a kind of dance commando force) has not gone unrecognized. On the eve of its departure for Europe in 1968, the premier of Manitoba presented the RWB with the Order of the Buffalo Hunt, "in recognition of attainment as a touring ballet of world renown." At the close of the 1968-69 season, the Kresge Foundation, of Detroit, Michigan, gave the company $6,000 toward the cost of a touring truck. The grant was given, the foundation stressed, "in recognition of the company's contribution to cultural life in North America, particularly for the benefit derived by audiences across the continent during its annual North American tours." Five years later, the Kresge Foundation gave the company a further $70,000 to pay for a touring lightboard.

The RWB has always boasted that it will perform in communities no other major ballet companies will consider, but it makes good on the boast at the expense not only of its programming and its choreography (which often must be trimmed or adapted to fit the performance space) but, most significantly, at the expense of its dancers. They are grossly overused, but there can be no question of understudies, and two incapacitated dancers can mean instant calamity. Regularly, tour replacements are flown in from the company school. Stories of dancers performing on strained tendons and pulled muscles are commonplace. Under these circumstances, being a dancer can become an endurance test. Richard Rutherford remembers how sickness hit the company in Russia. "Shirley New we almost lost . . . she got so sick. She got so dehydrated she lost about 15 pounds—she'd run off stage, throw up in a bucket, then run back on and do a few more steps. I became very ill, too, with a temperature of 103. But there was nobody else who could do my roles, so there was just no question. I had so much fever in my muscles that I couldn't do a class, but somehow I got on stage and I forgot. Until that final curtain came down and I realized, and it all came rushing back and I was sick again. But for a few moments there . . . it's like, you don't cough on stage or you don't hiccough . . . you don't yawn—you become something else, totally."

For the RWB, the show must always go on, and for years the company claimed it had only missed one performance, and that through no fault of its own: fog delayed a flight from Halifax, Nova Scotia, in 1965 and the company's opening in San Juan, Puerto Rico, had to be postponed for a day. (They preferred, of course, not to recall the Sudbury engagement that was cancelled early in 1954 for fear the company would be branded "red.") In recent seasons, however, adverse weather conditions and union disputes have marred that record.

The stage crew, currently under associate general manager Bill Riske, long ago learned to anticipate the unexpected.

Concrete flooring is a frequent problem. The dancers' contracts specify surfaces of a certain resilience (1 ⅝ inches of air beneath the performers) and the crew is so often called on to lay a new stage over the existing surface that they keep a note in the camper of exactly how much lumber and plywood sheeting the job needs. As far as stages are concerned, though, 'twas ever thus. On the company's first-ever visit to Brandon, Manitoba, the dancers were billeted in what was then the Brandon asylum, and inmates on their best behaviour were let out to help get the stage ready. As therapy, it must have been of dubious help: the stage was so pitted and worn that the parolees were treated to the spectacle of dancers chewing Kleenex to make filler for the holes. And when, in the early 1950s, dancer Kay Bird complained about a fall she took on a badly sanded stage surface in Fargo, North Dakota, the theatre manager told her not to worry —"When Roy Rogers was here, Trigger fell, too."

Small-town touring means small-town problems. In Kamloops, B.C., the crew once had to deal with a piano whose pedals fell off in the middle of a show. On another occasion they had to build new *legs* for a piano. Regularly, they are called on to strengthen or rebuild backstage flying equipment. Just as regularly, things go wrong—anchor pins pull out of walls, curtains jam and trip, light booms get stuck in full view at half hoist.

International touring presents problems of a more complex kind. When the company went to South America, the impresario insisted on attaching an aide to the company for the entire trip. The reason soon became apparent. Without his constant greasing of official palms, the company would never have mounted half its shows, and might be struggling around the continent still.

Weather can create havoc. The dancers' touring schedule takes them through some of North America's roughest winter country. Almost always, they manage to make it. Sometimes, they wish they hadn't. In Huntingdon, West Virginia, in the winter of 1976-77, they found themselves performing in a temperature of eight degrees centigrade. The audience was asked to enter the theatre early to help warm it with their body heat, and oil heaters were placed on the stage.

Inevitably, there are touring stories that have become RWB legends. They still talk, for instance, about the Orchestra That Couldn't Quite. It happened in Ottawa, in 1960. The company was dancing Brian Macdonald's *The Darkling*, which is set to Benjamin Britten's *Variations on a Theme of Frank Bridge*. The locally recruited orchestra played so atrociously that, according to Sheila Mackinnon, "it sounded, to be rude, like a barnyard passing wind." At one point, the music actually stopped entirely, and the dancers were left to fend for themselves. "We were all hysterical," she says. "I don't know how we kept going. The conductor sang, he whistled, we'd yell cues to each other . . ." Marilyn Young, who was dancing the lead, recalls: "At the end, my partner and I were just guessing what we were doing, talking to each other, saying things like 'I'll meet you in the corner because they've just jumped 10 bars.' Someone had to slap me to take a curtain call."

There was the case of the Laughing-Boxes. Someone in the orchestra thought it might be a good idea to encourage audience response at an Akron, Ohio, performance of Paddy Stone's *Variations on Strike Up the Band* by setting off an automatic laughing machine. Somehow, the machine was tripped too early and as the audience watched the *Don Quixote pas de deux* in solemn silence, raucous mechanical laughter came booming from the pit. No one, recalls pianist Linda Lee Thomas, was able to stop it—"the cellist kept trying to spike it"—and it became so ridiculously intrusive a little old lady in the front row of the stalls kept leaning over into the pit and whispering "Sssh." (Audience response, though, is never predictable. In Adelaide, Australia, a woman in the front row found the Stone ballet so hilarious she kept leaning over at each new joke and slapping conductor Neal Kayan on the back in congratulation.)

Then there was the story of Peter Garrick's Flying Glass Eye. It was Richardson, Texas, 1971, and the company was doing George Balanchine's *Pas de Dix*. Garrick, who has been sightless in one eye since birth, did his double *tour en l'air* at the end of the men's variation, and out his glass eye flew. It rolled to the middle of the stage, and sat there. Panicking in the wings, Garrick was reprimanded by Richard Rutherford for making so much fuss "over a jewel off your costume." "Over what?" asked Garrick, turning to face him.

By the middle of a season, the strains of touring are visible in the dancers' sallow skins and dark-rimmed eyes. On the road, one person's cold or infection can turn immediately to an epidemic, and, with no doctor conveniently to hand, there is often a temptation to share around prescribed medicaments. Romances and disputes flare up, flame briefly, and gutter. Phenomena like insomnia or forgetfulness tend to run in company-wide rhythms. A whole dressing room full of women can find their monthly cycles synchronized.

The company jokes that anyone wanting to get in touch with a dancer in the RWB is best advised to send mail to the head office, marked Please Forward, but for the dancers the need for a sense of personal base becomes increasingly acute as a tour progresses. If the company is playing at or near someone's hometown, the visiting relatives are "shared" by the whole company. By the end of a tour, the return home is a genuine relief. As Bonnie Wyckoff put it, "rediscovering a closetful of forgotten clothes, one's own bed, refrigerator, books, music . . . even the banging radiators and dripping faucets are a comfort, because they're familiar."

The stress of touring, she once wrote, is monumental, the pace relentless. "The feeling is that of being constantly pressed forward from behind, straining what feel to be the very limits of endurance." But those who stick it out would have it no other way. "There is a real sense of urgency and a certain restlessness in dancers' natures that is somehow quieted by the travelling and the constant performing. Time loses some of its threatening value, and much can be accomplished during tours in terms of developing and maturing as a dancer and person . . . things are appreciated from a different level, a broadening perspective, on each return."

3 The Choreography

You cannot relate to all people.
Life is full of personal taste.

ARNOLD SPOHR

The Royal Winnipeg Ballet grew and flourished because it offered beer and skittles for the people. It was a successful pop dance company—that is, it gave its audiences entertainment-dance rather than serious explorations of the art—long before pop dance became fashionable in the repertoire of the major ballet companies. While other companies built cool museums for the reverent display of classical masterpieces, the RWB was busy rigging carnival side-shows. The purists looked on from a distance, purse-lipped, but the people came. Well, the mass audience always has had money and time for flash and novelty in any art, and the RWB has had its share of black-velvet paintings. It has had proportionately less than its share of old masters, but then, the argument has always gone, for the deliberately pocket-sized RWB, they would be imprac-tical.

Eclecticism and saleability have always been the joint cornerstones of the company's programming policy. No one else carries a repertoire quite so delightfully, ridiculously diverse, and while other companies copy the format, none carry it off with quite the same innocent insouciance: the Joffrey Ballet looks too *knowing* these days; American Ballet Theatre is too *big*.

227

What to Do till the Messiah Comes, *1978 cast*. *(Jack Mitchell)*

For a company as remote from the real centres of civilization as the RWB is, this diversity has been a matter of survival. There's no point in offering encyclopedias if your buyers want comic-books. Arnold Spohr and his colleagues want desperately to be taken seriously by their peers, and in the past decade there has been a noticeable change in the RWB's programming policy. The emphasis on trendy flippancy has lessened. It is a more adult, more sophisticated company than it used to be—and, in terms of repertoire, a far better one. Steadily, the old principles of catering to a low common denominator in the audience are being replaced by principles of artistic seriousness. And inevitably, selling tickets has become a far more difficult business.

The ballets that were danced in the company's first decade were made wholesale, to a purpose. They made no great technical demands on their interpreters—how could they, when the dancers were just beginning?—but they entertained. They seem to have been perfectly serviceable works, appearing (thanks to Gweneth Lloyd's remarkably fertile imagination) at the rate of three or four a year, programmed always on the something-for-everyone principle: a classical "white" ballet, a futuristic ballet, a mimed comedy.

She had sensitive musical tastes, she was alert to the current of fashion in the arts, and she had a handy choreographic versatility that served her purposes well. For her time she was probably daring and innovative (though one observer remembers most of her ballets as "naïve English girl-school pieces"), and she doubtless gave encouragement to the flowering Winnipeg visual-arts scene in commissioning sets and drops from young artists like Robert Bruce (whose drop for *Dionysos* caused a furore), Charles Faurer, and Joseph Plaskett. But she never went to unacceptable extremes. She and her associates knew their audience and always bore its needs in mind.

The notebooks in which she created certain of her later ballets have been preserved, but few of her works survive in any other recorded form. One exception is *Shadow on the Prairie*, perhaps her most famous composition, which she made in 1952. This was filmed, and shown to great acclaim across the country. Its value today is historical: it was one of the first works of dance art to speak seriously of the Canadian experience. This was not her first ballet on a Canadian theme, however. *The Shooting of Dan McGrew*, a comic ballet derived from Robert Service's Yukon poetry, was a popular favourite for years after its appearance in 1950. Other popular comic and melodramatic works of their era were *Triple Alliance* (1941), *An American in Paris* (1943), *Pleasure Cruise*

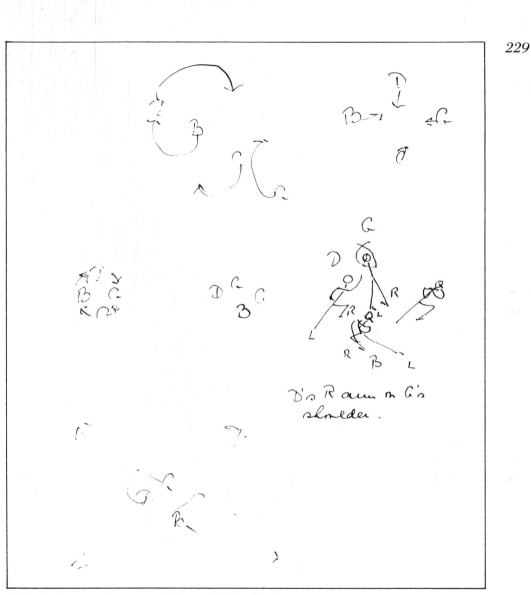

A facsimile page from one of Gweneth Lloyd's choreographic notebooks.

(1946) and *Chapter 13* (1947). Dramatic and modernist creations that made particular impact in their time were *The Wise Virgins* (1942—later remounted as *Parable*), *Allegory* (1948—a Greek-symbolist piece that showed, according to the program note, "the need of spiritual regeneration of mankind through the medium of the arts in the broken post-war world"), and *Visages* (1949—described at the time as "a vastly important contribution to Canadian art. . . . The presiding spirit of the Winnipeg group has never evolved anything so starkly daring, so controlled in its evocation of anguish, and so boldly designed."). Pure dance works that are specially remembered include *Etude* (1943), *Concerto* (1947), *Arabesque I* (1947), *Arabesque II* (1949) and *Romance* (1949).

This ability to create in so many diverse styles, a distinct boon to the growing company, was a product of Gweneth's background. She was a specialist in "the revived Greek dance," but while she had given herself adequate classical-ballet coverage for teaching purposes, she was less than secure as a choreographer in strict classicism. At the 1949 Canadian Ballet Festival, S. Morgan-Powell in the Montreal *Star* said Gweneth's choreographic style "appears to be working towards a ballet of freer movement, based upon, but in no way subservient to, classical technique." Marilyn Young, who danced with the company in the early days, remembers an early version of act two of *Swan Lake*. "I guess Gweneth had set it from her memory, and the little swans, instead of doing *piqué* in the opening step, were jumping it. When Margot Fonteyn was on tour, she watched our version of it, and when we started off, she said, 'What's this, it's all wrong!' and we said, 'Well, that's how we were taught.' We had no great Russian geniuses to hand things down to us at that time."

The fact that Gweneth's choreographic style was a product of her own limitations may have been fortuitous at the time, but its effect on the company was far-reaching. She established a stylistic pattern that has endured, with various modifications, for four decades—a pattern of blending elements of classical ballet with elements of contemporary work to produce a dance style that expresses more clearly than either single element could the spirit that has always moved the Winnipeg company.

Over the years, various members of the company tried their hand, as dancers will, at choreography, with varying degrees of success. One of the earliest was Arnold Spohr, whose *Ballet Premier,* made in 1950, was only the third non-Lloyd ballet to enter the repertoire. It won him high praise. Herbert Whittaker, in the Toronto *Globe and Mail,* picked it out as the highlight of the Fourth Canadian Ballet Festival in 1952. Anatole Chujoy considered it had been composed with "a fine feeling for the choreographic line, and a good, perhaps intuitive knowledge of the requirements and possibilities of spatial dancing." Spohr's *Intermède,* the following year, was received with similar—

perhaps slightly less flattering—enthusiasm, "and so I thought I was pretty good. Everyone said my work was like Balanchine's." So he went to see what Balanchine's work was like, "and I thought, goodness, if I could choreograph like that I'd be quite all right. But who needs two Balanchines?" His future choreographic forays were only intermittent. He says now he doesn't miss choreographing—creating was always so much fear and agony. He prefers, he says, teaching and coaching and keeping *other* choreographers' work alive: Spohr the facilitator.

Between Spohr's departure and return the company went through the hands of Ruthanna Boris and Benjamin Harkarvy. Each contributed four or five works to the repertoire, and in the opinion of one longtime Winnipeg ballet-goer they moved the company steadily toward a sense of class: art as well as entertainment. But the company has always needed to be run by someone who understands the city's innocent, small-town mix of conservatism and love of novelty. It needed Spohr. He reintroduced the old principles, and added a sense of showbizzy contemporaneity. Fired by his personal dreams of making the company one day look like American Ballet Theatre, he began to buy and commission ballets from established and promising choreographers throughout the Western world.

He has stuck always by Lloyd-Farrally first principles. "I'm trying mainly to get a classical style," he says. "That's the basis of everything—but I've kept the Gweneth and Betty tradition of a diversified rep, because it's important to me that you have the communication with the public. Our company should be saying what's happening today and tomorrow. We've got to stay with it. The great classical companies already exist. We should have a base, but be of now."

His stress on diversification and staying "of now" has left the company, in fact, noticeably weak in the classical style. And it has certainly not done very much to help the company shape any distinctive character or individuality. But it has certainly kept the product saleable.

Saleability has often seemed the single abiding principle at the heart of pop or entertainment ballet, which is one reason why it is so little regarded by critics. Another more important reason for that, however, is the fact that under what is often a glittering surface of razzle-dazzle theatrical effect these works too frequently have nothing of interest to say in actual dance terms: the art has sacrificed its own expressiveness to become a vehicle for sensory massage. Audiences become caught up, unavoidably, in the visual and auditory excitement of the *effects* in a work like Vesak's *Messiah* or Macdonald's *A Ballet*

High, and they leave the theatre convinced they have had a dance experience, when in fact all that has happened is that they have had their senses stroked.

Cream-puff ballets, too, play a significant role in the RWB repertoire—"you can't knock box office," Spohr always says, and frothy, frilly pieces that do no more than offer pretty, superficial entertainment still enter the repertoire at the rate of one or two a year. Paddy Stone's two most recent works, *Variations on Strike Up the Band* and *The Hands* are examples (Stone has made a career out of bright-and-breezy television variety choreography, and it shows). Others are Michael Smuin's *Pulcinella Variations,* Brydon Paige's *Rigodon,* Larry Hayden's *Moments* and *The Whims of Love,* and Stuart Sebastian's *The Seasons.* All are enthusiastically wolfed down, and there has never been any denying that Spohr's finger-on-the-pulse common touch has always paid off in terms of audience response.

However, his main thrust in repertoire-building has been much more broadly contemporary than this, and it is fascinating to see how the basic Lloyd principle of a classical-modern blend has been maintained and amplified.

Ana Maria de Gorriz and Winthrop Corey in Paddy Stone's Variations on Strike Up the Band. *(Martha Swope)*

The Darkling *(left to right): Ted Patterson, Beverley Barkley, Jim Clouser, Marilyn Young, David Shields, Rachel Browne, Richard Rutherford, and Sheila Mackinnon. (Campbell and Chipman)*

The first choreographer after Gweneth Lloyd to be involved with the RWB in any milestone way was Brian Macdonald, whose career has been inextricably interwoven with the developmental years of Third Stream (that is, contemporary-classical) dance. When his ballet, *The Darkling*, entered the repertoire in 1959 he was already well known in Canada as a versatile man of television and theatre, but it was at the RWB that he made his first significant forays into serious choreography. *The Darkling* dealt with the way in which individuals' inner problems and characteristics can disrupt even the happiest of love affairs. Roy Maley, in *The Winnipeg Tribune*, called it "the most provocative ballet yet produced by the RWB," though Frank Morriss, in the *Free Press*, thought Macdonald was being "much too clever for his own good. . . . When he sheds mannerisms and makes use of his evident dramatic gifts, Mr. Macdonald will go places."

Morriss's words were to find many echoes thereafter. A fierce individualist, and a difficult man to get to know, Macdonald has always had a magpie eye for trends and fancies. His work is clever, slick, and strong on bravura effect. But his emphasis on gimmickry often detracts from any genuine human communication his work might make. His ballets can come across as brittle, superficial, and mannered, as if he is unprepared to dare a simple honesty. One dancer who

While the Spider Slept.

worked with him for years says: "I don't think Brian is able to show his human emotions. He retains too much of himself away from people, in order to create an image."

Macdonald has always prided himself on his all-round versatility. "You must not let yourself get in the position of so many choreographers of cutting the same piece of cloth over and over again," he once told an interviewer. In the dozen years of his on-again-off-again collaboration with the RWB, he brought to it or created for it 14 works, each with its own distinctive (if sometimes derivative) character. They provided the hard core of a recognizable repertoire that carried the RWB through Europe—not English, not American, not Russian or European: *Winnipeg*. At the same time, through the challenge of their technique, his ballets allowed the company to grow in performance.

His work for the RWB ranged from comedy (*Les Whoops-de-Doo*, from 1959; and *Pas d'Action*, a clever and witty send-up of classical story-ballets—in Sheila Mackinnon's words, "one of the best farces ever done") to dramatic narrative (*Rose Latulippe*, 1966) and populist schlock (*A Ballet High*, 1970, in which the company was accompanied by a live rock group).

Throughout his choreographic career, Macdonald has been fond of embrac-
ing causes and espousing social principles. *While the Spider Slept* (1966) was
another treatment of the alienation of 1960s youth, inspired by poetry written on
the death of John F. Kennedy; in it, one critic thought, the RWB might find its
soul. *Five over Thirteen* (1969) was an artless, obvious, and naïve attempt to
show the joy that could result if the individual would abandon his shell of
self-defence and embrace his fellows.

His imagination has often been at its best under someone else's influence, or
in collaboration with other artists. *Aimez-vous Bach?*, which won a gold medal at
the Paris Festival in 1964, combines something very close to the cool, strict
Balanchine style with modern dance-hall movements; it was created the
summer after he spent some months in New York on a Canada Council grant,
observing Balanchine and his company. The London critic Peter Williams
summed up this aspect of Macdonald's work succinctly in a roundup article in
Dance and Dancers on the company's 1965 London season. He was unable to
find any kind of personal style in Macdonald's work, he said. "They all seem too
tailor-made to certain needs with far too much impersonal reference to what
others have done. I hope soon that I am going to see a work about which I can say,
'*This* is Brian Macdonald, this is the way he thinks, he feels, and this is the path

Five Over Thirteen.

along which he is obviously moving.' . . . He worries me because all the time I have the idea that somewhere there is the creative artist trying to break through outside influences."

Nevertheless some of the company's most fruitful years were those when Macdonald, Spohr, and Sergei Sawchyn were together: the three ignited among them a vital spark. The careers of company and choreographer had intertwined at a crucial time for all of them. But he was by no means alone in the lists. Spohr, tireless in his hunt for new choreographic talent, gave a variety of homegrown choreographers their head concurrently with Macdonald—Robert Moulton, Don Gillies, and particularly James Clouser, whose work was at one time lauded by Walter Terry as "amazingly versatile and exceptionally talented"—and he also brought in a wide variety of outsiders. By no means all of his gambles have paid off—the repertoire is littered with the residue of choreographic experiments that have guttered out after being given their brief chance to flame, but Spohr vigorously defends his practice of allowing young choreographers the right to fail before an audience, "because otherwise how are they ever going to learn and how are we ever going to discover them?" Some of his gambles have paid handsome dividends in terms of company image and audience excitement, and when this has happened it has been interesting to watch other, less adventurous companies jump onto his sometimes rickety bandwagon. Currently, about a dozen companies in the U.S. and Europe dance ballets originally made for the RWB.

Of all the early imports, the most significant by far was Agnes de Mille. The relationship, which was to bring the company five ballets in just over a decade, began in 1962. Miss de Mille had already been a shaping force in the 1940s "revolution" of the American musical theatre with her imaginative and innovative choreography for such musicals as *Oklahoma!, Carousel* and *Brigadoon*—suddenly, dancing became an integral part of the whole work, rather than something arbitrarily imposed—and her purposeful blend of dance, theatrics, emotional communication and psychological exploration was to prove ideal for the evolving style of the RWB. The first of her works to enter the RWB repertoire was *The Bitter Weird*, a dramatic tale of love and death in the Scottish highlands, set to music from *Brigadoon*. This was vigorous ballet-drama enriched by clearly-stated psychological overtones, and it showed off the company's vitality and high spirits. At the close of its première performance, it was given, in the words of *Saturday Night* reviewer Ralph Hicklin, "a prolonged, screaming, shouting ovation, the like of which I've not heard anywhere else in Canada." (On

Sheila Mackinnon, Richard Rutherford, and Jim Clouser in The Bitter Weird *by Agnes de Mille. (Campbell and Chipman)*

the same program, by way of contrast, was the Winnipeg première of George Balanchine's *Pas de Dix*, a buoyant plotless romp to Glazunov's *Raymonda* music. Its demanding classicism—the grand Russian manner with an added Hungarian tinge—quite defeated the company, as it still tends to do.)

The de Mille-RWB association strengthened through the 1960s. In 1965 came a comic-dramatic entertainment titled *The Rehearsal*—a narrated presentation detailing in graphic form the joy, disappointment, and relentless hard work that *may* lead to on-stage success in dance. Miss de Mille herself delivered the narration at the work's Winnipeg première. "Contrary to rumour," went one of her most popular lines, "*choreography* is the oldest profession." And in 1967 she created for the company *The Golden Age*, to music of Genevieve Pitot—another narrative ballet, built around a story of prostitution in the European opera houses of the mid-nineteenth century.

All three of these works were made specifically for the RWB, and to each of them de Mille brought her unique flair for instantly accessible themes and bold characterization through dance. They were followed into the company's repertoire by two de Mille narrative-dance classics from the 1940s—her *Fall River*

Fall River Legend.

Bonnie Wyckoff as the Cowgirl and Terry Thomas as the Champeen Roper in a scene from Rodeo.

Legend, which deals with the story of Lizzie Borden and the axe-murder of her
parents, and *Rodeo*, subtitled *The Courting at Burnt Ranch*, which tells the tale
of how a cowgirl gets her man. The ballets of de Mille are often spoken of
disparagingly as simplistic dramatic vehicles of negligible dance content, but
their immediate impact is seductive: the drama, brilliantly manipulated, always
intrigues. Their success at the box office is undeniable. Audiences everywhere
love them. When a survey of the Winnipeg home-season audience was taken late
in 1977, the all-time favourite from the company's repertoire proved to be
Rodeo. (Its runners-up provide as clear an indication as any of hometown
audience preferences: after *Rodeo*, in order, came *Swan Lake*, and the two
Paddy Stone light-entertainment pieces, *The Hands* and *Variations on Strike Up
the Band*.)

The de Mille contribution to the RWB repertoire is unique; Spohr has never
been able to hit on anyone else who combines quite the same instinctive sense of
mass appeal with the ability to make it work in choreographic terms. But there
have been significant contributions, of varying durability and in other styles,
from a number of other imported outsiders.

New works by four of these were seen on a remarkable single bill in the fall of
1968. To celebrate the opening of the city's new concert hall, the company
brought together the talents of four U.S. choreographers—Eliot Feld, John
Butler, Anna Sokolow, and Todd Bolender—and the evening's content might be
seen as a crystallization of all that Spohr was aiming for in his push for "of now"
programming.

Feld's work, *Meadow Lark*, is one of the few made-for-the-RWB ballets that is
likely to endure as a minor dance classic. It is set to selections from the flute
quartets of Haydn, and Feld, who works in a vigorous neo-classic style with
some traces of modernism, matches the bucolic good humour of the music with
dance of a flowing and sprightly charm. There is a sense of spring about it; we are
witnessing some kind of eighteenth century country festivity. The ballet has no
narrative, but glimpses of relationships emerge and fade. It was the 26-year-old
choreographer's third work, and while it has been superseded in importance by
later Feld creations like *Intermezzo*, it remains a splendid example of his
musicality, his sense of form, and his lively choreographic imagination.

Butler was probably the most overtly Third Stream choreographer the RWB
had to that date encountered. He was originally trained in modern dance, but his
works are products of the experimentation in cross-breeding ballet and modern
dance that first became popular in the late 1950s and early 1960s.

His contribution to the RWB repertoire on that 1968 program was *Labyrinth*, another made-in-Winnipeg work. It dealt with the individual's loneliness in society, a common Butler theme; a lone male was thwarted by a crowd in his attempts to find happiness. It was an important example of the heavy, dramatic spectacle (spectacle in place of depth) that was becoming increasingly popular among the new cross-breeders. In 1971, the RWB added to its repertoire Butler's *Sebastian*, an intense sweeping melodrama (very effective when well danced, as it is by both Aiello and Shim) about a Venetian slave who saves the life of the woman he loves at the cost of his own.

Anna Sokolow contributed her jazz ballet, *Opus '65*, made to music of Teo Macero. Sokolow, whose brilliantly theatrical work is generally heavily laden with despairing commentary on modern man's condition, was the originator of what *The New Yorker* critic Arlene Croce was later to call "the Sokolow stare"—"devised . . . as a theatrical expression of the Age of Confrontation. Once an evening, the performers come to the footlights and stare out accusingly." The performers did more than stare out accusingly in *Opus '65*. They roared toward the audience on make-believe motorbikes, shouted and jeered at the passive watchers on the other side of the proscenium arch, then one by one leaped in despair into the orchestra pit. The non-balletic element was strong.

Todd Bolender, the other choreographer whose work was seen on that 1968 program, is yet another who has worked on both sides of the dance fence. His 1956 piece, *The Still Point*, to the first three movements of Debussy's String Quartet, entered the company repertoire in 1966. It was a tender examination of a young girl's search for happiness, and as was the case in many of the new works of the period it placed more emphasis on expressiveness in movement than on virtuosic dance-demonstration. However, his *Donizettiana*—the 1968 offering—was a much less adventurous work. A series of *divertissements* to music of Donizetti, it was described by Clive Barnes at the Winnipeg performance as "a dull ballet—one of those Balanchine-style works which have everything to offer except Balanchine." Predictably, the company looked terrible in it.

But then, the company rarely looks its best in purely classical works—partly, of course, because of the consistent lack of emphasis on classicism in the RWB repertoire. There has been a push in recent seasons to move the company in the direction of white ballets like *Giselle*, *Swan Lake* and *Les Sylphides*, and privately Spohr says he would love to see the company take on works like these. But he has stayed away from them for two reasons: his company is too small to carry them off effectively, and Canada already has a major classical company (the National Ballet of Canada) that can do them far better.

Nevertheless, he has made a practice of keeping a variety of shorter classic or neo-classic works in the repertoire, both to satisfy the traditionalists and to keep his dancers on their classical toes. Balanchine's *Pas de Dix* was an early example, and others are Benjamin Harkarvy's *Grand Pas Espagnol*, the Bournonville *Napoli*, Frederick Ashton's *Les Patineurs*, even Anton Dolin's restaging of Jules Perrot's nineteenth century *Pas de Quatre*. And, over the years, there has been a steady flow of showpiece *pas de deux*, both imported and homemade. These date back as far as the company's first decade, when David Adams went to London and brought back *Le Spectre de la Rose* and bits of *Swan Lake*. Most of the various ballet masters and mistresses who have passed through the company have added this or that classical bit to the repertoire, and a number of visiting guest dancers have taught and left behind the things they know, so that the classical side of the company's repertoire tends to look like an untidy dumping ground of mismatched leftovers gathered from some choreographic Salvation Army stall. But they never fail to delight the RWB's audiences, however much they might distress the purists and outstretch the company.

Far more serious attention has been given by Spohr to the development of the company's contemporaneity, though it was not until the arrival of Norbert Vesak and John Neumeier that he found choreography that would give the company the same strong sense of identity it had derived from Macdonald.

Vesak is another Third Stream cross-breeder, and, like Macdonald, he has a distinct penchant for the theatrical effect. His first two ballets for the company, *The Ecstasy of Rita Joe* and *What to Do till the Messiah Comes*, have been two of the most successful ticket sellers in the RWB history, though as ballet, both have dated. (*Messiah*, indeed, was made on a theme of sensitivity awareness that was passé even before the ballet was launched.)

Rita Joe is a message-ballet about the plight of the North American Indian. (Chief Dan George was once asked whether he agreed that the money spent on the ballet could have been better spent on social amenities. On the contrary, he said: the white public badly needed educating about the Indian plight, and *Rita Joe* was one of the best methods of education he knew.) A young Indian girl goes to the city, is seduced by its ways, is unable to cope, is brutally treated, and finally dies. It is an indictment of human callousness; but then, so was the George Ryga play on which the ballet was based. After concept, there must be

Ana Maria de Gorriz as Rita Joe and Salvatore Aiello as Jaimie Paul in the love scene pas de deux *from* The Ecstasy of Rita Joe.

form, and for much of the ballet, the danceform evolved by Vesak is desultory stuff: bland, unimaginative group work that merely serves as space-fill around the songs and the films and the theatrics. The ballet's saving grace is a long, expressive love *pas de deux* for Rita Joe and her man, Jaimie Paul.

The situation was repeated with *Messiah*. The work's highlight, standing out

from a morass of cliché group movement lacking either subtlety or imagination,
was a *pas de deux* (the "Belong" section) that today is occasionally danced as an
entity outside the complete work. Again, though, the ballet was tricked out with
all manner of visuals—lighting effects, projections, gleaming tubes, sheets of
tinfoil, and a strange ellipsoidal object not unlike a giant potato chip that rose
from the centre of the stage and hung at various angles throughout the
ballet—and it won a warm reception from audiences everywhere.

Neumeier's *Rondo*, which was introduced on the same program as *Rita Joe*, is
far simpler, but, in terms of choreographic and interpretative demands, far
heavier. Vesak was out for the broad effect, the theatrical impact. Neumeier
approached dance as an expressive and communicative vehicle. His style suits
the RWB handsomely. Like Gweneth Lloyd, Brian Macdonald, and Norbert
Vesak before him, like Oscar Araiz after, he was trained in both classical and
modern technique; like them, he has evolved his own particular mix of
modernity and classicism. He is interested in using dance, he says, to explore
human relationships through movement alone, not through literary plots; the
five movements of *Rondo*, for instance, crystallize in non-narrative dance
metaphor the travails the individual is forced by society to suffer. Six grey-clad
dancers, representing the individual, undergo various brutalities at the hands of
brown-clad, mechanistic others. Neumeier ends (unlike, for instance, Butler)
on a note of cautious optimism: the individual survives, but is changed.

John Neumeier's Rondo. *(Colette Masson)*

Rondo made new demands on the company as interpretative artists. Neumeier wanted them to bring their own approaches to their roles, rather than simply carry out steps that had been arbitrarily imposed. Some of the dancers, accustomed (perhaps even preferring) to be treated like dancing machines, were shaken by the novelty of the experience. Not all of them welcomed it. The process intensified, however, with *Twilight*, in 1973, a far more subtle and complex work—the fulfilment of the promises *Rondo* had made. Its original German title, *Dämmern*, is impossible to translate into a single English word. It means the time between darkness and light, both at dawn and dusk; it also implies a potential for unreality. More than any other work in the RWB repertoire, *Twilight* is a piece of psychological exploration. Using 16 solo-piano compositions by the Russian composer Alexander Scriabin, it probes, in the words of Neumeier's program note, "unconscious states of mind. In an atmosphere between sleep and waking, between darkness and light, between events happened and imagined we look, as it were, inside the dancers—as they listen to this music." He has since said that he tried to create in this work a ballet that was based, like Jerome Robbins' *Dances at a Gathering*, on the interweaving relationships within a group or a community of individuals. The dancers are on stage as the audience arrives; they warm up, and the pianist begins to play. What eventuates is a series of enigmatic solos, duos, and sequences for ensembles of various sizes—subtle, sometimes seemingly whispered statements about living, loving, and longing.

The flash and noise of *The Game* (which made up, with *Rondo* and *Twilight*, an evening-long presentation called *Pictures*) was a complete contrast to the introspection of the two works that preceded it, though the ballet dealt with similar preoccupations—the individual, existing in and coming to terms with his social setting. But if *Twilight* dealt with the human interior, and if *Rondo* dealt with generalized mass forces, *The Game* focussed squarely on one person, as he struggled through the "game of life," expressed here as a giant pinball machine. "As in life, key figures recur," said Neumeier's note. "As in life, the essential and senseless are juxtaposed; as in life, there is no absolute winner—the game has no end." The work was undeniably theatrical. The pinball machine came complete with 360 flashing lights, slide-screens, fashionably trippy movies—all the hysteria of modern existence—and the soundtrack was a rock-and-orchestral collage of a variety of versions of Moussorgsky's *Pictures at an Exhibition*. For anyone who might have missed the message of the previous two segments in the full-evening program, *The Game* certainly brought them crashing home. For many who had been captivated and intrigued by Neumeier's previously demonstrated thoughtfulness, however, it seemed too heavy-handed. Was it a pointer to the damage we do to ourselves by our slavish attention to faddism and cults-of-the-moment—or was it the product of someone who had succumbed to faddism himself? The answer was uncomfortably unclear.

Neumeier's *Nutcracker* is arguably the freshest, certainly the most progressive, version of the ballet on view today. Inspired by a 1966 John Cranko

Bonnie Wyckoff and David Peregrine in Nutcracker. *(Jack Mitchell)*

Marina Eglevsky as Maria in Nutcracker.

version, Neumeier first sketched it on his own Frankfurt company in 1970, but revised and completed it on the RWB in 1972.

There have been, of course, dozens of variants on the basic Nutcracker ballet. More than 100 companies in North America alone have a *Nutcracker* in their repertoire, all slightly different, all using more or less the music that Tchaikovsky wrote for the original Petipa-Ivanov version that was presented in Leningrad at the end of the last century. But Neumeier effected major changes. The ballet became a less pretty telling of Hoffman's fairy tale and more a touching and amusing psychological study of childhood on the brink of maturity. He wanted, he said, "to celebrate that classic moment, childhood's end." He makes his central character, Maria, no longer seven years old, as in the original version, but 12. It is no longer Christmas, but her birthday. Drosselmeier, the mystery man who in the original version magically transports the little girl to the dream-world Land of Snow and Land of Sweets, is no mystery at all—he is the ballet master for the local Hoftheater where Maria's older sister is a dancer. Drosselmeier gives Maria not a nutcracker toy but a pair of *pointe*-shoes—and when she falls asleep and dreams, he takes her first to his ballet studio and then to the theatre stage. The cherished nutcracker doll is a gift from her sister's military boyfriend—and it is the boyfriend who reappears in the dream to partner both Maria and her sister.

Neumeier's modifications—far more sweeping than those of the much-lauded Baryshnikov version of 1976 for American Ballet Theatre—have disconcerted more than a few, and the work's extreme technical challenges have often proved major stumbling blocks for its performers. But it gives new dignity to what too often has been allowed to become an exercise in cheap mass-manipulation and sugary sentimentality.

Netting Neumeier gave the RWB a certain cachet, and reinforced the image of Spohr as a spotter of fine new choreographic talent. For several years the RWB was the only company in North America to list a Neumeier work in its repertoire (the National Ballet of Canada subsequently did his *Don Juan*) and many believe that, by acting when he did, Spohr was able to obtain the very best of Neumeier's work. There are those who think his work is over-intellectualized, and certainly he doesn't need to give his ballets the lengthy program notes they often carry, but it would be difficult to overestimate his value to the company—not only at the box office (his *Nutcracker* has become the biggest money-maker in RWB history) but also in setting a tone, contributing to the cooler, more serious image the company developed in the 1970s.

Equally valuable in this regard has been the work of the Argentinian Oscar Araiz. His background, like Neumeier's, is mixed (he studied both modern dance and ballet from his teens) though he goes further in his dissociation of his work from any conventional narrative or even conceptual sense. "Movement," he said once, "should create a sensation, not tell a story. The audience must learn to receive and enjoy dance directly, without first sifting its supposed content through their brain."

The first Araiz ballet that entered the RWB repertoire, his brief *Adagietto pas*

Bonnie Wyckoff and Joost Pelt in Oscar Araiz's Adagietto. *(Jack Mitchell)*

de deux to the fourth movement of Mahler's Fifth Symphony, was an early hint of that non-objective principle in dance. It is an expression of togetherness that speaks far more clearly of some kind of elemental, natural closeness and interdependence than it does of the romantically human. His *Rite of Spring* went further. Savage and erotic, performed in brief rehearsal costumes on a bare stage, it is a stripped-to-essentials dance rendering of what Dylan Thomas called "the force that through the green fuse drives the flower," the atavistic life-impulse. Its imagery is often prehistoric—reptiles, crawling creatures, a bloody darkness—and it is filled with agonized rolls and curves, a compulsive bodily spasticity, an animal tempestuousness. The dancers crawl like insects, they fight like animals, they slither like mammals in mud. Not everyone enjoys

The 1978 cast of Rite of Spring. *Above (left to right): Bill Lark, Michael O'Gorman, Ronn Tice, David Herriott, Baxter Branstetter, Harry Williams, Rodney Andreychuk, and Eric Horenstein. Below: Bonnie Wyckoff is figure at top. (Jack Mitchell)*

Sheri Cook as the Earth Spirit in Rite of Spring. *(Jack Mitchell)*

it. It challenges preconceived ideas about what dance must be. But it has become a staple of the RWB repertoire.

Family Scenes (to Francis Poulenc's Concerto for Two Pianos) attempts to depict relationships within a family group—Araiz calls it "a sequence of loose portraits or melodramatic pictures . . . a stage game." In jerky, silent-movie images, in an old-fashioned era, mother, father, son, and two daughters interweave complex patterns of love and displeasure, happiness and hate—as if Louisa May Allcott were being rewritten by Sigmund Freud. Below the surface, disquieting undercurrents simmer and bubble. It is an effective work, though somewhat undernourished (like much of Araiz) in terms of choreographic invention.

Mahler 4: Eternity Is Now has become one of the two or three most precious jewels in the RWB's choreographic crown; some writers have called it a masterpiece. Araiz has taken the shortest and happiest of Mahler's symphonies (the fourth, subtitled *Ode to Heavenly Joy*) and created with and on it a richly romantic image for the transience of earthly concerns and the permanence of eternal happiness. The ballet evokes a dark-lit, beautiful otherworld, floating in space and time; it is about the indestructibility of innocence. The opening movement sets us in a forest of bare trees. Sleigh bells usher in participants. There is a slow-motion time-suspended chase through the woods, a girl and her lover, and a crowd following; we meet a happy family. In the second movement, Death—a charming, handsome figure—invites various persons to heaven. One of them is the girl. The slow movement expresses earthly anguish and yearning at the loss. The finale transports everyone to eternity—and heaven, we discover, is a family picnic, back in the woods (now rich with foliage) where we began.

Like Neumeier, Araiz tends to over-explain in his program notes, and he complicates this ballet with an unnecessary array of allegorical figures. Nor does he invent much movement that is new. In the opening two movements, he

Mahler 4: Eternity Is Now; *Marina Eglevsky and Roger Shim (foreground) and the 1978 cast.*

seems swamped by the music's size; he runs out of things to say. But what is important here is his ability to take simple elements from the whole range of dance and forge them into a seamless unit that appears, for the moment of its viewing, as if it could have been expressed no other way.

The work of Araiz, in Spohr's eyes, is very much an expression "of now," and Araiz works dominated the company's programming in New York in 1978, as they dominated the touring and hometown programming in that and previous seasons. This Araiz emphasis was by no means unanimously popular, particularly in Winnipeg, where audience members complain frequently about the "modernistic" slant taken by programming in recent years (by which they mean, chiefly, Neumeier, Araiz, and Vesak). "I like to have a properly varied program," says one board member. "I think that's what we always had and when it isn't properly varied or when it's just plain bad . . . well, I think the Winnipeg audience ruddy well knows when it's seeing a bad show and they know the company can do better, and if it isn't going to they're not going to waste their time."

Spohr rarely shows anger, but this is a question that hits a nerve. "We're moving ahead," he says, "and I feel I've maybe gone a little beyond them. I'm leading them on and they're being left behind. We're not in our early days; we belong to Paris, to London, so Winnipeg should get with it. And if they're not prepared to, they shouldn't give me slander for my 'terrible' programming. I do try to please the public, but I'm trying to move ahead."

Eva Christiansen and Sheri Cook (foreground) and Margaret Slota (left rear), Bonnie Wyckoff, and Marina Eglevsky in Women. *(Jack Mitchell)*

Appendix of Ballets

Choreographers are listed alphabetically. Their works for the RWB are listed chronologically. Titles in bold type are works created for the company. The date immediately following the title is the year the work was first performed; if it entered the RWB repertoire at a later date, the entry year is shown in parentheses.

Abbreviations: M = music (* signifies an original score); D = designer; S = scenario; C = costumes. First casts, or their principal members, are shown for most major ballets.

DAVID ADAMS

Ballet Composite
1949. M: Brahms (*Variations on a Theme of Haydn*). D: David Adams with David Yeddeau. C: David Adams. A neo-classic ballet attempting to fuse geometric choreographic patternwork with romantic music. First cast: Jean McKenzie, David Adams, Viola Busday, Joyce Clark, Reg Hawe, Carlu Carter, Leslie Carter.

Geschrei
1951. M: Milhaud. D,C: Joseph Chrabas. A satire on the Charleston era, set in a "speakeasy." First cast included Roger Fisher, Sheila Killough, Jon Waks, Viola Busday, David Adams, Sheila Henderson, Eva von Gencsy, Arnold Spohr and Lillian Lewis.

Masquerade
1951. M: Khachaturian (from his *Masquerade* Suite). C: David Adams and Clarice Hardisty. A light classical *pas de deux*. First cast: Lillian Lewis and David Adams.

LEO AHONEN

Daydream
1967. M: Minkus. C: Ted Korol. A *pas de deux*.

SALVATORE AIELLO

Solas
1976. M: Villa-Lobos. A woman laments. First performed by Marina Eglevsky.

OSCAR ARAIZ

Adagietto
1971 (1974). M: Mahler (fourth movement, Symphony no. 5). C: Oscar Araiz. A *pas de deux* depicting "the weaving of bodies, the meeting of emotions, the changing of atmosphere from tenderness to ecstasy."—Araiz. First RWB cast: Louise Naughton, Craig Sterling.

Rite of Spring
1966 (1975). M: Stravinsky. D,C: Oscar Araiz. A choreographic rendering of the ballet suite evoking a ritual of pagan Russia. Principals in the first RWB cast: Sheri Cook, Bill Lark, Betsy Carson, Salvatore Aiello, Bonnie Wyckoff.

Family Scenes
1974 (1976). M: Poulenc (Concerto for Two Pianos). D,C: Susana Otero Leal. Melodramatic dance "pictures" capturing the complex emotional interplay between members of a family. First RWB cast: Salvatore Aiello, Ana Maria de Gorriz, Bonnie Wyckoff, William Starrett, Marina Eglevsky.

Magnificat
1969 (1976). M: J. S. Bach. D: Gwen Keatley, Bill Williams (lighting). C: Oscar Araiz. A setting of Bach's choral masterwork. First RWB performance involved 24 dancers, five vocal soloists, 60-voice choir.

Mahler 4: Eternity Is Now
1976. M: Mahler (Symphony no. 4). D,C: Oscar Araiz. A lyrical evocation of the essence of the music's statements about temporal and eternal happiness. First RWB principals: Bonnie Wyckoff, Sheri Cook, Mauricio Wainrot (guest), David Peregrine, Gary Norman, Salvatore Aiello.

The Unicorn, the Gorgon and the Manticore
1964 (1977). M: Gian-Carlo Menotti's madrigal fable. D,C: Mabel Astarloa. An allegorical treatment of the plight of the nonconformist artist (in this case, a poet) whose work becomes fashionable. RWB first-cast principals included: Bill Lark, Roger Shim, Marina Eglevsky, Bonnie Wyckoff, Harry Williams.

Festival
1976 (1977). M: Flavio Venturini. C: Mabel Astarloa. A bright and joyous program-opener with a jazz-dance base.

Women
1974 (1977). M: Grace Slick. C: Mabel Astarloa. Five women reveal their characters and hopes; jazz-tinged in style.

FREDERICK ASHTON

Les Patineurs
1937 (1966). M: Meyerbeer. C,D: William Chappell. A *divertissement* in which the dancers are supposed to be skating on ice.

GEORGE BALANCHINE

Pas de Dix
1955 (1963). M: Glazunov. C: Constance Officer. An entertainment with a strong Hungarian flavour, to music from the last act of *Raymonda*.

Glinka Pas de Trois
1955 (1977). M: Glinka. A *divertissement* in the classical style.

TODD BOLENDER

The Still Point
1955 (1966). M: Debussy (String Quartet op. 10, first three movements). C: Constance Officer. A lonely and rejected young girl searches for (and eventually finds) love.

Donizettiana
(1968). M: Donizetti. C: Doreen Macdonald. A bright, classically oriented *divertissement*.

RUTHANNA BORIS

Pasticcio
1956. M*: Vittorio Rieti. D: John Russell and John Graham. *Pasticcio* is an Italian word meaning stew. The basic ingredient here is the thought of love.

Roundelay
1956. M: Carl Czerny/Stephen Heller. A plotless ballet "just for fun . . . its essence is the open quality of friendliness peculiar to youth."—Boris.

Le Jazz Hot
1956. M: popular tunes of the 1920s, arranged by Paul Keuter. A nostalgic look at the "roaring twenties," made in the style of a vaudeville act.

The Comedians
1952 (1956). M: Dmitri Kabalevsky. C: Alvin Colt. A modern-styled evocation of the traditions of the travelling players of the *commedia dell'arte*.

Cirque de Deux
1946 (1957). M: Gounod. D,C: Robert Davison. The ballerina and the principal dancer, as king and queen of the balletic circus arena, assisted by their pages.

The Wanderling
1957. M: Schubert (Wanderer Fantasy). A little girl's macabre imaginings.

JOHN BUTLER

Labyrinth
1968. M*: Harry Somers (*Five Concepts for Orchestra*). D: Rudi Dorn. C: Stanley Simmons. "A man enters the labyrinth of the world today, a landscape of unreasoned terror and violence."—Butler. First cast principals: David Moroni, Christine Hennessy, Dianne Bell.

Sebastian
1966 (1971). M: Gian-Carlo Menotti. D:
Lawrence Schafer. C: Stanley Simmons. A
seventeenth-century Venetian slave dies to save
the life of a courtesan he loves. RWB first-cast
principals: Winthrop Corey, Louise Naughton,
Salvatore Aiello, Teresa Bacall, Maria Lang.

JOY CAMDEN

Baba Lubov
1951. M: Dmitri Kabalevsky. D,C: John
Graham. A children's ballet based on a Russian
fairy tale.

JACK CARTER

Pas de Deux Romantique
1961 (1972). M: Rossini. C: Norman McDowell.
A *pas de deux* in the romantic style. First RWB
cast: Marina Eglevsky, Sylvester Campbell.

JOHN CLIFFORD

Concert Fantasy
1971. M: Tchaikovsky (Concert Fantasia in G
major). D,C: Thomas Pritchard. A classical tutu
work. First cast: Christine Hennessy, Winthrop
Corey, Alexandra Nadal, Walter Bourke.

JAMES CLOUSER

Recurrence
1961. M*: James Clouser. D: Peter Kaczmarek.
C: Constance Officer. The sweet and bitter
growing pains of the transition from adolescence
to maturity.

The Little Emperor (and the Mechanical Court)
1962. M: Léo Delibes. D: Ted Korol. A
children's ballet.

Danse Bohème
1963. M: Bizet. "An essay in lyricism and
gentle bravura."—Clouser.

Quartet
1964. M*, C: James Clouser. Four dancers meet
to rehearse a modern-day choreographic
recreation of the Theseus legend. First cast:
Richard Rutherford, Donna-Day Washington,
Kit Copping, Patrick Crommett.

Tribute
1964. M: J. S. Bach, Grieg, Saint-Saëns. D:
Peter Kaczmarek. C: James Clouser. A
three-part tribute to the company's founders, to
celebrate the company's twenty-fifth
anniversary.

Sylvia Variations
1965. M: Léo Delibes. A fusion of
nineteenth-century ballet deportment and
twentieth-century technique.

Out of Lesbos
1966. M*: James Clouser. Sappho, the Greek
poet, looks back on her life.

Riel
1966. M*: James Clouser. D, C: McLeary
Drope. A narrative ballet based on the story of
Louis Riel; created to mark Canada's
centennial.

Note: Clouser also contributed a number of
choreographies to music from classical ballets,
among them *The Land of Snow* (from act one of
The Nutcracker), 1963, and a *Coppelia* (M: Léo
Delibes), 1963.

MICHEL CONTE

Variations for a Lonely Theme
1960. M: Brahms (*Variations on a Theme by
Haydn*). D: Claude Jasmin. C: Jacques de
Montjoye and Fernand Rainville. A young man's
life is chronicled. First performance principals:
Marilyn Young, David Shields.

Un et Un Font Deux
1961. M,C: Michel Conte. D: Jacques de
Montjoye. A classroom flirtation.

GLORIA CONTRERAS

Moncayo 1
1959 (1966). M: José Pablo Moncayo. A
fast-paced ballet in Latin-American spirit.

PETER DARRELL

Mayerling
1963. M: Fauré. D: Roy Izen. C: Grant
Marshall. A ballet based on the life and loves of
Crown Prince Rudolf, of Austria.

Chiaroscuro
1959 (1963). M: Darius Milhaud. D: Roy Izen. C:
Grant Marshall. Impressions of the light and shade
of human behaviour.

AGNES DE MILLE

The Bitter Weird
1953 (as Ballad). (1962). M: Frederick
Loewe/Trude Rittman. D: John Graham. C:
Motley. Music and dances from the musical
Brigadoon form the basis for this narrative drama of
love and death in the highlands of Scotland. First
RWB principals: Richard Rutherford, Marilyn
Young.

The Rehearsal
1964. M*: Morton Gould. A narrated-and-danced glimpse into the process of making dances.

The Golden Age
1967. M*: Genevieve Pitot, "after Rossini." D: Rudi Dorn. C: Stanley Simmons. An exposé of corruption in the European opera houses of the 1860s. Principals: Christine Hennessy, David Moroni, Richard Rutherford.

Fall River Legend
1948 (1969). M*: Morton Gould. D: Oliver Smith. C: Stanley Simmons. Based on the case of Lizzie Borden, who was accused in 1892 of murdering her parents with an axe, the ballet "explores the passions that lead to a violent resolution of the oppressions and turmoils that can beset an ordinary life."—program note. RWB first-cast principals: Christine Hennessy, Shirley New, Dick Foose, Petal Miller, Sheila Mackinnon, Richard Rutherford.

Rodeo
1942 (1973). M*: Copland. D: Oliver Smith. C: Frances Dafoe. How the cowgirl got her man at Burnt Ranch. RWB first-cast principals: Peter Garrick, Terry Thomas, Bonnie Wyckoff.

ANTON DOLIN

Pas de Quatre
1941 (1968). M: Pugni. D: Tom Lingwood. C: Morley Wiseman. A reconstruction of the famous 1845 coming-together of the four great Romantic ballerinas of the era, Taglioni, Grisi, Cerrito, and Grahn. RWB first cast: Christine Hennessy, Alexandra Nadal, Donna Frances, Sheila Mackinnon.

ELIOT FELD

Meadow Lark
1968. M: Haydn. D: Robert Prévost. C: Stanley Simmons. Aristocratic late-eighteenth-century gambols in an open space. First-cast principals: Richard Rutherford, Sheila Mackinnon.

JOSE FERRAN

Pastiche
1967 (1967). M: Francisco Alonso, Soutullo y Vert. D,C: Jean Robier. A light ballet with a Spanish-Hungarian flavour.

DON GILLIES

Ballet Three
1961. M: J. S. Bach.

The Golden Phoenix
1962. M*: James Clouser. D,C: Don Gillies. The French Canadian fairytale.

WALTER GORE

The Light Fantastic
1963. M: Chabrier. A lively abstract work.

The Last Rose of Summer
1971. M: Lord Berners. D,C: Osbert Lancaster. A comedy in a Victorian setting.

BENJAMIN HARKARVY

La Primavera
1957 (1957). M: Vivaldi (from *The Four Seasons*). D: Benjamin Harkarvy. C: Donald McKayle. A lyrical ballet with emotional undertones.

The Twisted Heart
1957. M*: Richard Wernick. D: Murray Simpson. C: Grant Marshall. Love, jealousy, and revenge in a group of strolling players, based on the *Pagliacci* story.

Four Times Six
1957 (1958). M: Walter Mourant. D: Benjamin Harkarvy. C: Jack Prince. A light ballet alternating playful and romantic moods.

Fête Brillante
1958. M: Mozart. C: Benjamin Harkarvy. A lively bravura showpiece.

Grand Pas Espagnol
1964 (1973). M: Moritz Mozkowski (*Five Spanish Dances*). C: Joop Stokuis. "A look back with affection" (Harkarvy) at the nineteenth-century Russian-Spanish ballet style.

LARRY HAYDEN

Moments
1973 (1974). M: Dvořák. C: Doreen Macdonald, Maryka Gawron. A lyrical and romantic mood piece.

The Whims of Love
1977. M: Adolphe Adam (*Le Diable à Quatre*). A celebration of the romantic style of ballet in the Paris of the 1840s.

HEINO HEIDEN

The Chinese Nightingale
1959. M: Werner Egk. D. C: Robert Prévost Hans Christian Andersen's fairy tale about an emperor and a nightingale with an enchanting song. RWB first-cast principals: Frederic Strobel, Marina Katronis, Rachel Browne, Sonia Taverner.

First-performance principals: Edith Jamieson, Paddy Stone, Jean McKenzie, Mary Gwen Reid.

FRANK HOBI

Dance of the Sabra
1957. M: Haim Alexander. "Israeli children are called sabra (cactus) because they are said to have as thorny a shell and as sweet an inside as the cactus fruit."—program note.

KURT JOOSS

The Green Table
1932 (1974). M*: F. A. Cohen. D: Hein Heckroth. S: Kurt Jooss. Masks: Hermann Markard. A dance of death, showing in bitterly satirical style the horrors of war and the survival of diplomacy. RWB first-cast principals: Bill Lark, Roger Shim, Peter Garrick, Frank Garoutte, Terry Thomas, Bonnie Wyckoff, Ana Maria de Gorriz, Louise Naughton.

NENAD LHOTKA

The Devil in the Village
1956. M*: Fran Lhotka. D,C: Ted Korol. An abridgement and rearrangement of original choreography by Pia and Pino Mlaker, this ballet used national dance steps and the rhythms of folk music to tell a Yugoslavian variant on the old tale of the enslavement of a man's soul by the Devil.

Slaveni
1965. M. Dvořák. D,C: Peter Kaczmarek. Separation and reunion in a Central European country under foreign domination just prior to the First World War. First-cast principals: Richard Rutherford, Lynette Fry.

GWENETH LLOYD

Kilowatt Magic
1939. M: Smetana (extracts from *Ma Vlast*). D: John Russell. C: Gweneth Lloyd, Betty Hey. A depiction of the development of hydro-electric power on the Canadian prairies.

Grain
1939. A five-minute ballet depicting the grain cycle from sowing to marketing.

Divertissements
1940 (original title: *Theme and Variations*). M: Tchaikovsky, Arensky. C: Ruth Haney. Interpretations in the classical style.

The Wager
1940. M: Mozart. D: John Russell. C: Mary Morriss. A three-act comedy in which a demure young miss is saved from marriage to a rich roué by the wiles of her sister, a "heartless minx." First-cast principals: Jean McKenzie, Betty Hey, Paddy Stone, Gordon Hill, Grace McFettridge.

Beauty and the Beast
1940. M*: Barbara Pentland. D: David Yeddeau. C: Pauline Boutal and Betty Parker. A two-act ballet-pantomime based on the popular fairytale.

Triple Alliance
1941. M: composite ("Street Scene," by Newman; "Rhumboogie," by Ron Raye and Hugh Prince; "Jalousie," by Jacob Gade and Vera Bloom; "Under the Spreading Chestnut Tree," by Weinberger; "Adios," by Eddie Woods and Enrico Madruqiera). D: Charles Faurer. S: Betty Hey and Peggy Jarman. C: Robert Bruce. A three-act comedy contrasting the manner in which, "with toil forgotten and pleasure in view," the people of Canada, England and the U.S.A. "gather together with the tankard or glass as the link which joins the circle of congeniality." First-cast principals: Paddy Stone, Betty Hey, Nancy Eyden, Gordon Hill, Jean McKenzie.

Backstage 1897
1941. M: Glazunov (*Scènes de Ballet*). D: David Yeddeau. S: Betty Hey. C: Betty Parker. Behind-the-scenes glimpses of a ballet in the making. First-cast principals: Patricia Litchfield, Paddy Stone, Jean McKenzie.

Les Preludes
1941. M: Liszt. D: John Russell. C: Lady Tupper. The journey of a man through life, and his reaction to the emotional incidents in which he becomes involved. First-cast principals: Paddy Stone, Jean McKenzie, Mary Gwen Reid.

Façade Suite
1941. M: William Walton (extracts from his two *Façade* suites). C: Robert Bruce. "A satirical ballet based on superficial nonsense in seven divertissements."—Lloyd.

The Wise Virgins
1942. M: J. S. Bach (arr: William Walton). D,C: John Russell. An abstract interpretation of the Biblical parable. First-cast principals: Paddy Stone, Jean McKenzie.

Finishing School
1942. M: Johann Strauss. D: John Russell. S: Josephine Blowe (Betty Hey). C: Dorothy Phillips.

A comedy set in a French finishing school in 1870. First-cast principals: Jean McKenzie, Patricia Litchfield, Betty Hey, Paddy Stone.

Queen of Hearts
1942. M: Haydn. D: John Russell. C: Dorothy Phillips. A children's ballet based on the old nursery rhyme.

Through the Looking Glass
1942 (later known as *Alice*). M: Deems Taylor. D: John Russell. C: Robert Bruce. An adaptation of Lewis Carroll's stories of the adventures of Alice. First-cast principals: Jean McKenzie, Patricia Litchfield, Paddy Stone.

Ballet Blanc
1942. M: Arensky. D: David Yeddeau. More *divertissements* in the classical style.

An American in Paris
1943. M: Gershwin. D: John Russell. C: Shirley Russell. A light comic entertainment set in Paris shortly before the Second World War. A visiting American feels nostalgia for his home. First-cast principals: Paddy Stone, Betty Hey-Farrally.

The Planets
1943. M: Holst. D: John Russell. C: Shirley Russell. An abstract interpretation of the music. First-cast principals: Paddy Stone, Betty Hey-Farrally.

Russalki
1943. M: Glinka, Liadov. D,C: Dorothy Phillips. Peasants and wood-sprites in old Russia.

Etude
1943. M: Chopin. D: David Yeddeau. C: Ruth MacGregor. "A choreographic poem danced in the classical tradition."—Lloyd. First-cast principals: Jean McKenzie, Paddy Stone.

Kaleidoscope
1945. M: traditional. D,C: Dorothy Phillips. A *divertissement* of national dances arranged for ballet.

Les Coryphées
1945. M: Tchaikovsky. D: David Yeddeau. C: Josephine Blowe (Betty Hey-Farrally). A classical ballet inspired by the paintings of Degas.

Dionysos
1945. M: Rachmaninov. D,C: Robert Bruce. The god descends to join his followers in frenzied celebrations of the vintage. First-cast principal: Paddy Stone.

Pleasure Cruise
1946. M: Ibert, Shostakovich. D: Dennis Carter. S: Joe and Josephine Blowe (David Yeddeau and Betty Hey-Farrally). C: Dorothy Phillips. A comic ballet built around a group of holidaymakers on board the *S.S. Penelope* in the 1890s. First-cast principals included: Lillian Lewis, Viola Busday, John Waks.

Arabesque I
1947. M: Robert Schumann; Tchaikovsky. (arr. Giaccomo Rossini). D: John David Phillips, C: Dorothy Phillips. A classical ballet in traditional *grand-divertissement* style. First-cast principals: Lillian Lewis, Arnold Spohr, Jean McKenzie.

Object Matrimony
1947. M: Schubert. C: Dorothy Phillips. A two-part version of Jane Austen's *Pride and Prejudice*.

Concerto
1947. M: Rachmaninov (Piano Concerto in C minor). D: David Yeddeau. C: Josephine Blowe (Betty Hey-Farrally). "The deep surge of rhythm reveals the concerto as fluctuating patterns of swirling motion and colour."—Lloyd.

Chapter 13
1947. M: initially Gershwin; rescored in 1948 by Robert Fleming. D: John Phillips. S: Joe Blowe (David Yeddeau). C: Dorothy Phillips. A melodrama of love, jealousy, vengeance, and death on a New York sidestreet. First-cast principals: Lillian Lewis, John Waks, Jean McKenzie, Reg Hawe.

Allegory
1948. M: Franck. D,C: John Russell. Shelley's poem "Music" inspired this ballet calling for the help of the arts in the spiritual rebuilding of the post-Second-World-War world. First-cast principals: Arnold Spohr, Lillian Lewis, Jean McKenzie.

Visages
1949. M*: Walter Kaufmann. D: Joseph Plaskett. C: Dorothy Phillips. A young girl and her lover are assailed by dissonant emotions (Lust, Jealousy, Fear, Greed, Hate, Indecision) and succumb eventually to Tragedy. First-cast principals: Jean McKenzie, Arnold Spohr.

Arabesque II
1949. M: Glazunov. D: John Phillips. C: Dorothy Phillips. A classical ballet in traditional *grand-divertissement* style. First-cast principals: Joan Anderson, David Adams.

Slavonic Dance
1949. M*: Walter Kaufmann. C: Malabar. A Slavonic dance for five.

Romance
1949. M: Glazunov. D: Susan Morse. C: Clarice Hardisty. A romantic ballet in traditional style. First-cast principals: Jean McKenzie, Arnold Spohr.

The Rose and the Ring
1949. M*: Walter Kaufmann. D,C: Pauline Boutal. A full-evening telling of Thackeray's story about the adventures of the bad princess Angelica, who wears a magic ring, and the good serving girl Betsinda, who is saved by a magic rose.

The Shooting of Dan McGrew
1950. M*: Eric Wild. D: John Russell and Joseph Chrabas. S,C: David Yeddeau. "The story of what might have happened the night the boys were whooping it up down at the Malamute Saloon." First-cast principals: John Waks, Fred Anthony, Jean McKenzie, Leslie Carter, Arnold Spohr.

Rondel
1951. M: Vivaldi. D: John Russell. C: Pauline Boutal. A troubadour captures the hearts of three beautiful sisters who live in a castle in olden-day Provence, but he runs away with the kitchen maid. First-performance principals: Arnold Spohr, Jean Stoneham, Eva von Genesy, Barbara Finlay, Sheila Killough.

Shadow on the Prairie
1952. M*: Robert Fleming. D: John Graham. C: Stuart MacKay. A young settler and his wife establish a home on the prairie, but she is unable to accept her new life and "in an agony of nostalgia and fear of the great snowy wastes dies."—program note. First-cast principals: Carlu Carter, Gordon Wales.

BRIAN MACDONALD

The Darkling
1958. M: Britten (*Variations on a Theme of Frank Bridge*). D,C: Peter Symcox. A lyric and dramatic ballet examining the way in which secret inner pressures can prevent individuals from finding happiness together. First-cast principals: Marilyn Young, Michael Hrushowy.

Les Whoops-de-Doo
1959. M*: Don Gillis. D,C: Ted Korol. "A whoop-up dedicated to the misalliance of

classical ballet and the Western myth."—program note.

A Court Occasion
1961. M: J. S. Bach (Brandenburg Concerto no. 2). D,C: Robert Prevost. RWB first-cast principals: Sonia Taverner, Fredric Strobel.

Prothalamion
1962. M: Delius. C: Ted Korol. A hymn for the wedding eve, dedicated to the memory of the choreographer's first wife, Olivia Wyatt.

Aimez-vous Bach?
1962 (1964). M: J. S. Bach. A setting of four works of Bach, developing from a dance lesson to a large ensemble, with a surprising and comic conclusion—the imposition of a jive-and-twist sequence on the D minor Toccata and Fugue. RWB first-cast principals: James Clouser, Richard Rutherford, Donna-Day Washington, Sonia Taverner, Leo Guérard.

Pas d'Action
1964. M: Franz von Suppé. D,C: By Chance. S: Brian Macdonald. "A story-ballet to end all story-ballets."—program note. A spoof, purporting to tell a tale of political chicanery in a fictitious imperial court. First cast: Sonia Taverner, Richard Rutherford, Fredric Strobel, Leo Guérard and Bill Martin-Viscount.

Swan Song
1964. M: Duke Ellington. A jazz-influenced work to parts of Ellington's *Peer Gynt* suite. RWB first-cast principals: Eva von Genesy (guest) and Richard Browne.

Rose Latulippe
1966. M*: Harry Freedman. D,C: Robert Prevost. S: William Solly and Brian Macdonald. A full-evening narrative-ballet presentation of the eighteenth-century French Canadian legend about a girl who danced with the devil to her doom. First cast principals: Annette de Wiedersheim (guest), Richard Rutherford, Sheila Mackinnon, David Moroni, Lillian Lewis.

While the Spider Slept
1966. M: Maurice Karkov. D: Rolf Nordin. C: Adèle Engard. "I have tried to reflect on stage something of the tremendous disintegration of modern life . . . of the need and effect of the 'peace-figure' and of how too often such a figure must operate in the telescopic eye of violence . . ."—Macdonald. RWB first-cast principals: Beatrice Cordua, Fredric Strobel, Sheila Mackinnon, Richard Rutherford.

Songs Without Words
1967. M: Schubert (*Octet*). C: Ulf Gadd.

Five Over Thirteen
1969. M*: Harry Freedman. D: Walt Redinger. C: Suzanne Mess. Joyous communication with others is possible, if we will only abandon our shells of prejudice and self-protection.

Canto Indio
(1970). M: Carlos Chavez. C: Doreen Macdonald. "A Mexican Indian song that is all brio."—program note. First RWB cast: Christine Hennessy, Winthrop Corey.

A Ballet High
1970. M*: Lighthouse (co-leaders Skip Prokop and Paul Hoffert). C: Doreen Macdonald. A semi-improvized experiment in blending jazz and rock music with ballet. First-cast principal: Christine Hennessy.

The Shining People of Leonard Cohen
1970. Performed to a reading of poems of Leonard Cohen, with additional electronically manipulated sounds by Harry Freedman. D: Ted Bieler. C: Brian Macdonald. A tender evocation of the moods and interactions of two persons in love. First cast: David Moroni, Annette av Paul.

DAVID MORONI

Etude: Printemps
1973. M: Krein, Yarulin, Minkus, Hertell. C: Doreen Macdonald. A lyrical exercise in *pas de deux* technique.

ROBERT MOULTON

Grasslands
1958. M: Virgil Thompson (*The Plough That Broke the Prairie*). D,C: Robert Moulton. The joys and hardships of life on the great plains, in three parts—"Quilting Bee," "Saturday Night," "Drouth."

Brave Song
1959. M*: original Indian, orchestrated by James Aliferis. D: Peter Kaczmarek. S: David Thompson. C: Robert Moulton, Gwynyth Young. Authentic music and dance of the Plains Indians, "heightened, re-choreographed and coloured to be more meaningful as theatrical work."—program note.

The Beggar's Ballet
1963. M: traditional. D: Peter Kaczmarek. C: Robert Moulton. An adaptation of John Gay's *The Beggar's Opera*, set to traditional English airs.

JOHN NEUMEIER

Rondo
1970 (1971). M: William Cornysshe; Ian Bark, Volka Rabe; Gustav Mahler; Jan Mortenson; Simon and Garfunkel. C: John Neumeier. An evocation of the way in which an individual can be changed by the pressures of society.

Nutcracker
1972. M: Tchaikovsky. D,C: Jürgen Rose. A full-length production of the classic, with many Neumeier modifications. First-cast principals: Violette Verdy (guest), David Moroni, Ana Maria de Gorriz, Sheila Mackinnon, Salvatore Aiello, Sylvester Campbell.

Twilight
1972, original title: *Dämmern* (1973, original RWB title: *Scriabin*). M: Scriabin. C: John Neumeier. "In an atmosphere between sleep and waking, between darkness and light, between events happened and imagined we look, as it were, inside the dancers—as they listen to this music."—Neumeier.

The Game
1972 (1974). M*: collage by Gerhard Peter and John Neumeier, based on Moussorgsky's *Pictures At an Exhibition*, as recorded by Stokowski and by Emerson, Lake and Palmer. D: Gunther Kieser. The chance and competition of life seen as a giant pinball machine. RWB first-cast principal: Craig Sterling.

BRYDON PAIGE

Rigodon
1974. M*: Michel Perreault. D: Ronald R. Fedoruk. C: Doreen Macdonald. French Canadian folk music blended with classical ballet technique.

STUART SEBASTIAN

The Seasons
1977. M: Glazunov. D,S: Gwen Keatley. "In this abstract classical ballet the dancers react to each season's characteristics and their inevitable change."—program note.

MICHAEL SMUIN

Eternal Idol
1969 (1972). M: Chopin. C: Marcos Paredes. A duet created in tribute to the sculptor Auguste Rodin—"an essay in concepts of form, from mass to shape to movement to flight."—Walter Terry. First RWB cast: Attila Ficzere, Madeleine Bouchard.

Pulcinella Variations
1968 (1972). M: Stravinsky. D,C: Marcos
Paredes. A plotless evocation of the mood and
style of the *commedia dell'arte*.

ANNA SOKOLOW

Opus 65
1965 (1968). M: Teo Macero. A jazz ballet that
examines—often with anger and with
desperation—the alienation of 1960s youth.

ARNOLD SPOHR

Ballet Premier
1950. M: Mendelssohn (Piano Concerto in G
minor). D,C: Grant Marshall. An abstract ballet
in a free classical style.

Intermède
1951. M: Cimarosa (a concerto for oboe and
strings). D,C: John Graham. "An abstract
modern ballet employing classical technique and
depicting the interplay of musical moods and
themes in terms of visual patterns."—program
note.

Children of Men
1953. M: Franck (*Prelude, Chorale and Fugue*).
D: John Russell. C: Eric Byrd. An allegorical
treatment of the theme of good versus evil, with
Faith and Light overcoming the Power of
Darkness.

E Minor
1958. M: Chopin. D: John Hirsch. C: Grant
Marshall. An interpretation in free classical
style of the composer's Piano Concerto no. 1, in
E minor, op. 11.

Hansel and Gretel
1960. M: Humperdinck. D,C: Clare Jeffery. A
version of the famous children's tale.

PADDY STONE

Zigeuner
1943. M: Zoltán Kodály. D: John Russell. C:
Elaine Hill and Elizabeth Edgar. A colourful
narrative ballet in a gypsy setting.

Clasico
1955. M: Latin American, arranged by Robert
McMullin, D,C: Jack Notman. A modern
classical ballet with a Latin flavour.

Variations on Strike Up the Band
(1969). M: Gershwin, arr. David Lindup. D:
Lewis Logan. C: Sue le Cash. A comic novelty
piece in which the dancers become musical

instruments. First-cast principals: Ana Maria de
Gorriz, Winthrop Corey, Teresa Bacall, Richard
Rutherford.

The Hands
1975. M: collage (Denise Levertov; Malcolm
Arnold; Wood, Forde, Finden; Eric Clapton; the
Beatles; Mozart). C: Tim Goodchild. Musical
works whose titles refer to hands are the basis of
this popular novelty number.

NORBERT VESAK

The Ecstasy of Rita Joe
1971. M: Ann Mortifee. D,C: Norbert Vesak.
Lyrics, dialogue: George Ryga (on whose play
the work is based). Film direction: Don S.
Williams. A dramatic narrative ballet of the
tragedy that befalls a young Indian girl who
leaves the reservation for the city. First-cast
principals: Ana Maria de Gorriz, Salvatore
Aiello, with voices of Chief Dan George and
Peter Haworth.

What to Do till the Messiah Comes
1973. M: collage (Chilliwack; Syrinx; Phillip
Werren). D: Robert Darling. C: Norbert Vesak.
Inspired by Bernard Gunther's touch-therapy
sensitivity-awareness book of the same name.
"Catch the joy as it flies . . . this you owe
yourself, this you must allow yourself, if you
can."—program note.

In Quest of the Sun
1975. M: Gregory Martindale. D: Ming Cho Lee.
A ballet based on the story of the conquest of
Inca sun-king Atahuallpa by Francisco Pizarro
and 40 soldiers-of-fortune. First-cast principals:
Richard Rutherford, Ana Maria de Gorriz,
Margaret Slota, Anthony Williams, Frank
Garoutte.

CLASSICAL WORKS

A variety of works and extracts from the classical
repertoire have been mounted on the company by
company members and guest teachers. Included
among these are:

Le Corsaire (pas de deux)
M: Drigo. Choreography: Alexander Gorsky.

Don Quixote (pas de deux)
M: Minkus. Choreography: Petipa, reproduced by
Mary Skeaping.

Flames of Paris (pas de deux)
M: Asafiev. Choreography: Alexander Vainonen.

Flower Festival at Genzano (pas de deux)
M: Helsted. Choreography: August
Bournonville.

*Giselle (*peasant *pas de deux)*
M: Adolphe Adam. Choreography: Leonid
Lavrovsky.

Napoli, Act Three
M: Gade, Helsted, Paulli, Lumbye. Choreography:
August Bournonville, staged by Kirsten Ralov.

The Nutcracker (grand pas de deux)
M: Tchaikovsky. Choreography: Rudolf
Nureyev/Lev Ivanov.

Paquita
M: Deldevez. Choreography: Petipa, reproduced
by Jorge Garcia.

The Sleeping Beauty
M: Tchaikovsky. Choreography: Petipa. Various
excerpts, reproduced by David Adams, and later
Eugene Slavin.

Le Spectre de la Rose
M: von Weber. Choreography: Fokine, reproduced
by David Adams.

Spring Waters
M: Rachmaninov. Choreography: Asaf Messerer.

Swan Lake
M: Tchaikovsky. Choreography: Petipa/Ivanov.
Various excerpts, staged by Gweneth Lloyd, David
Adams, Eric Hyrst and others.

Les Sylphides
M: Chopin. Choreography: Fokine.

Capsule Chronology

1938 *Spring:* Gweneth Lloyd and Betty Hey (Farrally) leave England and take up residence in Winnipeg.
Fall: Winnipeg Ballet Club founded. First contacts established with Lady Tupper, David Yeddeau, John Russell. First dancer-members include Paddy Stone, David Adams, Jean McKenzie.

1939 *June:* ballet club's first performances, as part of "Happy and Glorious" pageant. Two brief Lloyd works: *Grain*; *Kilowatt Magic*.

1940 *June 11:* club's first major performance, with full orchestra. Three Lloyd works: *Divertissements*; *The Wager*; an expanded *Kilowatt Magic*. Financial disaster, critical success.

1941 *June 6:* second major presentation, again with full orchestra. Three new works (*Backstage 1897*; *Triple Alliance*; *Les Preludes*); more critical success, more financial disaster. First contacts with Richardson family.

1942 *January:* Arnold Spohr sees his first ballet.
March: three new Lloyd ballets, to recorded music.
November: two new Lloyd ballets, including *The Wise Virgins*.

1943 *May:* two new Lloyd works. Company now known as Winnipeg Ballet.

November: two new Lloyd Ballets (including *An American in Paris*) plus Paddy Stone's choreographic debut, *Zigeuner*. Arnold Spohr makes his performing debut.

1945 *February:* company's first "tour"—to Ottawa for two performances.
November: first Western tour (Regina, Saskatoon, Edmonton).
December: three new Lloyd ballets, including the controversial *Dionysos*.

1946 *January:* Paddy Stone leaves for New York.
July: David Adams goes to England. Association between Winnipeg Ballet and Banff Centre School of Fine Arts begins.
September: "farewell" performances for Paddy Stone, passing through *en route* from New York to England.

1947 *March:* three new Lloyd works, including *Concerto*. Company invited to take part in international choreographic competition in Copenhagen. Fund drive launched.
May: plans to go to Copenhagen abandoned due to lack of funding.
October: Chapter 13 new.
November: tour to Regina, Moose Jaw.

1948 *March: Allegory* new.
April/May: First Canadian Ballet Festival, organized by Winnipeg Ballet, attended by Governor-General and companies from

265

Toronto, Montreal. National Ballet Association set up.
October: Adams returns as guest.
November: major tour of Eastern Canada.

1949 *January:* two new Lloyd works.
March: company attends Second Canadian Ballet Festival, in Toronto. Company incorporated as a non-profit cultural organization.
May: David Adams makes first choreographic foray (*Ballet Composite*); one new Lloyd work, *Romance*.
October: month-long nine-city Eastern Canada tour.
November: all debts have been cleared, a small surplus exists.

1950 *May:* Arnold Spohr makes choreographic debut with *Ballet Premier*; first performance of Gweneth Lloyd's *The Shooting of Dan McGrew*.
October: Gweneth Lloyd moves to Toronto; remains artistic director.
November: Third Canadian Ballet Festival, Montreal. Spohr's *Ballet Premier* acclaimed best of entire festival.

1951 *March:* gala benefit production, with two new works by Adams. First company performance at which no Lloyd work featured.
May: première of *Intermède* (Spohr).
October: command performance for Princess Elizabeth and Duke of Edinburgh.
November, December: *Rondel* (Lloyd), *Les Sylphides* (Fokine).

1952 *Spring:* Western tour, first time to Pacific.
May: Fourth Canadian Ballet Festival; Eastern tour as far as Maritimes.
June: Hurok, Columbia offer tours. Company moves to new headquarters.
October: Shadow on the Prairie (Lloyd).
November: company signs contract to tour U.S. for Columbia

1953 *January-March:* company's first full cross-Canada tour (including three performances in U.S., marking first time a Canadian company had crossed border).
February: Queen grants company permission to call itself "Royal."
June: company's first professional administrator, Henry Guettel, appointed.

September: company anticipating major deficit.

1954 *January:* Alicia Markova appears with company in Winnipeg.
January-March: 28-city tour of Eastern Canada and Central U.S., including Washington (with Markova). Tour loss: $13,000.
June: costumes, sets, choreographic records, original scores destroyed in major fire in downtown Winnipeg. Operations suspended.
December: major fund drive launched to re-establish company.

1955 *April:* Kathleen Richardson appointed to RWB board.
June: Betty Farrally appointed artistic director, Nenad Lhotka ballet master.
November: Royal Winnipeg Ballet returns. Program includes new version of *The Wise Virgins*, classical extracts, new works by Stone, Lhotka.

1956 *January:* Ruthanna Boris arrives to set *Pasticcio*.
March: $30,000 fund drive launched. Why subsidize "a bunch of galloping galoots"? asks city alderman.
September: Ruthanna Boris, Frank Hobi, return as guest principals; will also help train and build the company. Lhotka resigns. Five new Boris ballets seen this season.

1957 *April:* Ruthanna Boris, Frank Hobi, leave Winnipeg.
May: Betty Farrally's connection with the company ends. She moves to British Columbia and is joined there in less than a year by Gweneth Lloyd. They establish a dance-school business.
August: Benjamin Harkarvy appointed artistic director. Arrives with music director Richard Wernick and six dancers, including Richard Rutherford, Rachel Browne.
November: two new Harkarvy works seen. First Canada Council grant: $20,000.

1958 *January:* two more Harkarvy works, plus a revival of Spohr's *Intermède* (1951).
February: Harkarvy resigns; so does Wernick. Arnold Spohr asked to mount upcoming March shows.
March: Spohr's shows "best for years." Spohr invited to take over as artistic director. He accepts.

August: Spohr makes contact with Brian Macdonald. He agrees to make *The Darkling* for the company that fall.

1959 Spohr's first full season closes after 42 performances for a total audience of 33,500 (compared with the previous season's 10 performances for 5,768). Budget almost balances.
July: Command performance for Queen, Duke of Edinburgh.
September: Macdonald returns after success of *The Darkling* to make *Les Whoops-de-Doo.* Robert Johnston joins company as manager.

1960 *January-February:* tour of Western Canada.
October-November: 10,000-mile tour of Eastern Canada.
December: Olga Moiseyeva and Askold Makarov, from Leningrad's Kirov Ballet, make guest appearances with RWB.

1961 Total attendance, 1960-61: 63,732. Net loss: $5,000.
October-November: tour of northern and midwest United States.
December: Bolshoi Ballet stars Rimma Karelskaya, Boris Hohlov, join company for guest appearances in Winnipeg, Western provinces.

1962 *March:* new works by Agnes de Mille (*The Bitter Weird*) and George Balanchine (*Pas de Dix*).
Net loss, 1961-62: $35,000.
September: official school of the RWB opened, Jean McKenzie in charge.

1963 *January:* company performs in Jamaica.
January-March: Western tour, U.S. tour. Accumulated deficit tops $100,000.
December: Kirsten Simone, Henning Kronstam, from Royal Danish Ballet, make guest appearances.

1964 *January: Aimez-vous Bach?* by Brian Macdonald enters RWB repertoire.
March: Macdonald makes *Pas d'Action* for RWB; appointed first official choreographer to the company.
July: company is "crown jewel" of Jacob's Pillow season. "That's where we became famous," says Spohr. Sergei Sawchyn joins company as manager. Jim Cameron's aid is enlisted for promotional writing.

September-October: small-town midwest tour, major Eastern Canada tour.

1965 *February:* $259,000 three-year fund drive launched.
March: Western tour.
September: appearances at Commonwealth Arts Festival, Britain.
October-December: company's first tour for Sol Hurok, circling North American continent.

1966 *January:* Caribbean tour.
August: Rose Latulippe, by Brian Macdonald, given first performances at Stratford Festival.
November: fund drive tops $200,000.

1967 *January-February:* 40-city U.S. and Eastern Canada tour.
April: Rose Latulippe, 90-minute CBC-TV special.
August: week engagement at Expo '67.
October: Western tour.

1968 *January-March:* 52-city U.S. and Canada tour.
April: Canada Council grant now $170,000.
October: company opens city's new Centennial Concert Hall with new works by Eliot Feld and John Butler, and Canadian premières of works by Anna Sokolow and Todd Bolender.
November: RWB is voted best company at International Festival of Dance in Paris; principal dancer Christine Hennessy wins gold medal for best female interpretation.
December: company acclaimed in USSR, Czechoslovakia.

1969 *February:* Jim Cameron joins full-time staff.
June: Spohr receives trio of major awards.

1970 *January-March:* Eastern Canada and U.S. tour.
June: company returns to Paris, also performs in Italy.
July: Macdonald's new works, *A Ballet High,* and *The Shining People of Leonard Cohen* first seen.
October: Richard Rutherford, David Moroni retire from dancing, Rutherford to become RWB associate director, Moroni to head professional training program.
December: Patrice Bart, Francesca Zumbo, of Paris Opera Ballet, make guest appearances.

1971 *January-March:* U.S. tour.
March: Lady Tupper dies.
July: Norbert Vesak's *The Ecstasy of Rita Joe* and John Neumeier's *Rondo* first performed.

1972 *February-April:* RWB tours Australia, with Bart and Zumbo as guests.
April: Sergei Sawchyn resigns; is replaced by Robert Dubberley. Cameron quits.
May: Richard Rutherford takes one-year leave of absence.
June: Vernon Lusby appointed associate director, Frank Bourman appointed ballet master.
December: première of John Neumeier's *Nutcracker,* with Violette Verdy as guest star.

1973 *January:* Vesak's new ballet, *What to Do till the Messiah Comes,* given first performance.
January-February: Western Canada tour.
February-March: Eastern Canada tour.
April: John Neumeier officially appointed choreographer to the RWB—first since Macdonald. His ballet *Twilight* added to repertoire.
June: Richard Rutherford officially rejoins company.
September: Margot Fonteyn, Heinz Bosl, guest artists.
November: Agnes de Mille's *Rodeo* enters repertoire.
December: Dubberley resigns; Cameron invited back.

1974 *January:* Western Canada tour.
February: U.S. tour.
March: Cameron returns, as general manager. Company is nearly $300,000 in debt; 1973-74 losses of $200,000-plus four times as great as any previous loss.
April-June: company tours Latin America. Spohr "discovers" Argentinian Oscar Araiz.
August: province of Manitoba gives RWB $250,000.
September: RWB given $70,000 by U.S. Kresge Foundation.

October: Araiz's *Adagietto* enters RWB repertoire; Mikhail Baryshnikov and Gelsey Kirkland appear as guests.
November: Kurt Jooss's classic anti-war ballet, *The Green Table,* enters repertoire.

1975 *February-March:* Eastern Canada and U.S. tour.
April: première Norbert Vesak's *In Quest of the Sun,* starring Richard Rutherford.
August: company appears at the Israel Festival, with Valery and Galina Panov as guests.
October: RWB première of Araiz's *Rite of Spring.* Vesak appointed official choreographer to RWB, alongside Neumeier.
November-December: Western tour.
December: Panovs appear as guest artists.

1976 *April:* Araiz's *Family Scenes* enters RWB repertoire. Ballet's accumulated deficit now up again, to $180,000.
October: Araiz added to company's roster of official choreographers. Two Araiz works enter RWB repertoire: *Magnificat,* and *Mahler 4: Eternity Is Now.*
October-December: Western Canada and U.S. tour.

1977 *January:* Cameron resigns. Edward Reger becomes general manager.
January-February: Eastern and midwest U.S. tour.
March-April: Eastern Canada tour.
April: Richard Rutherford resigns.
June: Frank Bourman resigns.
October: Hilary Cartwright joins RWB as company teacher. Principal dancer Salvatore Aiello becomes *régisseur.*
November-December: Western Canada tour.

1978 *March:* company undertakes one-week stand in New York; highly praised.
April: Western Canada tour. Cartwright, Aiello and Moroni promoted to associate directors.
By end of 1977-78 season, ballet deficit tops $300,000.

Index

Numerals in italics indicate photographs.